REA

ACPL

DISCARDED

YO-BYA-603

11-30-72

THE WORLD OF YOUNG SHOLOKHOV

THE WORLD OF YOUNG SHOLOKHOV

Vision of Violence

By

MICHAEL KLIMENKO

THE CHRISTOPHER PUBLISHING HOUSE

NORTH QUINCY, MASSACHUSETTS

COPYRIGHT © 1972

BY THE CHRISTOPHER PUBLISHING HOUSE

Library of Congress Catalog Card Number 70-189367

ISBN: 1–8158–0282–X

PRINTED IN

THE UNITED STATES OF AMERICA

1723906

To
Marianna
Andreas
Marcus
Anna
Martha

PREFACE

There is really not a great deal that can be said of this book. Rather, the book should speak for itself, to prevent the Preface from serving as a further expansion of the author's thoughts. It should be noted, however, that this book in no way makes a pretense of being a complete investigation of Sholokhov's early work. A total investigation of any author or, by the same token, a complete mastery of any literature is hardly ever possible. A work of this nature should include not only the given author's life and his work, but should at the same time be cognizant of his time and his society in all its aspects and relations, systematically and chronologically presented.

On second note, this author would like to add that almost every sentence in this book could have been annotated. This, however, would not be of help and would place an unnecessary burden upon the book. Also, the writer admits that at present it would not be possible for him to annotate all references. In several places he makes general references and assertions, such as "critics say" or "it was said." This generalization can be explained by the fact that he has studied Sholokhov and his work for many years. In fact, he started this study long before deciding to expand it into book form. Although having read many books and articles pertaining to Sholokhov in Russian, German and English, he made few notes at the time. Thus, when he did begin compiling material for the present book, many of the books he had read previously were no longer available to him, and it became impossible to find and annotate all the references he needed. This explains, for the most part, why general allusions are made to many references.

For the same reason, it would be impossible to present a complete bibliography and, thus, only those books on Sholokhov which were used directly are listed herein. Since a bibliography on Sholokhov would by this time embrace a good-sized volume in itself, it would be quite useless to try to present here even a selected list of titles. The works of Sholokhov which the author thought were necessary for reference are indicated in the Notes and References at the end of each respective chapter.

In addition, the quotations from Sholokhov's works which are used in this book are taken from the latest editions available: *Collected Works* (Russian) in eight volumes, Moscow, 1962, and the English language edition of *The Quiet Don.* published by the Foreign Languages Publishing House in Moscow. As it is known, the text of *The Quiet Don* has a long and very complicated history of revisions and alterations which could easily be the subject of a separate investigation.

Last, but not least, for practical reasons it was necessary for the author to adjudge the term *Early* Sholokhov to the completion of *The Quiet Don,* He is aware that chronologically, since the first volume of *Virgin Soil Upturned* was completed prior to the last volume of

The Quiet Don, this classification cannot be completely justified. But, inasmuch as *Virgin Soil Upturned* displayed a different concept of reality, its inclusion into Sholokhov's early period would burst the frames of this investigation out of all proportions. For this reason, having included a chapter on Sholokhov's start, the author has limited the subject matter of the investigation to *The Quiet Don* only.

In regard to the spelling of Russian names, the most widely accepted and practical system is utilized, that of the Library of Congress. However, in a few instances, such as Gorky and Mayakovsky, which have established their own spelling, exceptions have been made to the above cited system.

It is this writer's pleasure to mention the American Philosophical Society in Philadelphia, whose grant no. 5541 from the Penrose Fund made it easier to complete the present work in a shorter time than had been previously anticipated. Their support is herewith gratefully acknowledged.

Michael Klimenko

CONTENTS

THE WORLD OF YOUNG SHOLOKHOV

Introduction I

THE CANON AND ITS REQUIREMENTS

The main object of this book is to investigate Sholokhov's concept of reality, as it was represented in his early work, including the fourth volume of *The Quiet Don*, i.e. to go the way that Sholokhov himself once went when he described the reality of his Cossacks' life.

The investigation will thus, by necessity, also include Sholokhov's own attitude to reality, as it was perceived and expressed by him. The author is here following the method shown by Erich Auerbach in his excellent book *Mimesis*, to study the text and to try to find that place at which the author usually stands and from which he looks around at the events described in his works. In other words, our investigation is conducted from inside of the work. The object of the investigation is then not so much what the work is about or what is in the work, but rather how the author has presented the outside world with its people which populate the work.

We said that the object of the book is the concept of reality. As it happens, the literary criticism of Socialist Realism has the same object when it studies literary art. It is known that the ideal concept of Socialist Realism's aesthetics is the close connection between art and reality, and the dependence of art upon reality.[1]

1

Literature, accordingly, should reproduce the reality of life. The task of literary criticism is then to investigate the reality of life as it is presented in the given work.

In spite of this external similarity of our objectives, there is, however, one basic difference between this author's object and that of Socialist Realism. The difference exists in our methods of understanding reality. For Socialist Realism there exists only one reality of life: the reality as it is seen and understood by the Marxist-Leninist philosophy.

It was Lenin who developed the philosophical concept of reality as it was subsequently accepted by his party-fellows and later followers. According to this concept, it is not the reality of real, everyday life that is the reality of our perception, but rather the reality seen in its strict revolutionary and dialectical development. This means that we have to perceive reality not as it is now, but as how it should be in prospective. In practice then, the reality that counts is not the everyday reality perceived by the "average" man, but rather the reality as the theoreticians of the Party would like it to be. It is not the reality of today, but reality as the theoreticians hope it will be in the future, in its historical and materialistic development.

This concept of reality became obligatory for the literature of Socialist Realism. In Soviet literature, this concept is described as Lenin's party principle, or *partiinost'* in Russian.

Life as presented in the literature of Socialist Realism must be seen and judged strictly from the positions of Lenin's party principles. This is stressed and repeated again and again in manifold ways by literary critics, by the writers themselves, and by ideological leaders in their speeches.

Socialist Realism has then nothing to do with the realistic representation of the reality of life, but rather with that specific philosophical or ideological view of reality. There is, and there cannot be, any other reality but the reality that was understood and interpreted by Lenin and his followers. And since every writer and every critic has to be a follower of Lenin and a Marxist, the slightest deviation from Lenin's point of view is not possible. The Marxist philosophy does not tolerate any deviation from its official interpretation.

What happens if an author's concept of reality does not coincide with that of the Marxist-Leninist concept? In theory, this should not happen. Since there is only one party, consequently there is possible only one party principle, and there is only one reality.

When it nevertheless does happen in practice, it is then worse for reality. The reality of life has to conform to Lenin's concept of reality and his principles.[2]

What then is required from the writer is that he understands and adapts his concept of reality to that of Lenin. No author can be allowed the luxury of having his own concept of reality. This usually results in the authors' twisting and adjusting their own, real concept of reality to that of the Marxist-Leninist concept, as long as their reality is molded to fit into the pattern.

It must also be said at this point that there can be nothing wrong with Socialist Realism, provided, of course, that the given author himself is a Socialist Realist, i.e. that he is a Marxist of Lenin's breed.

The Quiet Don in many respects represents an exception in Soviet literature. It occupies a really unique position in the theory and practice of Socialist Realism. The first three volumes of it were written at the early stage in Soviet literature when Socialist Realism was not yet proclaimed to be the prevailing theory of literature and when every writer could express his concept of reality as his personal opinion, relatively freely. And this was done by young Sholokhov. There can now be no doubt that Sholokhov's concept of reality deviates in many ways from that of the official interpretation, for which he was severely criticized by his colleagues in proletarian literature. Yet as of now, his work is recognized in the Soviet Union as a classic work of Soviet literature, as the highest expression of the method of Soviet Realism, and as a standard of its aesthetical ideals.

It now became a recognized fact that Sholokhov had difficulties with the publication of his masterpiece. Editorial boards of the Proletarian Literature refused to accept the novel without some cuts and shortenings. Only the insistent demands of Serafimovich, the old friend and well-wisher of beginning writers, enabled the first two books of *The Quiet Don* to be published without cuts. And, the third book of *The Quiet Don* and the first of *Virgin Soil Upturned* were published in the magazine *New World* only after intervention by Gorky and the Central Committee of the Party. Sholokhov more than once recalled this help with gratitude.[3]

It is unknown up to the present, why they supported the publication. We have no other explanation than this one: Probably, the people who favored publication of the novel had recognized its value and greatness. It was indeed not difficult to see that *The Quiet Don* was, so to speak, a first rate work of art. In any case, they did not suppress the work.

Later, in 1934, the theory of Socialist Realism was formulated. If the theory, with its rigid requirements, had been established prior to the publication of *The Quiet Don*, it undoubtedly would have made this great work of literary art unfit for the literature of Socialist Realism, because its representation of reality does not coincide with the concept of reality as it is required by the norm of Socialist Realism. The work would have been declared wrong in its conception and harmful to the interests of the people in the Socialist country.

Fortunately, *The Quiet Don* had established its reputation as a great work before the canon came into existence. And once the work, which did not express the official concept of reality, was published and recognized by the authorities as a masterpiece, not only in Russia but also abroad, literary criticism and interpretation had to do the rest of the job in adjusting it to the norm of the official canon. The critics had to interpret and re-interpret Sholokhov's concept of reality until it was moulded to the desired degree of acceptability to the officially recognized concept of reality. So, it happened that in this case, not the author—Sholokhov—has adapted his reality to the Marxist-Leninist party principles, but rather his concept of reality was adjusted by literary critics to the norm and standards of the required aesthetics. An attempt was made even by Sholokhov himself to change his novel in order to satisfy the demands of the canon.

In 1949 Stalin's letter, written twenty years earlier to Felix Kon, became known.   Felix Ia. Kon (1864-1941), known Polish revolutionary, joined the Bolsheviks in 1918, and since then had established his life and career in Moscow, occupying various editorial offices. Stalin's letter to Kon, dated July 9, 1929, was written on the occasion of a certain Russova's review of a booklet by an author of virtually unknown name from Ivanovo-Voznesensk, Mikulina (today completely forgotten) *Sorevnovanie mass, (Emulation of Masses).* Stalin furnished a foreword to this inconsiderable work by an author unknown in the literary world.   Apparently, it was a poorly written book, and as such was much criticized for its errors.   The reviewer accused the author of misleading Stalin in having him write a foreword.   Stalin, in his letter to Kon, tried to justify his foreword and Mikulina's booklet as having great value for the masses of the workers.   He wrote that the value of the book was to be measured not by individual details but by its general trends.   The tone of Stalin's letter seemed to be marked by a certain degree of tolerance.   He seemed to say that unknown authors and their unascertained works should be promoted rather than ignored.   Sholokhov's name was mentioned in the letter purely by accident, only as an illustration of the fact that even the mistakes of young authors should be tolerated.   This is what Stalin wrote in 1929:

> A famous author of our time, Comrade Sholokhov, commits a number of very gross errors in his *The Quiet Don* and says things which are positively untrue about Podtëlkov, Kryvoshlykov and others, but does it follow from this that *The Quiet Don* is no good at all and deserves to be withdrawn from sale?[4]

The letter was published for the first time in 1949. This time it produced quite a different effect than it had done twenty years earlier. Meanwhile, Stalin of course became the infallible expert in all fields—one whose authority could no longer be doubted. Apparently Sholokhov felt that he had to correct his errors in creating the Communist characters of Podtëlkov and Kryvoshlykov. He changed a great deal of his novel. The new *Quiet Don* edition of 1953 unmistakably bore the marks of the official taste and of the requirements of the canon. Sholokhov had to adjust his concept of reality to that of Lenin's party principles, by necessity assigning the leading roles to the Communist characters—as should befit the work of a Socialist artist.

Literary criticism in turn had to adjust its tastes and standards to the new text as changed by Sholokhov.[5]

Fortunately for literature, Sholokhov found enough strength in his new edition of 1956 to restore some passages of his original version. Others, on the other hand, were retained as revised in 1953.

The Quiet Don became the accepted standard of Socialist Realism's aesthetics. It became not only a custom but also a prerequisite to extoll the novel's merits. The critics cannot do otherwise. Once the work has been recognized, it has to be praised. By the way, the same story happened with Mayakovsky. Since the time when Stalin had pronounced Mayakovsky to be the greatest poet of the Socialist epoch, a critical attitude to him was no longer possible. A negative criticism of Mayakovsky can hardly be tolerated in the Soviet Union. The core of the matter is that the criticism itself must be moulded in accordance with the definite criterion of the same Marxist ideological scheme. The Marxist reality of life is the only standard for criticism.

In the case of *The Quiet Don,* the scheme of the literary criticism is seen in the interpretation of Grigorii Melekhov, the novel's main character. His rebellion against the Revolution is explained in such a way as if he were searching for truth and failed to find the only correct way of life shown him by the Communist Party. The critics seem not to notice the fact that Grigorii, as millions of other people with him, could not accept that "only correct way of life" because it was simply unacceptable to him. The Revolution, as it was revealed in the novel, was repulsive to the Cossacks' way of life.

Or another example of Grigorii's schematic interpretation: the critics assert that Grigorii fought against the people, while his antagonist, Koshevoi, fought for the people. Again the critics do not notice the simple fact that there were people *(narod)* on both sides of the Great Watershed, cut out by the Bolshevik Revolution. There were people with the Reds, as there were people with the Whites.

One other common scheme of interpretation beaten by criticism is the assertion that the Cossacks who fought the Soviets in the Don have finally understood and accepted the great, universally human truth of the Communists. And again, the critics seem not to notice the simple fact that the Cossacks were defeated with arms in their hands, that they in reality had no other choice but to reconcile themselves with the victorious Bolshevik forces. The victors imposed their truth upon the defeated Cossacks, and the Cossacks had to accept their defeat.

Sometimes literary critics may find certain short-comings in the novel, such as Sholokhov's weakness in presenting the Communist characters. Sometimes they find objectivism in Sholokhov's work, and digression from the Marxist concept of reality such as lack of clear ideological positions. These critics again seem not to see that Sholokhov in *The Quiet Don* had his own concept of reality, proper only to him and to no other writer.

What happened to Sholokhov was perhaps what he was most afraid of and against which he fought very hard in his life. On many occasions in his many speeches, he raised his voice against poor criticism in Soviet literature. He always spoke of high qualities of literature, and high qualities of literary criticism. He never defined what he meant exactly by the high quality. In literature, he probably had in mind the purity of language. In reference to literary criticism, he probably was indirectly protesting the fact that the critics have failed to evaluate his work properly and render it justice.

Once at an international conference, a Czechoslovak-ian Marxist scholar asked the author of this book why *The Quiet Don* was permitted to be published. Although this question had never occurred to this author, as it actually hardly ever occurs to the millions of other readers, it is, nevertheless, a revealing question. While it calls for further meditation, it invites also a negative answer. In the opinion of that Czechoslovakian Communist, who professed to be an ideal Marxist, *The Quiet Don* should not have been published. Apparently the ideal Czechoslovak Communist thought that the novel does not express the ideology or the criterion of the Soviet-Marxist concept of reality.

During the terror years of the mid-thirties, when Sholokhov worked on the last part of this novel, an attempt was made to eliminate him (see page 129f.). The attempt failed, through unexpected interference and unforeseen circumstances. The attempt can be interpreted as a fear that as long as the novel was not yet finished, the Soviet authorities had every reason to mistrust the young author. They were not sure how he would lead and conclude his hero, and wanted to prevent the undesired, i.e. un-Marxist, ending of the novel.

Sholokhov's masterpiece proves once more that talent cannot be restricted by one ideological or any other norm, that it breaks all the norms and standards imposed upon it, and re-evaluates all values and criterion anew. Sholokhov's strength lies in his very personal attitude toward his work, free of any external coersion, in his loving and inexorable presentation of his central character, and in his concept of reality as he himself saw and experienced it.

This we will seek to discuss and to prove in our presentation. At this point it must be said that *The Quiet Don* is the last and the only work by Sholokhov to which he gave the free course of his personal expression. His next novel, *Virgin Soil Upturned,* bears very strong marks of the Marxist-Leninist concept of reality. Saying this we do not give our judgment on the novel's artistic performance and qualities. What we are saying is only that Sholokhov, having assumed the Leninist concept of the party principle in art, was no longer free to express his very personal concept of reality as seen from his own vantage point. *Virgin Soil Upturned* expresses the point of view of his Party.

NOTES AND REFERENCES

1. Some important literature to the question of Socialist Realism is: A. Ivashchenko, "K voprosu o kriticheskom realisme i realisme sotsialisticheskom" in *Voprosy Literatury*, 1957, n. 4, pp. 46ff.; V. Shcherbina, "O sotsialisticheskom realisme," *Voprosy Literatury*, 1957, no. 4, pp. 3-30; E. Tager, "Spory o realisme," *Voprosy Literatury*, 1957, no. 4, pp. 71-82; D. Ta marchenko, "K sporam o realisme," *Zvezda*, 1957, no. 10, pp. 172-180; S. Petrov, "O edinstve literatury sotsialisticheskogo realisma," *Moskva*, 1958, no. 12, pp. 184-202; and his *Problemy realisma v khudozhestvennoi literature*, M. 1968, pp. 21, 216, 225, 244-245, 249, 270-273, 279ff.; L. I. Trofimov, *Osnovy Teorii Literatury*, M. 1959, p. 298ff.; V. Asmus, "O sotsialisticheskom realisme," *Voprosy Literatury*, 1957, no. 5, pp. 98-115.

2. Cf. Helmut Gollwitzer, *The Christian Faith and the Marxist Criticism of Religion.* Scribner's Sons, New York, 1970. "If reality contradicts the doctrine—then, in good Hegelian fashion—so much the worse for reality." Page 102.

3. V. V. Gura, F. A. Abramov, *M. Sholokhov, Seminarii,* Leningrad, 1962, p. 157.

4. Cf. Stalin, *Sochineniia*, vol. 12, M. 1949, p. 112. English edition, *Works*, M. 1955, p. 118.

5. About the new edition of *The Quiet Don* and its unreserved acceptance by the critics. See: L. Iakimenko, "Novoe izdanie Tikhogo Dona" in *Literaturnaia gazeta*, Aug. 10, 1954, pp. 3-4. Iakimenko expressed not only pleasure but also approval of the corrected version. To the question of the revised text see: Jürgen Rühle, *Literature and Revolution:* A Critical Study of the Writer and Communism in the Twentieth Century, New York, 1969. Translated from the West German edition of 1960. Cf. Chapter on Sholokhov, *The Epic of the Cossacks,*

pp. 58-77.   Cf. also David H. Stewart, "The Textual Revolution of *The Silent Don* in: *The American Slavic and East European Review,* vol. XVIII, April, 1959, pp. 226-237.

Introduction II

THE MAN AND HIS CRITICS

When written sources such as diaries, letters, drafts, and various other documents are not yet available, the author's intentions and motives remain hidden. It may prove then to be a difficult task to try to investigate the literary work of such an author. Sholokhov is one of these cases. Despite very numerous monographs and research articles about him, many facts about his life and activity remain unknown to this date. Many aspects of his life and work have not yet been researched.

Sholokhov is approached by his critics and reading audience with a definitive, preconceived opinion, perhaps more so than anyone else in Soviet literature. In Sholokhov's case, this opinion takes the form of a more or less official attitude toward him. As literary study in the Soviet Union is motivated more by the heart and sentimental attitude than by reason and objective analysis, to change the established opinion or to introduce a new aspect into it is barely possible. Sholokhov has continuously identified his literary work with all Soviet literature. Almost from its very beginning to recent years, he has stood like the voice or symbol of its flowering and its success. His name has been canonized and posed as the norm for the whole of Soviet literature. To change the opinion about him would mean to change the opinion about the whole of Soviet literature. No one would ever dare to take such a step. The canon is applied in practice, but not analyzed.

If the writer Sergei Timofeevich Aksakov, like many of his contemporaries, was afraid that every touch of the government to his literary fame, however benevolent, would darken it,[1] then Sholokhov, like the commanding majority of his contemporary writers fearlessly identified his name with the government and its official ideology, offering his literary talent to the service of the ideology.

Another writer, Boris Pasternak, an older contemporary of Sholokhov, took an entirely different position. In his address at the First Congress of Soviet Writers in Moscow in 1934, turning to his colleagues, Pasternak warned: "Don't sacrifice the person for the sake of a scheme. In the great warmth which the people and government surround us, the danger in becoming a literary official is too great. We should keep away from this favor in the name of the great, active, and truthful love for the native land and all the contemporary, great people."[2]   Setting on this thorny path, Pasternak remained faithful to the end.

Sholokhov entered into the Soviet literature when Soviet literature itself was being born. Being written or published at that time were works which subsequently became established as Soviet classics: Vsevolod Ivanov's *War Train* and *The Partisans* (1921), Fadeev's *The Flood, Against the Current* (1923), and then *The Rout* (1924), Furmanov's *Chapaev* and *The Mutiny*, Fedin's *Cities and Years* (1924), poems by N. Tikhonov, E. Bagritskii, and novels, tales, and short stories by L.

Leonov, A. Malyshkin, and many others. These works spoke of a new current of young strength in Soviet literature when Sholokhov appeared.

For a few years Sholokhov remained unrecognized by the RAPP critics (from the Russian Association of Proletarian Writers), the Formalists, or even Gorky.[3] After the first two volumes of *The Quiet Don* were published, RAPP critics saw in Sholokhov only an epigone, without his personal creative individuality. They attacked him for absence of ideological background, and even for being alien to proletarian literature, saying that he was serving as a conductor for hostile *kulak* ideology in Soviet literature, that he was justifying the White Cossack uprising. They saw in him a counterrevolutionary writer who was forcing harmful ideas into Soviet literature. The Formalists found in Sholokhov a direct pupil of Tolstoi and a continuer of the Russian nineteenth-century literary tradition. They found the peculiarities of *The Quiet Don* to be found only in its concern with the way of life *(byt),* physiological details and eroticism.

Gorky, having recognized Sholokhov's talent and seeing in him an author who had presented a truthful and talented picture of the Civil War and the great revolutionary events which kept pace with life, all the same saw in him only a chronicler of the Cossack province, interested only in his native Don. Like the *Rappovtsy* (critics from Proletarian Literature), Gorky saw Sholokhov's main fault in that he did not clearly isolate the author's position from the position of his hero, Grigorii Melekhov.

Closest to the understanding of Sholokhov came the

critics from *Pereval,* "The Pass" Association.   Judging
the novel to be a great work, they saw in it true artistic
achievements, though scoring it as merely a description
of a way of life.

Although Sholokhov himself was a *Rappovets* (he had
joined the RAPP in 1924), because he lived far from
Moscow, he remained aloof from literary groups and
from all the ofttimes bitter and cruel polemics which
were bursting out among the literary groups.   Even later,
after the dissolution of all literary groups and associ-
ations and the formation of a single Association of
Soviet Writers, Sholokhov deplored and criticized the
factionalism among the writers of the Association.

Recognition came to him only after the publication
of the first volume of *Virgin Soil Upturned* and the
third volume of *The Quiet Don* in 1932.   A decree of
the Central Committee of the Party "On the Rebuilding
of Literary Organizations" on April 23, 1932, also
played a fundamental role in the re-evaluation of Sholokhov's work.

Immediately, Sholokhov became known and recognized by everyone as one of the leading writers in the
method of Socialist Realism.   The former critics from
the RAPP went even further, proclaiming that he had
always been a writer of Socialist Realism.   He was proclaimed a pupil of Gorky and a follower of Mayakovsky.
Sholokhov at once became a writer of the Gorky school.
From that time on, his writing was taken to the service
of the country and its interest.   Critics proclaimed that
his works told the truth to the world about the Soviet
nation and armed the laborers with historical experience.   Party and Soviet workers who were assigned to

work in rural areas began to study Sholokhov's works attentatively, especially *Virgin Soil Upturned,* gathering from it the popular wisdom and experiences of Party guidance and imitating Sholokhov's hero, Davydov. The collective farm workers in their turn expected from the party functionaries the qualities depicted by Sholokhov in his positive, wise heroes.

As in its time the first volume of *Virgin Soil Upturned* fulfilled a large role in the policy of collectivization, the second volume in 1960 was taken as a means of arming the country in the struggle for upgrading the agriculture. Like the first volume, the second turned out to be very effective. *Virgin Soil Upturned* was looked upon as a textbook of life which told about the toilers of the country.

In like manner, Sholokhov's works were taken for arming the country during years of war with Germany. They seemingly taught and helped people to fight and conquer.

Moreover, the significance of the writer Sholokhov was not only that his works served the Soviet people, but also that they served other peoples of the world as well, such as the Chinese people in their struggle against Japanese invaders. In China, *Virgin Soil Upturned* taught the people vigilance, the skill of recognizing the enemy, courage before the enemy, and most of all, collectivization of agriculture. In Viet Nam Sholokhov's works taught the people to struggle successfully against foreign oppressors.[4] Sholokhov everywhere lent his fresh, fruitful support to the development of progressive literature in the whole world.

But criticism did not elaborate what his influence

actually was. Critics did not go beyond their declarative pronouncements. Briefly, Sholokhov's significance was measured in how he glorified his native land, and that with his works he seemingly demonstrated the fruitfulness of the connection of literature with the life of the people.

The text of Sholokhov's work was not studied carefully. Sometimes critics misconstrued his text, constructing their own ideal heroes and conceptions which were entirely different from those presented by the author, or else changed them beyond recognition. The critics were not interested in the real Sholokhov, but only in an author, who was fitted to their scheme.

The merits of Sholokhov's book, like those of all other writers, were determined by criteria or usefulness, actuality of theme, programmed actions, tendentious ideas. They were not judged by those internal qualities such as how they were written, but by criteria such as what they were written about. Such themes as collectivization, industrialization, the theme of the leader and teacher of the proletariat, defense of the fatherland were considered not only as timeless but a matter of honor for writers.

The works of Sholokhov, like those of his fellow writers, were considered as historical commentaries or illustrations of events. Thus, Lezhnev wrote that *The Quiet Don* must be studied collating it with the historical facts of the Civil War on the Don, that is, with the reality which was reflected in the multi-volumed novel.[5] Lezhnev reproached criticism because in studying *The Quiet Don* it left unaccounted for the historical reality of the past which the writer presented in the novel.[6]

If a work of literature thus reflected historical reality, then the task of the critic had no other function than to comment on those events according to the novel. A different historical reality besides the author's reality did not exist. Criticism inexplicably overlooked the fact that Sholokhov's works reflected not historical reality but only the author's own understanding of reality. In addition, criticism didn't see that a literary work in no case can distort nor present reality objectively. If criticism declared that Sholokhov recreated reality truthfully, it must be understood that this concept of ideal reality existed already in the minds of critics, independent of Sholokhov's presentation. In like manner, if critics often emphasized that a certain work distorts reality, then this must be understood as really saying that the critics created for themselves some kind of ideal concept of reality which did not, could not, and did not have to coincide with the author's concept of reality. In this case, criticism refused to accept the work as it was, and the author could not understand the critics.

Critics did not study Sholokhov's works in essence: they did not consider those essential questions such as the attitude of the author to his characters, or the formal questions of stylistic structure of his works. What interested criticism were only the questions raised by the author, basically of an ideological, intellectual or emotional order, such as how the heroes managed their problems, or how they fulfilled the tasks assigned by the Party. The attitude of the author to his heroes and the questions raised by the author did not interest the critics; they were interested in the problems and the heroes themselves. Thus, discussion of literary problems was always transformed into a discussion of ideological and political problems. This turned out to be much easier than literary study.

Having taken such a course, criticism turned away from literature itself, and was not able to gain an understanding of Sholokhov's work or of his characters, especially those of the characters who could not be placed in definite ideological categories.

NOTES AND REFERENCES

1. Cf. S. Mashinskii, "Introduction," in S. M. Akaskov, *Sobranie Sochinenii v chetyrekh tomakh,* vol. 1, Moscow, 1955, p. 57.

2. Boris Pasternak, *Stikhi, 1936-1959, Articles and Addresses,* Ann Arbor, University of Michigan Press, 1961, p. 218.

3. Data on Sholokhov discussed in this introduction are to be found in V. V. Gura, F. A. Abramov, *M. Sholokhov, Seminarii,* Leningrad, 1962. See also: Richard Hallet, "Soviet Criticism of *Tikhii Don,* 1928-1940" in *The Slavonic and East European Journal,* vol. XLVI, no. 106, Jan., 1968, pp. 60-74.

4. Gura, Abramov, p. 107.

5. Lezhnev, *Put' Sholokhova. Tvorcheskaia biografia,* Moscow, Sovetskii pisatel', 1958.

6. *Ibid.,* p. 11.

BEGINNINGS

Sholokhov is the man of one book and of one hero. All his works, with a few exceptions, are about the Don Cossack. He shows the Don Cossack in times of peace, in the German War, in the Civil War, again in time of peace, but filled with bitter social strife, in the years of collectivization, and again in war, and finally the fate of the Don Cossack after the war. Even when the hero is not a Cossack, like Stockman or Davydov, his life nevertheless is connected with the Don area.

His hero, again with a few exceptions, is the simple Cossack, a man from the soil, a laborer who is attached to his home and to his work, because it is his vocation in life. He is always a member of a certain family, and of a certain social class. Sholokhov's main concern is the social consciousness of his Cossack hero. He never depicts his hero outside of his social relations, never without a social issue. Sholokhov seems to have no interest for other aspects of people and their lives.

The theme of his work is thus limited, geographically and socially. It is not the quiet Don, but a very turbulent one, with its troubled and unquiet people, that serve as the main theme to Sholokhov's work.

Sholokhov is himself a son of this Don. But he is not a Cossack. However, he was adopted by the Don as he in turn has adopted for his home the Don which he loved so much.

Mikhail Aleksandrovich Sholokhov was born on the Don, in the hamlet of Kruzhilinin, Veshenskaia *stanitsa* (the former District [*oblast'*] of the Don Cossack Warriors, now the Veshenskii *raion*), into a family of *raznochinets,* natives of the Riazan province. His father worked as a clerk or manager in various business and industrial enterprises, at a steam mill and others. According to the testimony of the writer, his father, till his death in 1925, often changed professions. At one time he was a cattle buyer. Once he also farmed on land which he purchased. In autobiographies written at different times, Sholokhov spoke variously in each about his father's professions. Our data here is taken from the autobiography written in 1931. In the autobiography of 1934, Sholokhov stated only that his father worked as a hired man since his youth. This is understandable. With the growth of his fame as a Soviet writer, he had to stress those aspects of his origin which were closer to the proletarian ideal.

The writer's mother was half-Cossack, half-peasant. In later years, speaking on various occasions to Ukrainian audiences, the writer liked to stress that his mother was a Ukrainian from the Chernigov area. In one autobiography Sholokhov stated that he and his mother owned land: the mother as the widow of a Cossack, and he as a Cossack's son. In 1912 Sholokhov's father, Aleksandr Mikhailovich, adopted Mikhail.[1] Now Sholokhov became one of the petty bourgeois, a *meshchanin.* As such, he had to transfer the land to his mother. Non-Cossacks did not have the right to own land on the Don.

The writer's childhood was spent in various hamlets. Not much is known about his childhood, however. Either his biographers, to whom all data were accessible,

were not interested in the writer's childhood ye
there was much that they were unable to clarify. /
himself Sholokhov speaks very modestly. He has
given much information about his childhood years, or
about the schools where he studied, about his early
activities as a writer.

For the elementary education of the future writer,
his father was able to hire a private tutor. This was
not only unusual, but even impossible for a father
who worked as a hired man. In all likelihood, the
writer's father belonged to the upper middle class. Sholokhov's former private tutor, Timofei Timofeevich
Mrykhin, told about this much later, when Sholokhov
had already been glorified and "canonized."[2] The
memoirs of the former private tutor could have served
as a rich source of the writer's childhood, but, unfortunately, they are entirely biased. Just as the ancient
Russian Saints' Lives had to represent the unusual deeds
and saintliness of the ascetics from their very childhood
and even from the time they were in their mothers'
wombs, Sholokhov's former teacher presented his illus-
trious pupil in the same vein. Aside from a few general
uninformative remarks about the unusual aptitude and
diligence of little Misha, he stated nothing concrete
about the writer's parents or about the pupil himself.

In 1912 Mikhail was sent to preparatory school in
Karginovskaia *stanitsa.* From 1914 to 1918 he studied
in the boy's *gymnasias* of Moscow, Boguchar, and the
Cossack *stanitsa* of Veshenskaia. Here is how Sholokhov himself talked about his gymnasia days in conversation with various people: "Not having finished the
Karginovskaia school, I enrolled in the preparatory class

of one of the Moscow *gymnasia*. . .I studied in Moscow for two or three years, and then continued my studies in the Boguchar *gymnasia*. For a few months in 1918 I studied here in Veshenskaia."[3]

Here, one is struck most of all by his complete neglect of his days in the *gymnasia*. It is as if Sholokhov wants to completely forget them, or strike them out of his life. He is not able, or, more likely, doesn't even want to remember in which *gymnasia* he studied. He does not know the exact duration of time he spent in Moscow. Despite the customary keen interest of Soviet historiographers in the childhood years of famed people, none of Sholokhov's biographers has taken the trouble to look for the school notes which might have been preserved about the former pupil. What he read, what especially interested him, as well as many other facts, remain unknown to this day.

Practically nothing is known about the post-school years of the writer. In the autobiography of 1931 he wrote laconically: "During the Civil War I was on the Don." Probably in those years he had no time for school. However, he must have done something, read something, been interested in something. Up to 1920 the Don area was under the domination of the White Armies.

Beginning in 1920, that is, from the final consolidation of Soviet authority on the Don, Sholokhov set to work on various jobs in the community. Here is what he stated about himself: "From 1920 I worked and knocked about in the Don area. For a long time I was a food requisition agent for the government. I chased after bands. . .and they chased after me. Everything went as prescribed. I happened to be in several scrapes, but in present days this is forgotten."[4] Once he worked as a teacher in the program for the liquidation of illiteracy. His work as a requisition agent is reflected in several of his early stories.

In 1922 Sholokhov was 17 years old. Behind him were four years of gymnasia. With the final consolidation of Soviet power and especially after the country's transfer to the New Economic Policy, the job of food requisition agent was no longer needed. The youth had to find new work. In those years this was not difficult. Young Sholokhov's wishes and plans for the future are unknown to us, but whatever his motives were, in October of 1922 the seventeen-year-old youth suddenly appeared in Moscow. His wish was to enroll in the *rabfak,* i.e. worker's preparatory school, to continue studying. But for some reason he did not enroll in the *rabfak,* and had to work instead. Having appeared at the labor exchange agency, and being questioned as to his profession, he replied that he was a food requisition agent. But in Moscow at the end of 1922, there was really no demand for such a profession. Sholokhov had to work as a common laborer. In August of 1923, after a few weeks of unemployment, the labor exchange agency assigned him to the post of accountant on the management staff of an apartment house in Presna. In his 1934 autobiography Sholokhov briefly stated that he was pursuing intense independent studies to pass university level exams.[5] But as before, we know nothing about the nature and extent of his independent studies.

Also unknown is exactly when Sholokhov began to think about writing. In September, 1923, that is, less

than a year after his arrival in Moscow, his first feuilleton, "The Test" appeared in the Komsomol newspaper,
Iunosheskaia pravda under the signature "M. Sholokh."
After five weeks a second feuilleton, "The Three" appeared in the same newspaper. One must assume that
probably these first, printed stories determined the path
of the future writer. Later in a conversation with an
Izvestia correspondent in 1940, Sholokhov himself admitted that he first felt inclined toward literary work
only after he came to Moscow in 1922 and when his
first feuilletons were published.[6] At that time he had
become associated with the literary group of young
proletarian writers, the *Young Guard*. It was easy for
Sholokhov's generation to enter into literature. Besides
young Sholokhov, several other young beginning writers
with whom he often met, were close to the group:
Iu. Libedinskii, V. Gerasimov, M. Svetlov, M. Golodnyi,
and Artem Veselyi. The writer A. Fadeev sometimes
would join the group also. They were all concerned
with the questions of literary craftsmanship and plot.
The notable critics Viktor Shklovskii and O. Brik sometimes were invited for discussions and lectures to the
young writers. At that time Sholokhov was working on
his *Stories of the Don*.

Early in 1924, in the *stanitsa* Bukanovskaia on the
Don, Sholokhov married Maria Petrovna Gromoslava-
skaia, whom he had already known before his departure
to Moscow. After the wedding he again left for Moscow, but in May of that same year he returned to the
Don to collect material for his future stories.

In April 1924, his third and last feuilleton, "The
Inspector," appeared in the newspaper *The Young Len-*

inist. In December, 1924, the same newspaper published his first short story, *The Birthmark.* Later Sholokhov declared more than once that he considered his serious literary activity to have begun only with the publication of that story. In December of that same year, Sholokhov joined the membership of the Russian Association of Proletarian Writers, RAPP. At about that time his future seemed to be wholly determined. From 1925 he began contributing systematically to many magazines and newspapers that published his stories.

From May 1925, his stories began to be issued by the state publishing house as separate booklets for mass circulation. In the beginning of 1926, publishing house *New Moscow* brought out the first collection of his stories, under the general title *Stories of The Don,* with a preface by Serafimovich; and in the autumn of that same year a second collection, the *Azure Steppe* was published.

It is difficult to establish the exact date, but probably by the middle of 1925 Sholokhov had begun to think about a large novel. In the summer of that year, he left Moscow and settled in his wife's native *stanitsa,* Bukanovskaia, where he began to collect material for a projected epic canvas, *Donshchina,* in which he had thought to depict the Civil War on the Don. But he was soon forced to leave his projected novel and to begin a new one, in which he intended to depict the Cossacks' life more broadly, against an historical background of the Civil War on the Don. The new novel was to become *The Quiet Don.*

With the appearance of the first volume of *The Quiet Don* began a new period in his writing career. The

riting of short stories turned out to be only a prepara-
ory stage to the larger accomplishment of creating a
four volume work.

His three small feuilletons stand apart from the early
stories and from the whole work. In the feuilletons one
is struck not only by an unusual freedom in the selection
of themes, but also by the lack of any preconceived
conclusion. Thus, in the feuilleton "The Test," which
Sholokhov presented as a true incident taken from life
in the Dvinskii region, Tiutikov, as a former party member, was instructed to test the political reliance of
Pokusaev, the secretary of a local party cell. The test
was unusual. It ended with the one being tested sound-
ly thrashing the tester, and in this way he convinces the
former Communist of his reliability. Where the ending,
as well as the idea of the test itself, is concerned, the
author lets the reader be the judge.

In the feuilleton "The Three," a conversation takes
place between three buttons. From their different
worlds and after various incidents they turned up on the
windowsill in the room of a certain yardkeeper. All
three relate their bygone lives and experiences. It is
difficult to find out what the author wanted to say by
means of the innocent conversation of three lost buttons. Perhaps the interpretation may be found in the
fact that one of the buttons turned up on the sill after a
life in the aristocratic world, and now had to adapt to
the conditions of a simple life. Or perhaps even more
simply—this could be taken as the departure of the old
world with its established comforts.

The third feuilleton, entitled "The Inspector,"[7] re-
minds one of Gogol's *The Inspector General.* Kosobu-

grov, being assigned to work among farm laborers, was mistakenly accepted (as Gogol's Khlestakov once was) for the inspector general from the Workers-Peasants Inspection Administration. When it was discovered that he was not the inspector, he was beaten up and arrested as well.

There is neither heroic pathos, nor unusual revolutionary romance in the feuilletons. There are no messages, either. Reflected here simply is life, observed in the early years of Soviet authority, when much was still confusing and unclear in the system and society.

The three feuilletons, small and insignificant as they are, reveal, nevertheless, features which remain inherent in later Sholokhov as well. First, there is the absence of the author's characteristics, presented by his own words. Any given characteristic is achieved by means of the participants' actions and by their words. It is as if the author were not present in his stories.

One further feature of young Sholokhov is the individualization of his participating characters. The characters do not appear to be classified into certain groups and divisions. This is achieved not through the author's words, but solely through the actions of the characters themselves. There is also a certain reticence in his stories. The conclusion is never revealed by the author. The reader himself must form his own conclusions.

But of course it would be premature to try to detect in Sholokhov's early stories traits that are characteristic of the future author of *The Quiet Don*.

The young author was not concerned with polishing his first stories. The following fact testifies to this. In the early part of 1924, Sholokhov sent to the editorial staff

of the newspaper *Molodoi Leninets* one of his first
stories, which he entitled *The Beasts.* The story was
not accepted, but, as was the practice in those years, a
review appeared in the same newspaper, written by the
well-known proletarian poet Aleksandr Zharov, who at
the time performed the role of literary consultant and
manager of the newspaper's mailbox. Zharov wrote
that, though written in a rich, graphic language, the
piece was not quite a story, but more of a sketch.
Zharov advised the beginning literateur to work on the
story and to introduce more action.[8] In all likelihood
a long correspondence regarding this story ensued between Sholokhov and Mark Kolosov, editor of the newspaper *The Young Leninist,* a fact evident from a subse-
quent letter of Sholokhov to Mark Kolosov, written
from the Don in May of 1924. From this letter it is
evident that Kolosov saw the main deficiencies of the
story in the lack of ideological content. The story was
written "neither to them, nor to us," i.e. neutrally.
Sholokhov stubbornly protested against such an interpretation of the story. "I wanted to show that a man,
who had killed his father in the name of the revolution
and thus considered to be a 'beast', (of course, in the
eyes of the 'slobbering intelligentsia') died to save a
baby. That is what I wanted to show, but perhaps it
didn't come out as I wanted. The story definitely aims
at this goal. Read it in its entirety to the editorial staff,
and you will be able to alter it according to your own
competent judgement."[9] It follows from this quote, in
the first place, that the author himself was not sure of
the clear realization of his intention—"perhaps it didn't
come out as I wanted"—and, in the second place, that

he thought it wouldn't be hard to correct or alter his story. This story was published later in *The Young Leninist* in February of 1925, under the new title *Produce Commissar.*

This was not Sholokhov's first published story. The first was *The Birthmark,* which appeared in December 1924, in that same newspaper, *The Young Leninist.* As much as Sholokhov's three feuilletons did not appear in any earlier collection of his works, the critics considered that the literary biography of the writer must have begun with the story *The Birthmark.* Only in the publication of his collected works in 1962 did Sholokhov include his first three feuilletons in an appendix to the seven volume edition.

In the above quoted letter, one expression deserves our attention. I have in mind "the slobbering intelligentsia." This is a typical propaganda expression of those years, which has remained in use to this time. It expresses contempt toward the Russian nineteenth century intelligentsia. The refusal of the Russian intelligentsia to be guided by abstract ideas of the Bolshevik Party was and remains, in the eyes of the Bolsheviks, a refusal to serve the people. The Bolsheviks, having accepted the dialectic of expediency as the sole foundation of their decisive actions, were not able to understand the indecision of the Russian intellectuals, who as the sole criteria for their behavior and service recognized only their uncompromising conscience. The Bolsheviks called the intelligentsia "slobbering." Sholokhov seemed to have no need to repeat this propaganda slogan, which already in those years had become a trite expression. If he did repeat it, then it was only from ignorance on his part. How could a youth, having studied two or three years in one of the Moscow gymnasia, know about the selfless sacrifice and courage of the Russian intelligentsia? It was not at all slobbering.

If the young writer was not sure of the clear formulation of his intention in one of his early stories, then it must be said that it is striking how quickly maturity came to him.

At the foundation of the majority of the *Stories of the Don* the author laid his personal experiences, gathered by his first-hand participation in events having occurred during the Revolution and Civil War on the Don. Sholokhov did not need to represent the reality of the epoch, because the epoch, through his experience, was automatically and simply reflected in his stories. They literally smell of powder and blood. This was a time when man seemed to be only a blind toy in the hands of some great elemental and incomprehensible force. The storms penetrated to the remotest corners, affecting, first of all, the social relationships and conflicts of the population. The stories are built around the sharp conflicts between the social forces and their bearers. In respect to harsh reality, Sholokhov had much in common with his contemporaries, like Babel' or even Pil'niak.

It is possible to discern three major subjects in Sholokhov's early Don Cossack theme: first, the subject of the biological struggle for life, second, the social conflict, and third, the power of the Cossack soil. The author's theme, the Don Cossack and his life, being already limited in itself, revolved in his early stories mainly around these three subjects.

In the subject of the biological struggle for life, the most dominant note of the author was the cruelty of man to man. It seems that cruelty attracted Sholokhov in a special way. Very often Sholokhov's man was not able to account to himself as to what kind of struggle it was, and why it was waged. For his heroes this was not a struggle between the old and the new ideas, but simply a struggle for a place in life. In this exactly lay the tragedy of the times as reflected in the early Sholokhov.

Sholokhov did not pose any problems or assignment for himself. Thus, he did not need to draw any conclusions, or solve any riddles. Consequently, there are no answers in his stories. Nor was he seeking the meaning of life, its secrets, or its destination.

His realism is the realism of the naked eye. There are no depths or heights in his text. All is visible on the surface. Nor is there a hidden meaning in his text. Everything that the author saw, thought, and felt, he consecutively and consistently engraved on paper.

Sholokhov, it seems, created an apocalyptic picture, where man rose against man, brother against brother, son against father, and father against sons. Everyone became brutal and cruel to extremes, everyone followed his own laws. Everyone, it seemed, concentrated on one main interest, which is called the instinct to preserve a place in life, as well as life itself. Feelings of love or concern about the small and helpless gave way to that submerged but vital and strong instinct. It seemed that nothing more remained in man aside from that dark, blind force of instinct, driving him to the struggle. Brutality seemed to have reached its limits. Sholokhov's hero acts as if not of his own will. He is driven by some force urging him on to vengeance and murder. He cannot explain to himself why and for what purpose he leads such a life. The author, too, does not account for this life. It seems he hid nothing, turned everything inside out, but gave no answers. This absence of a single, definite answer bespeaks the later author of *The Quiet Don.*

Yet it was not cruelty as such that attracted the author's attention. The horror encountered in life is juxtaposed to the most ordinary routine and everyday calm. In this, the young author did not correct the world, did not make the world better, or worse. He remained aloof from any ideological scheme.

The first story *The Birthmark* already seems saturated to the limit with the tragedy of those years. A father was with the Whites and his son with the Reds. For seven years the father was not at home and did not see his son. Likewise, the son did not know anything about his father.

When they met on the field of battle, they did not recognize each other. Only after the father had killed his son and, having taken his boots from him, had seen the birthmark, did he recognize his son. Life for the father then turned abhorrently senseless:

"Son!. . .Nikolushka! My own! . . . My own blood. Say one word only! Speak if you have the strength! How did this happen?"
Pressing him to his breast, the *ataman* kissed the hands of his son, growing cold in death, and, clenching his teeth to the damp steel of the mauser, shot himself in the mouth. (*Sochineniia,* Vol. 1, p. 14.)

The author was not interested in the victory or the justice of the Reds or in the cruelty of the Whites, but was interested only in the tragic episode. The theme is perhaps not original. World literature abounds with such themes, but by means of the entire development preceding the story, Sholokhov made of it his own theme, one typical of those years. He did not heighten or embellish this epic theme. There is no moral here either. The theme of the heroic epos was transformed by Sholokhov's pen into the most ordinary of episodes.

It was not enough to have a tragic ending. Sholokhov had to emphasize that the tragedy was entirely in vain, and that it really wasn't a tragedy, but a simple, senseless, and brutal happening. "But in the evening . . . a buzzard unwillingly darted away from the torn head of the *ataman*. Darted away and melted into the grey, autumn, colorless sky."[10]

There is no affirmative pathos. Everything ends in nothing, there is no heroic death.

Here is another example of the blind struggle where, without hate or desire, man is driven like a child's toy in the hands of an incomprehensible and dark force. In the story *The Family Man* a father relates his sad story to a stranger who happens by. The father was mobilized by the Whites, whereas his two elder sons went to the Reds. First, one of the sons fell prisoner to the Whites. The Cossacks forced the father to beat his own Communist son in order that the father demonstrate his loyalty to "the quiet Don."

"I stood on the steps," the father said, continuing his sad story. "I was thinking, Holy Mother, can it be that

I am going to kill my son?"... I looked at him, and my soul turned cold. . . . I understood there: if I don't kill him, then my own village will kill me, and the small children will be left poor orphans." (*Sochineniia,* Vol. I, p. 165.)

Sholokhov relates this briefly, without an author's interpretation and sentimentalism. The man seemed unable to act differently in that situation.

After a short time the second son fell to the Cossacks where the father was serving: "Here they beat him cruelly," related the father, "and said to me":

"Here's the order, Mikishara. Take your son to the staff. He is safe with you. He won't run away from his father."

"And God gave me reason. I thought: they assign me to escort my son, and they think that I'll let him go free. Then they'll chase, catch him, and kill me. . . ." (*Sochineniia,* Vol. I, p. 166.)

In saving his own life, and even more, fearing for the lives of his small children, the father had to kill his own son:

"You take, Vaniushka, the martyr's crown for me. You have a wife and one child, but I have seven small ones. If I would let you go, the Cossacks would kill me, and the children would go about the world begging alms." (*Sochineniia,* Vol. I, p. 168.)

No one asks Sholokhov's hero whether he would have been able to act differently. Neither does the author ask. He did not try to condemn or justify his hero.

Here is another example showing that there were neither innocent nor guilty people in those years of beastliness. I have in mind the story *The Offence,* written in 1925, but first published only in 1962. The drama of this story is not that of the Revolution. It belongs to the time of famine after the Civil War. In the famine year before the Blessed Virgin's day in the fall, Stepan, falling from exhaustion plowed his bit of land. The land was unfaithful, had not yielded anything that year, and was therefore not worth sowing. However, Stepan came with a bow to the perfidious land because there was a family of eight that remained from the son who had been killed in the war. They suffered terrible hunger during the winter. For spring they were given seed loans. Stepan transported the seed home on a team of oxen. From the station to the farm it was one hundred and fifty *versts.* At night in the wild steppe he was attacked by the hungry Tauridians. These were the Ukrainians of the Don, whose ancestors had settled there from the southern Crimean steppes in the time of Katherine the Great. They took the seed away from Stepan. Thus, his land was not sown. Everyone around was planting, but Stepan had nothing to plant.

Then, hay mowing took place. A pair of Stepan's oxen disappeared during the night from the hay-mowing operation. Searching for the lost oxen in one of the villages, Stepan saw and recognized one of the men who had taken seed from him last winter. Stepan acts as if not of his own will. Vengeance, dumb and as if impersonal, drives him. This is the vengeance of the deserted, seedless land. Having been recognized, the Tauridian did not even try to defend himself or resist. He seemingly understood that justice was not on his side, and to resist was not worth his strength. "The

Tauridian unexpectedly sat by the legs of a halted, sweaty horse, put his palms in the dust, and looked up at Stepan."[11] The end of the story is horrible and cruel.

The author never said a word about the truth or justice of life. In view of such bitterness, any kind of moralization, even the smallest, would have been out of place. And Sholokhov restrained himself from this.

The Tauridian, not trying to justify himself, was only asking for mercy. But blind vengeance does not know mercy.

> "Pray to God!" breathed Stepan, and crossed himself.
>
> "Stop! Wait! In God's name, I beg! What about the boy?"
>
> "I'll take him to my place. . . .Don't trouble your soul about him."
>
> "I haven't carted away the hay. . .oh! My farm will go to ruin. . . . And how can. . . .
>
> Stepan raised the pitchfork, held it above his head for a brief moment, and, feeling a mounting roar in his ears, thrust it with a groan into the soft body, which was impalled with a shudder of the teeth.
>
> He threw a handful of hay onto the stern, yellowing face, pressed to the earth, then climbed onto the wagon and took into his arms the little boy, who had dug himself into the hay.
>
> He walked away from the wagon with reeling, drunken steps, going toward the lights of the settlement, glimmering on the horizon. (*Sochineniia,* Vol. I, pp. 196-197.)

Here it should be mentioned that the Soviet Sholokhovist Iakimenko, who knew the story only through the manuscript which was preserved in the files of the Central Government Archives of Literature and History, cited quotations from it in his monograph, using "khokhol" everywhere instead of "Tauridian."[12] It could be assumed that this was Sholokhov's first version. In the latest, the most complete edition of his works, Sholokhov in 1962 changed the derogatory "khokhol" into "Tauridianin."[13] It is apparent that Sholokhov wanted to obliterate signs of Great Russian chauvinism in relation to the neighboring Ukrainians.

Sholokhov's stories are full of the cruelty of life. It seems that Sholokhov has some special predisposition toward the cruelty of man to man. But he is not unduly fascinated by descriptions of cruelty. The scenes may be cruel to the extreme, but they do not appear to be the author's goals in themselves. They are only a small fraction of life presented by him. He mentions the cruelty only in passing. The author does not sensationalize the cruelty and, in addition, does not moralize about it with a definite intention. A father may beat his son till he draws blood, not because he is especially cruel or blood thirsty or because he wants to beat him up. It is not premeditated, but happens rather as an accident. Of course this does not lessen the cruelty, but the author does not dwell on it and does not ponder upon it. A father hits a worker because the worker has broken a tooth of a mowing machine. The son makes a remark to the father for this, calling him a scoundrel. In answer, the father knocks the son off his feet and whips him with the horse's saddle girth till blood comes. Then:

> In the evening, when they returned home from the fields the father cut off a cherry stick, whittled it, and stroking his beard, thrust it into Ignat's hands:

"Go, son, go into the world, and when you learn some sense, come back again"—and smirked. (*Prodkomissar, Ibid.*, p. 28.)

Or a husband beats his wife, but saves her new-born baby. The wife had admitted to the husband that she had passed information to the Whites about the Red army. Her admission came while she was giving birth. "My heart here boiled in my breast, and I couldn't bear any more—I kicked her with my shoe and blood came from her mouth."[14] The whole story is written in *skaz* form, related by the hero.

To the scenes of cruelty one must add also the descriptions of hunger in the country, and death by starvation. In *Aleshka's Heart,* one hungry winter, not having seen bread for five months, Aleshka acquired some dry meat from a dead foal.

> Towards evening, having eaten some of the stringy meat, Aleshka's younger sister, the dark-eyed one, died.
> The mother lay for a long time face down on the earthen floor, then rose, turned to Aleshka, with trembling lips:
> "Take her by the legs."
> They took her! Aleshka by the legs, the mother by the curly hair, they brought her out to the garden into the ditch, and lightly covered her with earth.
> The next day a neighboring lad met Aleshka, who was crawling along an alley and said, picking his nose, and looking to the side:
> "Lesha, at our place a mare dropped her colt, and the dogs gobbled it up."
> Aleshka, leaning against the gate, was silent.
> "And the dogs also dug out your Niuratka from the ditch and ate up her insides. . . ."

Aleshka turned and went, silently, not looking around.

The lad, hopping on one leg, shouted after him:

"Our mama says that those buried without a priest and not in a cemetery, those the devils will eat in hell!. . .You hear, Lesha?" (*Aleshka's Heart, Sochineniia,* Vol. I, p. 47.)

There is a merciless and cruel consistency in this description. It is probably in this consistency that the strength and attractiveness of Sholokhov, the writer, is hidden. He steps back from nothing, hides nothing, and embellishes nothing. What is necessary to say, or what he wants to say, he says in full strength.

There is also humaneness in his descriptions of inhuman cruelty. A son, who had sent his father to execution for the concealment of grain, running from the pursuit of rebellious Cossacks, saves from certain death a baby, which was lying frozen along the road. He himself later falls into the hands of the Cossacks, where certain death awaits him.[15] This story was spoken of earlier. Sholokhov, in a correspondence with Kolosov, defended his tendencies from attacks of the RAPP group. (See above, p. 30.) Sholokhov himself insisted on the tendency in this story which his critics failed to see. In seeking a tendency, he, however, did not resort to idealization or easy moralization. In one other story, his hero saved a colt but he himself perished.[16] Here it is again apparent that the author did not choose to involve himself or his personal feelings in the events he described, thereby preserving a certain distance and aloofness through the work.

It was probably this kind of cruelty that British readers of Sholokhov's works had in mind when they reproached him for excessive cruelty.[17]

In conclusion, it must be said of the struggle of the biological instinct for life in Sholokhov's early work that the author in no way perceived the cruelty of human existence described by him as the natural regularity of life. A man acts brutally to his fellow man only when circumstances force him to act this way. He takes no pleasure in acting brutally and cruelly. Sholokhov's work does not create an impression that cruelty of life is a law-governed existence, but rather that it is a violation of this phenomenon we call life. Man should not be cruel to his fellow man. There is no reason for senseless cruelty. On the other hand, he did not preach the easy way out of the atrocities of life, either. He did not show the way, did not prescribe a program to improve life. He remained an artist, with his own subjective view of life and man.

The hero does not act blindly, as if not in control of his own will, in all of Sholokhov's early stories. Sometimes he realizes his own strength and often his weaknesses, and he struggles consciously, but still not less savagely, searching for a place in life. It is the struggle between the rich and the poor, between the general principles of wealth and poverty, which attracted Sholokhov's attention in his early work. Social inequality was the central conflict of the epoch. The Revolution and the following Civil War saw class rising against class, thus aggravating the social differentiation among the Cossacks. From here Sholokhov took his second theme: that of social conflict. He did not need to invent or especially sharpen this social conflict. Like every artist, he observed the conflicts in his everyday life and then registered them in his work. As a proletarian writer he could not look at life in any other way. It would be unrealistic to expect from him a different perspective of social life in the Don area during the Soviet power's first years there. An impartial perspective does not exist in regard to social conflicts. The young author's sympathies, as they should be, are on the side that was supported by the Soviet power: on the side of the poor. The secret of his art, however, is that he did not thrust out too much of his sympathy towards one side. At times he could even present the social conflict of the two sides equally, without justifying or disapproving either of them. Thus, under his pen the social conflict is then turned into a struggle for existence, where there is no right or wrong, but only the rich and poor, the people as they are.

Often Sholokhov's hero does not realize that this has to be a class struggle of the new against the old, and that he is the bearer of a certain ideology or idea. Thus, the social conflict in Sholokhov is again transformed into a struggle for a place in life and does not appear to be a struggle for betterment of the social conditions in life.

Here is one of his earliest stories, *The Shepherd,* in which social struggle should stand in the foreground, but in reality it does not. The representative of the local village committee propounds to appoint as shepherd a young lad, Grigorii, a *Komsomolist,* because he does not have any means of making a living. The village does not want Grigorii as shepherd because he is a Komsomolist, and does not believe in God, but the representative insists. Grigorii goes herding cattle with his sixteen-year-old sister, Duniatka. He herds and dreams how he will earn his bread, and how in autumn he will go to the city to study.   Grigorii wants to enroll in the Worker's School.   He would put Duniatka in some course of learning, too.   "In the city there are many various books."

But it did not happen that way.   Cattle began to die of sickness.   The elders tried to use their home remedies on the cattle.   They blamed the young shepherd because he did not believe in God.   Grigorii even wrote about this in the newspaper.   He wrote about the loss of cattle, about curing by sorcery, and about the injustice of the division of land in the village.   And one night, when Duniatka had gone to the village for provisions, two of those about whom Grigorii had written in the newspaper came to him and had their revenge by shooting him on the spot.

Duniatka goes away to the city alone, where there is Soviet authority, and where the proletariat is studying to govern the Republic.

"So it is said in Lenin's book."[18]   There is nothing in this story which could not have happened in those years.   But the matter is not so much what Sholokhov described, as *how* he described it.

The story is framed in such a way that the social conflict does not obtrude.   The struggle is more like a response to the deep, hidden, elemental forces unleashed by social inequality than like a conscious class struggle for a new social structure.   Of course, social inequality has always existed in the country.   What Sholokhov emphasizes here is not the struggle for a new system, but rather a moment in the general struggle, elemental and cruel, against social inequality.

The cruel and again elemental struggle is observed in

the story *Aleshka's Heart,* mentioned above. In the village there is hunger. Aleshka's fourteen-year-old body is swelling from hunger, for he has not seen bread for five months. Aleshka's younger, dark-eyed sister died, and they buried her in a ditch. The older sister was beaten to death by a rich neighboring woman, Makarchikha, who caught her stealing on her property. She beat her and threw her into a well. Aleshka saw this happen. He himself had been beaten half to death by that same rich neighbor when he had stolen into her cellar to drink milk. Now his mother also dies. At this time the rich neighboring woman is planning to buy the house from Aleshka's mother, which she wants to fix up for her son-in-law.

Aleshka was saved from certain death by starvation only because he was hired to herd the State procurement agency's horses. Later he was hired by one of the rich villagers, where he worked for food. Because Aleshka visited the community center, the master beat him. One night Aleshka overheard a secret conversation between his master and some strangers about a planned uprising in the village. Secretly, Aleshka conveyed this information to the political commissar in the procurement office, which of course, forestalled the success of the planned uprising.

What matters in this story is not that there is an obtrusive purpose, a tendency. After all, it is impossible to remain without some kind of proclivity when speaking about social conflict. Even when presenting social conflict as objectively as possible, one cannot remain entirely without some kind of sympathy or antipathy. It may be possible to pass over social conflict in silence, not to notice it, and not to write about it. But if a writer writes about conflict, he cannot write as if there were no conflict at all.

Sholokhov wrote at a time when the country was saturated with social conflicts. And he wrote about those conflicts. He could not write without exhibiting certain tendencies. The question is again *how* he presented his tendencies. Sholokhov took one very concrete event and presented it precisely as an event, without the broad generalizations so characteristic of Soviet literature, where every generalization acts not only as a conspicuous tendency, but as a program or idea. Sholokhov enclosed his instance of social conflict in a tight, rigid plot structure and stayed within that frame—that is, he did not generalize this single happening. By thus limiting the action of the story, he strengthened and intensified the plot and the action of the story that did take place. On the other hand, by limiting the action, Sholokhov seemingly narrowed the social conflict and reduced its significance. Neither Aleshka nor the rich local folk stand out as bearers of a social idea, or as fighters for a new or old social order. They act separately. individually, as the moment demands, not recognizing themselves as active participants in some kind of programmed struggle. These conflicts might have been described not only in Russia after the Civil War, but in other countries as well. These are universal human themes. Nowhere does the story raise a claim to be an obvious truth whose demands are unappealable, irrefutable, and intolerable.

Only very few stories did Sholokhov saturate with moral content. A conflict very much like the previous conflict, but more recognized by the participants as a class struggle, is observed in the story *Farm Laborers* (1926). A newly widowed mother said to her teen-age son Fedia: "Go son, hire yourself out to good people as a worker. I will go into the world. . .maybe in a year or two we'll knock about, collect enough money to buy a horse and then live our own life. . . . What do you think?"[19]

But to break away from poverty was not easy. And this is not so only on the Don. This is a universal theme. The poor man dreams of how he could earn more, but the rich man dreams of how to receive a worker's strength cheaply. Once Sholokhov's Fedia becomes a farm laborer, it is hard to break out. He had to work hard, but he earned trifles. "I'll work according to conscience; I'm not afraid of work. Salary—what you'll give," said Fedia to his employer, a rich Cossack.[20]

Fedor is taught to stand up for his rights not by some principled hero who has recognized the Soviet justice, but by another farm laborer like himself who, in addition, was a drunkard. This man's advantage was that he was a qualified machinist, indispensable for threshing. He demands good pay for himself, teaches Fedor to do the same, and sends him to the Komsomol cell. But for some reason the machinist himself was not a member of the Komsomol.

The Komsomol cell from a neighboring farm did, of course, stand up for Fedor. They instructed Fedor to sue his master for hiring a worker without a contract. They also accepted Fedor into their membership and guided him in organizing a new cell among other farm laborers. However, a new life did not begin for Fedor.

Again he had to become a farm laborer. But this time he had a good master. He continued to make plans to earn enough money and live by his own means as his own master, delivering his mother from poverty.

In this story there are many commonplace events which might fit any other situation or any other story. But there is also a concreteness of situation. One of the commonplace events is Fedor's acceptance into the Komsomol. The scene of acceptance is the same everywhere—devoid of individualized features. Other such scenes are the law-suit, the bitterness of the village's rich men against Fedor, and his beating.

But aside from these commonplace events there are original scenes in the story, such as the dreams of Fedor and of his mother of rising from poverty. Sholokhov noted these dreams very precisely, and individualized the characters.

On the whole, this is one of Sholokhov's few early stories in which he stands up as a social critic, a propagandist for social justice, and a fighter for a new life. This is practically the only story by the young author written in this vein, where his tendentiousness obtrudes while at the same time depicting the struggle between the old life and the new Soviet power.

Sholokhov's every story is saturated with struggle, but very rarely with that conflict between the new and the old orders of life. When the new order does appear, it does not stand out didactically as an advertisement for the new power.

Sharp family conflict saturates the story *Wormhole*, one of Sholokhov's best early stories about the Cossacks' peace-time way of life. Iakov Alekseevich's fifteen-year-

old son Stepka joined the Komsomol without the per-
mission or advice of his father. Another Cossack would
have taught Stepka with a club. But Iakov Alekseevich
is a cautious Cossack. Here is how Sholokhov draws
Iakov Alekseevich:

> Iakov Alekseevich—a man of the old make: wide-boned,
> stooping; a beard like a new millet broom,—resembling to
> a T those *kulaks* whom the artists with nothing else to do
> draw in the back pages of the newspapers. One thing not
> in common, however—his dress. Because of occupational
> necessity *kulaks* without fail are supposed to have a vest
> and squeeky shoes, but Iakov Alekseevich in the summer
> goes around in a sack-cloth shirt, unbelted, and barefoot.
> (*Sochineniia,* Vol. I, p. 237.)

With this characterization, Sholokhov seemingly wants
to say that not all *kulaks* have to look alike. In fact,
his hero resembles not a genuine *kulak,* but rather the
usual stereotyped caricature of a *kulak* drawn by an
idle artist. It is more like a satire on those artists who
portray *kulaks* as always being identical, and who do
not distinguish individual features. In addition, Sholokhov narrates that after Iakov Alekseevich had sold
an extra pair of oxen and dismissed a hired man, the
local Soviet had transferred him to the middle class
peasantry.

And now Iakov Alekseevich's younger son became a
Komsomolist. He does not stand for prayers any more,
does not observe fasts, and does not take the blessing
of the cross from the priest. From the story it is
obvious thus, that at first the influence of the Komsomolist on the family was very negative. There was no new

life in Stepka, but only a negation of the established
order. He broke away from his family. Iakov Alekseevich decided not to beat his son. In relating this decision
Sholokhov probably thought to comment on his hero's
prudence, that he was unlike other people who would
immediately administer a cruel beating. Iakov Alekseevich decided to reeducate his son: "From day to day
he made fun of the new authority, order, laws. . .he
thought to open the eyes of Stepka."[21]

The older brother also spoke to the younger:

> What plague do you need in the Komsomol?. . .This is all
> nonsense! It's a suitable trick of factory workers; they'll
> work eight hours—then off to the club or Komsomol, but
> we corngrowers can't do that. In summer, in work time,
> you'll drag through the night, but what kind of worker are
> you going to be the next day? Say, truthfully: do you
> want to get a job from the Komsomol? Did you join them
> for this purpose? (*Sochineniia*, Vol. I, p. 239.)

The reader cannot avoid feeling the fairness and justice in this reproach to the youthful *Komsomolist.* But
Sholokhov refrained from giving an answer to the repri-
mands, as if he wanted to let the reader himself draw
his own conclusions. Of course, looking at those times
when the Komsomol and the Soviet system had been
established in Russia, now, forty years later, a dispassionate answer is hardly possible. Today every reader
would be obliged to say that the Komsomol in those
years was a progressive factor and a guarantee for the
victory of the new life over the old. But at the time
when Sholokhov wrote this story, 1926, when the victory of the new system was not yet apparent, not to

give an answer to his brother's reproach, meant to remain neutral. And perhaps it was not for nothing that overzealous critics from Proletarian literature often attacked Sholokhov for his sympathy with the *kulak* ideology. In this story Sholokhov indeed did not disclose any new tendencies in the life of those years. New in the story was the presentation of the theme itself— concrete, saturated social inequality in the village, with detailed events.

And when at the end of the story the father and the eldest son beat Stepka, this happened not because he was a Komsomol member but because they were afraid that Stepka and his neighbor Prokhor had lost or maybe sold a pair of his father's oxen.

In conclusion it should be emphasized once more that the young author saturated every one of his stories with sharp conflict. It seems that Sholokhov did not know man outside conflict. His conflict was social, based on population stratification in the country and the traditional struggle of the poor against the rich from time immemorial. Sholokhov was not interested in anything else. If in Sholokhov there is tendentiousness—and it could not have been otherwise—then it is expressed indirectly—not by the author's interference in his heroes' lives or by the author's judgments and generalizations, but through the heroes themselves. As they are drawn into the actions of the story, Sholokhov's conflict loses its didactic and propagandistic significance. Struggle becomes more unconscious, elemental, as if without qualification. The heroes often do not understand the conflict and the world in which they live, and therefore act not according to any convictions or ideology but as they want, often instinctively, blindly, and cruelly.

There is something in Sholokhov's early stories which attracts the reader. In Chekhov, for example, there was something in his plays which made his audience, both men and women, weep, and which made youths kiss roses from his garden simply because they were from Chekhov's garden. In Chekhov this *something* was a definite tenderness of feeling, a helplessness which made the heart beat faster. Perhaps in Sholokhov it is the crudeness and straightforwardness which attracts the people of our time. In Chekhov's tenderness there was a definite helplessness and tragedy; in Sholokhov there can be felt a definite respect toward the victims of his brutalized men and toward man himself.

In regard to the third subject in Sholokhov's early work—the power of the soil—it seems that his heroes have a special, (I would like to say) Sholokhovian relationship to the land. The land plays a special role in the life of his Cossacks. The land is not only a source of food on which the Cossack works and for which he cares, but it is also the meaning of his existence. When he is deprived of the possibility of working on his land, the Cossack's life loses its meaning and full value. A twenty-five-year-old Cossack left as a cripple after the Civil War suffers, not because he is a cripple, but because he is not able to go about the land any more. Here is how his father tells about him:

. . .I noticed once. In the spring. I was herding sheep not far away. I looked and saw my Anikei crawling along the plowed ground. I thought, what is he going to do? And see: Anikei looked around, saw that there were no people near, so he fell down to the earth, faced down, embraced the lumps of dirt turned by the plowshare, squeezed them to himself, smoothed them with his hands, and kissed. He's twenty-five years old, and he never will plow in his life. Hence, he is suffering. (*Sochineniia*, Vol. I, p. 260.)

To a Cossack land, which does not yield a harvest is like a barren wife or, even worse, like an unfaithful wife. But the Cossack does not think of getting rid of a barren plot of earth. He will go to it with a bow and a kiss. He will embrace it and weep in the hope that some day it will give him life. A bad harvest paces along the earth with iron hoofs. The earth does not bear fruit. There is no grain even for seed. Nevertheless, the Cossack goes to the field secretly at night to look at the earth which has deceived him.

It was terrible for Stepan to go out beyond the burial mound, to gaze at the black plowed land, sprawled out like a corpse. He stood, hands loose, with trembling fingers, sighed, and cut the sigh short with a wheeze. (*Sochineniia*, Vol. I, p. 194.)

And so it was every night.

Describing this attitude to the land, the author again escaped the temptations of sentimentality. Nowhere did he stoop to cheap sympathy toward the poor Cossack whose family was deprived of food by the unfaithful land. Nowhere did he sink into a didactic tone.

As if to emphasize this special connection with the soil, the author not only makes his heroes kiss the earth, but also eat it. To confirm his oath, the Cossack must eat soil; a verbal oath is not enough. Only when ιe Cossack eats earth can one believe his oath. "Swear that you aren't for the Reds. And don't cross yourself, but eat the earth!" orders the chief of a band to one of the Cossacks.[22]

Only in one area did the author fail to escape emotional impregnation of his stories: in the description of his child heroes. One of these stories is *The Rascal* (1925). In the autobiography of November 14, 1932, Sholokhov himself recalled his early stories rather unflatteringly, calling them naive and childishly helpless. If it was possible, he would have repudiated the majority of them, thought the twenty-seven-year-old Sholokhov.[23]   At that time he had just published the third volume of *The Quiet Don* and the first volume of *Virgin Soil Upturned,* and thus had reached the climax of his literary glory. Later, however, he himself included all his early stories in all three editions of his collected works.

If the terms "naive and childish" are applied to his early stories, then *The Rascal,* in which adolescents or children act as heroes, might be first to deserve such a designation.

It seems that children as heroes in Soviet literature should not be treated as a part of the plot, taken directly from life and related to life, but rather should be used as a literary device.   Wherever they appear in Soviet literature, they unmistakably play only one role— to strengthen the author's ideological tendencies.   No author can remain impartial in relation to young heroes. Children in Soviet literature must perform heroic deeds, suited to their age of course, but which nevertheless are unusual deeds.   They must help the Red partisans or even Red Army detachments. Their dreams, too, are not ordinary dreams, but about Lenin, or revolutionary brotherhood. Sholokhov was not able to escape this scheme.

That from which the author refrained while dealing with grown-up heroes—personal involvement in events—he put into the mouths of boys. In the dialogue of the two boys in *The Rascal* it is impossible not to feel the ideological strain and, therefore, falsity. The son of a priest must be weak, sickly, malicious, vindictive, and a braggart. The son of the Red Army soldier, though also a braggart, is a truthful, heroic, direct braggart. It is incomprehensible why the Sholokhovist Iakimenko saw a purity and faithfulness in tone in precisely this story.[24] Having recognized an emotional tone in the story, Iakimenko himself imbued his analysis of Sholokhov's work with an emotional approach to literature. Thus, speaking about the story *The Rascal,* Iakimenko only reaffirmed the fact which had been narrated, eulogistically exalting Sholokhov's understanding of life and his heroes' attitude toward life.

The critic's task is not to elucidate the relationship of heroes to life. Such relationships are evident by themselves in the story: they are sewn with white thread everywhere, so to speak, and every reader sees them without the help of the critic. For this reason, literary criticism which analyzes the relationships between the heroes and the reader seems to be superfluous. The task of the critic is not to explain what the author has depicted, but more to explain how he depicted his hero and then to explain the relationship of the author to his hero.

In the story *The Rascal* there is none of that human charm of which Iakimenko speaks,[25] and neither is there any high psychological activity in the father's story about Lenin and the Revolution. Rather, in this story is reflected that legendary, apocryphal, posthumously created concept of Lenin's personality as a kind of all-Russian *bogatyr*. In the stories of the father to his seven-year-old son, and then in the child's understanding, Lenin appears to be omnipresent, omniscient, omnipotent, and, of course, always able to help in the personal misery of the boy's life.

This small hero accomplishes a feat worthy of his understanding of Lenin. First he helps the food requisitioning detachment find grain hidden underground at the priest's house, and then he reports the appearance of bandits in his village to the Red Army men. For this the seven-year-old boy had to gallop on a horse at night to a neighboring village. He dies with Lenin's name on his lips from an accidental bullet of the Red Army men, having succeeded, of course, in reporting the appearance of the band. This is very schematic, simple, unreal, and, almost anecdotal.

In regard to the language of the early Sholokhov, and the later Sholokhov as well, one may say simply that basically he neither created nor employed special linguistic means or a scheme to convey an impression or to attract the attention of the reader. Not serving as a means to achieve an effect or a goal, his language appears to be the goal itself, the self-sufficient essence of that which the author wanted to say. With very minor exceptions the new trends of search and modernism in the literary language of the Twenties did not touch the young author. He remained faithful to the language of traditional realism. The exceptions comprise only small fragments, subject to the influence of rhythmical prose. But they are too minor to merit any independent significance in discussing the language of the author.

The language of rhythmic prose is most evident in his first published story *The Birthmark*: *"Tianet narochnyi v koniushniu loshad', potom goriachim oblituiu."*[26] Here the rearrangement of the usual order of words in the sentence creates an impression, a diverse effect and melodiousness. This bears the stamp of poetry. Or, here is still another example of rhythmic prose. Usually Sholokhov creates such prose in descriptive pictures. *"Po kochkovatomu letniku, po koleiam, vetrami oblizattym, myshastyi zhidorozhnik kucheriavitsia, lebeda i pyshatki gusto i makhrovito lopushatsia."*[27] This is a description of a steppe road.

But soon Sholokhov freed himself from this experiment. The last stories were free of rhythmic prose.

Out of the twenty-five early stories published in Sholokhov's latest *Collected Works*, four are written in the genre of *skaz*, and three are partially *skaz*, that is, partially narrated by the hero himself. The author as an observer and narrator is absent in the *skaz*. In the *skaz* the hero himself, from his own point of view, though created and formulated by the author of course, tells the story. Usually this gives the author more freedom to operate with the language and with the motivation and theme of the story. The language becomes more individualized, as the author may stoop to somewhat crude and folksy speech. And the hero himself appears more colorful against the background of his language. Usually, stories written in the *skaz* form are shorter than the ordinary author's narration. It is as if the storyteller does not allow his speech to drag out and lose itself. Chronologically, the first of Sholokhov's stories written in *skaz* form was *Shibalkov's Seed.* A Red Army soldier, Shibalkov stands with his year-old son in the children's home and narrates to the manager his unhappy story. He wants to put his son in the care of the children's home. The story is written on many levels. Shibalkov delivers not only his own speech, but also the words of the Cossacks of his detachment and the words of Daria, the mother of his child, whom he had been forced to kill on the orders of his Red detachment. The purpose of Shibalkov's speech seems to be to persuade the manager to accept the child into the children's home. But in the course of the story, the emphasis is shifted and another theme of the story emerges: the treachery of Daria and the fate of the child.

> "Do you know, Iasha, who told the band that we didn't have any cartridges?" —and she looks at me serious like.
> "Who?" I ask her.
> "Me."
> "What have you done, you fool, got rabies? There is no time to talk. Be quiet, lie down."
> She starts again.
> "Death is standing at my head, I will confess before you, Iasha.... You don't know what a serpent you have warmed at your bosom."
> "Well, confess," I say. "The hell with you."
> There she lays it out. She talks, and beats her own head against the ground.

"I," she says, "by my own will I was with the band and slept with their chief Ignat'ev. . . . A year ago he sent me to your squadron, so I would communicate to them all the intelligence. Thus I pretended to be raped. I am dying, otherwise later on, I would have ruined your whole squadron."

Then my heart boiled over in my breast, and I could not stand it—kicked her with my boot and bloodied up her mouth. Then the seizures begin in her again, and I see— between her legs appeared a child. (*Shibalkov's Seed, Sochineniia*, Vol. I, p. 36.)

The stories *Family Man* and *The Azure Steppe* are written in semi- *skaz,* as is his much later story, *The Fate of a Man.* First the author created the appropriate setting. In *Family Man,* as in *The Fate of a Man,* the author needs a ferry on the Don. The ferry man uses the opportunity to relate to the passenger, a stranger, his woes. When the setting is created, the *skaz* begins. Once begun, the *skaz* is not interrupted by the author.

The Azure Steppe presents the same combination of the author's outward description and the personal story told by the hero. The author again has created the needed setting: the Don steppe, burning heat, a herd of sheep, "Grandfather Zakhar and Me." Grandfather Zakhar is the narrator of the simple story, which happened to his sons in the *Citizen's War.* His listener does not interrupt the grandfather's story in any way. Only in one place does the author allow Grandfather Zakhar to blow his nose; and at the end of the story the author again describes the Don steppe.

Despite the common theme and some common features, it was impossible to see features of the future author of *The Quiet Don* in his early works. The early stories lack the broad concept and all the complicated connections of life characteristic of the author of *The Quiet Don.*

On the methodological plan, nevertheless, his early work is indicative of a writer who succeeded in saturating his short stories with detailed and authentic conflicts and strains of life in the early period of the Soviet regime in the Don area. From the very beginning of his career Sholokhov appears as an author with a heightened interest in a concrete and detailed presentation of the human situation. From the specific, he leads his reader to the general, from the realistic and detailed to the model and ideal, from the unknown particular to the known habitual and accustomed universal. Such movement of thought and form from the concrete and detailed, from the banal, perhaps trivial to the author's own subjective understanding of life, which the reader can accept without large reservations as his own understanding, is also observed in *The Quiet Don.* In this sense Sholokhov is remarkable as a realist, free of schematic or dogmatic strain.

Because his early stories are saturated with concrete and detailed situations, they create a definite impression of being a part of a bigger picture of life. The subject matter of the stories can hardly stand by itself and for its own sake, isolated from the general social stream. Rather, the subject matter forms a fragment of a life unseen, which stands in the background.

As his stories cannot stand for their own sake, so are the characters which fill his stories with reality and agitation of life. Sholokhov's method of presenting man

appears not in depicting man for his own sake, as something finite or isolated, but always as a component of a
larger whole—of society, or of, indeed, life itself. In this
sense, Sholokhov's method of the presentation of life
is very much reminiscent of that of Tolstoi. For both
of them life flows like a mighty stream which has
neither a beginning nor an end. On the other hand,
there is a basic difference in their vision of life. While
for Tolstoi life, having a strong rational element, was
never a violent factor, it is a very violent, and indeed a
brutal experience for Sholokhov. Sholokhov's life
breaks through as if uncontrolled by rational human
senses, driven by primitive, elemental instincts, like a
violently rushing torrent, ending very often in senseless
killing or inhuman brutality.

NOTES AND REFERENCES

1. The complicated relationship of Sholokhov's parents is
explained in a book by D. K. Stewart, *Michail Sholokhov: A
Critical Introduction,* Ann Arbor, 1967, pp. 13-14.

2. T. Mrykhin, "Iz moikh vospominanii" *Donskaia pravda,*
Veshenskaia *stanitsa,* May 24, 1955. See V. V. Gura, F. A. Abramov, *Sholokhov, op. cit.,* p. 164.

3. See Gura, Abramov, *op. cit.,* p. 164.

4. *Ibid.,* p. 165.

5. *Ibid.,* p. 167.

6. *Ibid.,* p. 168.

7. Two of the feuilletons, "The Test" and "The Three," are
translated into English and can be found in the collection of
stories and speeches entitled *One Man's Destiny and Other*

Stories, Articles, and Sketches 1923-1963 by Michail Sholokhov. Translated by H. C. Stevens. Published by Alfred A. Knopf, New York, 1967.
8. See Iakimenko, *Tvorchestvo Sholokhova,* Moscow, 1964, p. 32.
9. Gura, Abramov, *op. cit.,* p. 168.
10. *Sochineniia,* Vol. I, *op. cit.,* p. 14.
11. *Ibid.,* p. 196.
12. Iakimenko, *op. cit.,* p. 72.
13. *Sochineniia,* 1962, p. 196-197.
14. *Shibalkovo semia, Sochineniia,* Vol. I, *op. cit.,* p. 36.
15. *Ibid., Food commissar,* p. 27.
16. *Ibid., The Colt,* p. 229.
17. Cf. Stewart, *op. cit.,* p. 46.
18. *Sochineniia,* Vol. I, *op. cit.,* p. 26.
19. *Ibid.,* p. 266.
20. *Ibid.*
21. *Ibid.,* p. 238.
22. *Ibid., The Birthmark,* p. 10.
23. Iakimenko, *op. cit.,* pp. 40-41.
24. *Ibid.,* p. 58.
25. *Ibid.,* p. 63.
26. *Sochineniia, The Birthmark, op. cit.,* p. 2.
27. *Ibid.,* p. 7.

GENESIS AND STRUCTURE OF THE NOVEL

No attempt is being made in this section to track the sources used by the author for his novel. That was done by Soviet Sholokhovists in sufficient degree.[1] It was shown by Vasil'iev that Sholokhov used very rich documentary material of Soviet and emigrant memoirists and historians.

Nor do we try to show how and where did the author find the prototypes of his characters. This kind of research, no doubt fully justified and necessary, was done by several critics in Russia.[2] This is more or less only an external history of the author's creative process.

This section on the contrary, would like to attempt to recreate the process of the novel's genesis, to trace the way which Sholokhov went. This would be then, more of an internal history of the novel. We would try to trace the author's concept, what it was from the beginning and how it was developing as Sholokhov was progressing with his novel. As a parallel work of this nature, we would like to point to the excellent book by Zhdanov, *Creative History of Anna Karenina.*[3]

Zhdanov traced Tolstoi's concept of *Anna Karenina* in all its changes and developments from the very beginning to the end. This was done by the extensive utilization of Tolstoi's many manuscripts and drafts. Studying and comparing them, Zhdanov retraced the movement of Tolstoi's thoughts. Using Sholokhov's manuscript, it would be possible to do a parallel work for *The Quiet Don.* Unfortunately, however, all of Sholokhov's drafts and manuscripts were lost during World War II. They were left in Veshenskaia and were burned when the house was destroyed under German bombing.

To try to retrace the movement of Sholokhov's thoughts, to find the leading principle by which his concept was guided, we have to employ here a different method. Since we have no external evidence based on the author's drafts and manuscripts as to how he adjusted the various parts to each other, or as to what was his original concept in regard to his characters, and how and in what directions the ideas and concepts of his characters were moving, we have to pursue our objective by the utilization of the text itself.

In the autumn of 1926, Sholokhov moved to his new residence in Veshenskaia *stanitsa,* where he has lived to the present. Since then, seen externally, his life has been quiet, almost uneventful. Through all these years, with the exception of the numerous trips which took him all around Russia and the world, and the interruption during the war, from 1941 to 1945, Sholokhov has resided in his native *stanitsa* Veshenskaia.

It is probably at the same time, when he settled in Veshenskaia, in the autumn of 1926, that he ceased his work on *Donshchina,* the large novel in which he wanted to show the part that the Cossacks played in the revolution. Having written about six printer's sheets in a year's time, he left *Donshchina* and began writing a new book, the novel *The Quiet Don.*

The main subject of *Donshchina* was the Cossacks'

participation in Kornilov's march on Petrograd in August, 1917. In the course of his work he understood that the Cossacks' role in the revolution would be difficult to understand if he did not, by way of background, supply information as to their previous way of life. A new novel was needed to fulfill this task. The new novel was *The Quiet Don.*

Having written three parts of the new novel, i.e. Volume One, he again returned to the manuscript of *Donshchina* and used it with some modification as Part Four and partially Part Five, i.e. Volume Two of *The Quiet Don.* The different concepts were thus used to build the foundations of the first and second volumes of *The Quiet Don.* That explains the break between them, before all in style and language, then in the design of the characters and in the geographic locations of the novel's main actions.

The work on *The Quiet Don* went on strenuously, intensely, with small interruptions for necessary trips to Moscow. Already at the end of 1927 Sholokhov sent the manuscript of the entire first two volumes to the editorial staff of the magazine *Oktiabr,* at that time under the direction of the *RAPP* group, the Russian Association of the Proletarian Writers. The members of the editorial staff, having looked over the novel, decided that it would be inappropriate for a proletarian magazine to print a novel about the prewar Cossacks, devoid of political acuity, without making some essential deletions and changes. For final approval the manuscript was given to Serafimovich, honorary editor of the magazine. But Serafimovich's conclusions were entirely different from those of the editorial staff members. Having read the manuscript, he ordered that the novel be immediately set, without cuttings or censorship.

The first volume (Parts One-Three) was published in the first four issues of *Oktiabr* (January-April) of 1928. The second volume (Parts Four-Five) appeared in the same magazine, May-October 1928 issues: Fame came early to Sholokhov. He was not yet 23 years old. At that time fame and success came easily to many in their early years or with their first publications. Twenty-eight year-old Pil'niak established his reputation as a writer with his first large novel, *The Naked Year,* in 1922. In 1924 everyone was in rapture over the first work of thirty-year-old Babel, *Cavalry.* In the 20's many considered him to be the leading writer in Moscow. The list of those to whom fame was kind during those years might be lengthened with the names of Vsevolod Ivanov, Fedin, Neverov, Libedinskii, Lavrenev, Trenev, and Fadeev. In addition one must remember Zamiatin and Olesha. Not all of them were able to keep their fame. Some of them were broken by collision with a brutal ideology, and some of them, having adapted their talent to the demands of the ideology, lost the favor of fame. Among the pleiad elevated in the 20's, Sholokhov almost alone having adapted his talent to the strict demands of the ideological canon, was able to hold on to the fame which visited him in his early years.

According to Sholokhov's own testimony, *The Quiet Don* in its final form was then not the author's original concept. With a few exceptions, Sholokhov did not transfer his characters from the *Donshchina* into his new novel. And the characters of *The Quiet Don* were not designed to be among the characters of *Donshchina.*

Thus the main character of *The Quiet Don,* Grigorii Melekhov appears in parts of the former *Donshchina* novel only for a short time and as if by chance. He is not connected with the rest of the characters in this part. There is no doubt that Grigorii Melekhov has been inserted into parts of the *Donshchina.* He does not participate in Kornilov's march. Little is stated about his part in battles of the German War, and absolutely nothing is stated about his promotion to officer's rank. Another plot line dominates the second volume of *The Quiet Don,* and other heroes occupy the author. Seen on the whole, Volume Two, i.e. former *Donshchina,* looks like an insertion into *The Quiet Don.*

As regards syntactic structure, the beginning of the second volume is rather reminiscent of Sholokhov's early stories, written in choppy prose. Here is the beginning of *The Quiet Don's* second volume

> The year One Thousand Nine Hundred Sixteen. Rain and wind. Poles'e. Trenches above the swamp, overgrown with alder. Ahead there are wire obstacles. In the trenches is cold slush. The wet gunshield of the observer gleams dimly. There are small fires in the dugouts. (*Part Four, Chapter I.*)

This passage was originally designed to serve as opening lines of *Donshchina.* Sentences, or rather fragments, are here brief and abrupt. Subsequently Sholokhov himself refuted such stylistic constructions, characteristic of his early work.

Seen as the whole *The Quiet Don* in its present form was started then from Part Four of Volume Two. In order to retrace the author's original concept and plan,

we, too, have to start our discussion here from Volume
Two, i.e. from the parts of Sholokhov's former novel
Donshchina.

The Quiet Don has eight parts. Parts Four and Five
among them fall in Volume Two. Sholokhov said that
he wanted to write a book about the Cossacks in the
Revolution. The novel *Donshchina* had to make up for
this.

In all probability Sholokhov's concept was to create
two main characters in the novel—one positive and one
negative. These had to be Bunchuk and Listnitskii.
Both of them were Cossacks who found themselves on
the opposite sides of the Revolution and the Civil War.

Part Four begins with the German War in October of
1916. The novel's two main characters, Bunchuk and
Listnitskii, are featured in full at the very beginning of
Chapter I. Both of them are officers. As Chapter I
opens we find them in conversation. Bunchuk reveals
himself as a Bolshevik and a member of the Russian
Social Democratic Worker's Party. He said that he
entirely shared the position of his Party faction in regard to the war—to transform the Imperialist War into a
Civil War. He was a defeatest, i.e. he worked for
Russia's defeat in the war. He joined the Army in
fulfillment of his Party assignment to conduct propaganda among the soldiers. To the question of his
officer-colleague as to what form of government should
exist in Russia after the war, Bunchuk said simply that
it should be the Dictatorship of the Proletariat. Those
who would not follow the Dictatorship were to be
destroyed. Then he read a long passage from one of
Lenin's brochures where Lenin delighted in expounding

on the organization of contemporary armies. The quotation from Lenin is addressed rather to the reader than to Bunchuk's partners in this conversation. The Cossack officers could neither understand nor accept Lenin's enthusiasm for military organization and discipline. The officers themselves were a living embodiment of that organization and discipline. Sholokhov used Lenin's words here for the sake of the reader. The reader should once more be convinced that Lenin was right, and that Bunchuk, who followed Lenin, was on the right path.

After this conversation, Bunchuk immediately deserted the front. At one of the conspiratory quarters of his Party, he was issued a false identification paper using the name of a private, Nikolai Ushakov, who allegedly was discharged from service on account of his chest wound.

Before Bunchuk deserted the front, Listnitskii, his opponent, wrote a report about Bunchuk and his propagandist role in the Regiment. By this Sholokhov wanted to stress Listnitskii's negative role in the Revolution. However, his report came too late, as Bunchuk had in the meantime escaped.

Then Sholokhov continues in this chapter with the Bolshevik leaflets among the soldiers in the regiments which called on the soldiers to turn their weapons against the government and the Imperialist War.

Listnitskii is revealed from the outset, ironically, as a devoted soldier who has no other ambitions or goals in his life except to serve his monarch. He could not tolerate the comrade-socialists. Bunchuk thought of him as a "stupid soldier, martinet." Undoubtedly, this was also the author's opinion.

No doubt, Sholokhov wanted to build his novel *Donshchina* on the background of these two characters. The protagonist Bunchuk, had to play a positive role; and his antagonist the monarchist Listnitskii had to be a negative character.   Sholokhov made both of them Cossacks.

They did not turn out, however, to be real Cossacks. Cossacks, like peasants elsewhere, were tillers of the soil and their only distinction from the peasantry was in the fact that they were homesteading landowners and had to fulfill military duty. Bunchuk, however, was a Russianized Cossack and a factory worker. For many years he lived in large cities: Moscow, Rostov/D, Tula. These data from his biography we learn, however, not from the opening chapter of the *Donshchina* but from previous chapters of *The Quiet Don,* written later. Likewise, from *The Quiet Don's* later chapters we learn about Listnitskii's social background. Although Sholokhov made him live among the Cossacks in the Don area, he was, nevertheless, not a real Cossack, but one of the small country gentry, with some ten thousand acres of land.

This was the beginning of the *Donshchina.* The plot develops here immediately, without a preliminary introduction to or acquaintance with the characters. Sholokhov brings his reader into the main conflict from the outset. Further on, however, the conflict featured so distinctly at the beginning, subsides.

Continuing our discussion, we come to Chapter III. This is a very long chapter, one of the longest in the entire novel, and represents, in all appearance, a combination of the former *Donshchina* and later *The Quiet*

Don. This serves as a clear indication that Sholokhov worked in parallel fashion on both his novels. True, he abandoned the *Donshchina* and started *The Quiet Don.* However, when the three parts of *The Quiet Don* were written, he connected them with the *Donshchina* parts not in a mechanical combination, but had to adjust them to each other so that their plots should work into one another. We shall see that he has interpolated several chapters of the *Donshchina* into *The Quiet Don* and that he has on the other hand also inserted many chapters of *The Quiet Don* into his former *Donshchina.* He did not achieve complete unity of *The Quiet Don,* but he did succeed in making one book out of the two. The fact that he presented for publication the two volumes together may also speak for our assumption as to their combination, and that he worked on them simultaneously.

The characters in Chapter III of Part Four are from *The Quiet Don*—all the Cossacks from the hamlet Tatarsk, now at the front of the War. We would have to mention here only those among them who interest us— Ivan Alekseevich Kotliarov and Valet. Sholokhov made both of them serve in two different regiments. Now, on the march they meet and speak of Stockman, whom they remembered from the fall of 1912 when he settled in their native hamlet. The chapter is timed, as are also the two previous ones, to October of 1916. After Sholokhov has described the meeting of the Cossacks from the hamlet Tatarsk, he presented documentary operations of military units and events of the Vladimir-Volynsk and Kovel sections of the front.

At the end of the chapter, Sholokhov depicts the

capture of a Bavarian soldier by Valet. At this occasion he brought in much of the German language spoken by the Bavarian. But since the Russian Valet did not understand German, the German speech here is addressed rather to the reader, than to Valet, as was also the case with Lenin's quotation. The German words, like—*In den zukünftigen Klassenkämpfen werden wir in denselben Schutzengräben sein, nicht wahr, Genosse?*—no doubt carry a propagandistic overtone. In the author's design, it is the reader who has to understand them, and not the hardly literate Valet, who took the German soldier captive and let him go free again.

Chapter IV was later written for *The Quiet Don*. It is an insertion into the fabric of the *Donshchina*. All the characters here—Grigorii Melekhov, Mishka Koshevoi, Stepan Astakhov—are those from *The Quiet Don*. As a matter of fact, it is the only chapter in Part Four where Grigorii Melekhov, the main character of *The Quiet Don* is mentioned. We see him here after his first vacation at home. The author does not let Grigorii act in events, in a deployed picture and in details, but rather the author himself narrates Grigorii's part. In all the previous parts the author let the hero himself play his part in all the events. The author only witnessed the hero's participation. In this chapter, on the contrary, the author rather in a cursory manner enumerated the events in which his hero was participating, as if he were only registering them. This chapter serves as a connecting link between Part Three and Part Five—i.e. between *The Quiet Don* and *Donshchina*—to complete Grigorii's service register in the War. It is compounded from many independent novellas: the encounter of Grigorii and Stepan Astakhov in the East Prussia, the Cossack Chubatyi, then the front in Rumania.

Chapters V, VI, VII, VIII and IX alike were undoubtedly written later for *The Quiet Don* and then inserted into Part Four, the former *Donshchina* fragment. Seen on the whole, this section is a larger insertion of *The Quiet Don* in the *Donshchina* part. It reports the affairs of the Cossacks in the hamlet Tatarsk either in their homes or on the front.

In the first two chapters of this section, we see the hamlet Tatarsk in the third year of the war, when life began to ebb away and to decrease. Everywhere was observed a picture of desolation. Even the fact that Natal'ia has borne twins to the joy and pleasure of her parents-in-law did not change the mood of a life decreasing. This event serves only as a contrast to the desolation. Stepan Astakhov's house may serve as a symbol of desolation. There is the usual Sholokhovian abundance of details and events of the life that has neither a beginning nor an end. It would be a sheer impossibility to enumerate even some of the plenitude of details.

The February Revolution of 1917 in Chapter VII is shown as it was seen by the local Tatarsk teacher Balanda, the Tatarsk merchant Mokhov and the Don landlords, the Listnitskiis, the father and the son. Not much is told about Aksin'ia in this section except for the mention of a few of her negative characteristics, like her cherry lips, her stout figure, and her non-Cossack manner of speech, acquired in the house of the lords whom she was serving.

Then Sholokhov takes his reader to the front, where the Cossacks from the hamlet Tatarsk perform their duties, and finally shows the impact of the February Revolution on the Cossacks of the front.

The rest of Part Four, from Chapter X on to the end, with the exception of Chapters XV and XXI, is devoted entirely to the events of the *Donshchina.* Sholokhov took these chapters, as they were written, from *Donshchina* and transplanted them into *The Quiet Don.*

The main characters of the former *Donshchina,* the opponents Listnitskii and Bunchuk, as representatives of the two opposing social and political forces, operate separately. The events unroll from the beginning of July 1917 in Petrograd and end with the defeat of Kornilov's march on Petrograd. Then we have the November coup, as experienced by Listnitskii, and finally the fate of the generals who supported Kornilov's march. The author's free fiction is here organically interwoven with historical events and persons. This required the study of the documents and memoirs. The author's objective was to present the passing away of the old world and the birth of the new. Listnitskii, the incorporation of the old world, remained even after the fall of the monarchy, faithful *ad absurdum* to the monarch. When the conflicts between Kornilov and Kerenskii arose, Listnitskii did not hesitate even for a moment in making his choice as to with whom to side. Kornilov meant for him the restoration of monarchy, or law and order as we would say today, and therefore it was easy for him to decide whom to support.

Bunchuk, on the contrary, served the Revolution and all that it represented as we know him to have done from the opening chapters of the former *Donshchina.* Sholokhov did not tell about his whereabouts since his desertion from the front. Now, at the end of August 1917 he reappeared among the Cossack soldiers, his former friends with whom he served at the front. He was assigned by his Party to dissuade the Cossacks from moving toward Petrograd. This was the famous Kornilov march against the Kerenskii government and thus against the forces of the Revolution. Sholokhov made Bunchuk a true revolutionary, as every revolutionary should be, devoted to his cause and not shrinking any obstacles. When it was necessary to kill an officer, Kalmykov, his former colleague, who now happened to be his opponent, Bunchuk did not falter.

Here Sholokhov inserted Bunchuk's conversation with the Cossack soldiers about Lenin, to show Lenin as a Russian *bogatyr,* the epic hero from old Russian folklore.

Also, new characters were introduced. One of these was Ivan Lagutin, native of the Cossack *stanitsa* Bukanovskaiia, who happened to serve in the unit under Listnitskii's command. Lagutin, while serving as a representative of the Soldier's *Soviet,* went through a good school and learned a great deal about the Revolution. Later, in Part Five, we will find him as one of the leaders of the Revolutionary Don, who together with Podtëlkov established the first Soviet government among the Don Cossacks. Lagutin's role in the novel was to present the Revolutionary sympathies of the Cossacks and to play against the interests of Listnitskii and other landed gentry.

Besides the fictitious characters there are hosts of historical personages, such as the Generals Kornilov, Krymov, Lukomskii, Denikin, Alekseev, Kaledin, Bo-

gaevskii and younger officers, Chernetsov, Popov, Spiri-
donov. To substantiate these accounts Sholokhov has
introduced a large amount of supporting documents,
telegrams, addresses, articles, leaflets, declarations, letters, resolutions and has incorporated all this into the
canvas of the historical events.

Chapter XV was undoubtedly written for *The Quiet
Don* and then later adjusted to the *Donshchina,* i.e. to
Part Four of *The Quiet Don.* It depicts a unit, with
Ivan Alekseevich Kotliarov, one of the characters from
The Quiet Don, marching against Petrograd. Sholokhov
was interested in the influence of revolutionary propa-
ganda on the Cossacks. So, he depicted the use of the
propaganda in order to show the participation of the
Cossacks in the famous Kornilov march.

The last chapter of this part, Chapter XXI, is obviously an insertion. It does not belong to the *Donshchina.*
With its action, geographical location and chronology it
stands closer to Part Five of *The Quiet Don.* It should
serve as a transition to *The Quiet Don.* We will discuss
it in connection with Part Five, after we have discussed
Parts One through Three.

We have to assume that the actual work on the *Donshchina* did not go beyond the chapters indicated here.
If we take out the insertions discussed above, the rest
would make up those six printer's sheets which were
written for the *Donshchina.* All the events of the
Donshchina took place far from the Don, far from Cossack life. *Donshchina* did not and could not become
the life of the Cossacks, as it was called for in Sholokhov's original concept. At this point Sholokhov obviously reached an impasse with his plot. His original

plan called for two Cossack heroes. These were created, however, with masses of the other Cossacks as their background. Besides being aloof from the real Cossack life, the two main heroes were lost amidst the nameless Cossack masses and many historical figures, far away from the Don. The role of the two main heroes in the novel was thus reduced to a minimum, or actually to naught. Neither Listnitskii nor Bunchuk become real leaders of the revolutionary and respectively counter revolutionary forces. Nor did they become principal characters in the novel.

No doubt, from here on, Sholokhov could not continue the *Donshchina.* There was no actual plot, as there was no real Cossack hero. He must have recognized that from the point he had reached so far, it would be very hard, or virtually impossible to combine and to further develop his heroes with the Don and the Cossack life. Thus, the *Donshchina* novel proved to be only a trial of the pen.

There arose a need for a new novel. Sholokhov abandoned his *Donshchina* and indeed started a different novel. It is to Sholokhov's merit that he was able to loosen himself from the *Donshchina* and to start a completely new work. When he recognized that he had reached an impasse in this work, he did not try to change or to adapt the *Donshchina* plot to his new concept.

The Quiet Don is an entirely new beginning, and a new concept. Here Sholokhov created the hamlet Tatarsk, on the right bank of the Don River, and the Cossack family Melekhov.

When *The Quiet Don* reached the chronology of the

Donshchina fragment, i.e. the end of the year 1917, Sholokhov must have recognized that he could use parts of the former *Donshchina* in his new book. And this he did. Thus, *Donshchina* is found to be an insertion into the new novel. It was not given its own independent plot line.

Because he was able to detach himself from his *Donshchina* beginning, Sholokhov made not two, but one book. With only very few exceptions, when it was necessary to combine them, did he interweave the actions and the characters of the *Donshchina* into *The Quiet Don* and conversely, from the new novel into what became a *Donshchina* fragment. We will discuss this interchange as we proceed with our work. Seen as a whole, his two concepts stand apart from each other; their characters and actions do not mingle together.

The central place in Sholokhov's new concept is undoubtedly occupied by the love affair between Grigorii and Aksin'ia. Although it is the only plot line of the new novel, it does not appear to be so exclusively. Sholokhov has framed the extra-marital love affair of the young Cossack Grigorii Melekhov in the whole plenitude of the Cossack life, in all its details and trifles, so that the love affair does not conspicuously appear as the dominant plot line in the novel. The love affair loses itself in the infinity of the life that surrounded it. From this point of view, we observe in *The Quiet Don* the same method that we previously saw in Sholokhov's early work. He never thrusted out one particular point in the plot to the degree that this point became a tendency. He rather subordinates the dominant plot line to many other events in his work.

First we hear of the love liaison as if only per chance, when Father Melekhov warned his son Grigorii against a love affair with Aksin'ia Astakhova, a married woman, their neighbor. By Grigorii's denial of the fact that he was having an affair with Aksin'ia, the author created an impression that there was and would be no love affair at all. The conversation between the father and son took place while they were fishing and is presented by the author in such a way as if what Grigorii's father had to say was not of any importance. About the beginning of this alleged affair, if there was one, we learn nothing.

In the next two chapters, III and IV, Sholokhov made Grigorii and Aksin'ia meet on two different occasions, but nothing is said about their love affair. The reader actually does not expect from their meetings any love affair such as that mentioned by Grigorii's father. On one occasion, Grigorii met Aksin'ia on the bank of the Don River. They were just good neighbors, as neighbors everywhere can be. From their rather joking, friendly conversation it is impossible to discern of their affair. Both of them acted as if they saw each other for the first time.

The next chapter then gives an account of a fishing expedition at night in stormy weather. Grigorii made rather a shy attempt to court Aksin'ia in the darkness of the night, but she resolutely pushed him away. These are only weak hints that Grigorii Melekhov, a lad about eighteen years of age, was actually not disinclined to joke with or court a married woman. These weak hints are framed into many other petty incidents from the Cossack life in the hamlet Tatarsk, so that the hints of the affair lose their independent meaning in the plot.

They are not depicted for their own sake as a goal of Sholokhov's art, but serve rather as means to another goal—to present a broad canvas of the Cossack life.

The next two chapters, V and VI, report about the Tatarsk Cossacks on their way to the Summer camps. Here Sholokhov has interlaced the chapter with a story about buried treasure, told by Khristonia. The next chapter narrates Aksin'ia's story of her hard lot. The author speaks very carefully about Aksin'ia's feelings toward Grigorii. He only says that Aksin'ia was a-fraid of her new feelings. Having sent Stepan off to the camps, she decided to see Grigorii as seldom as possible. This decision was strengthened even more when she saw that he tried to approach her when they were fishing together.

In Chapter VIII we learn again of a casual meeting between Grigorii and Aksin'ia. There is nothing that can be concluded from this meeting as to their relations, or Grigorii's love toward Aksin'ia.

In this chapter we also hear about young Listnitskii for the first time. The episode with Listnitskii is an obvious interpolation. He is the character taken from the *Donshchina* fragment. At the beginning of this chapter, the author depicts the partitioning of the meadows among the Cossacks in the hamlet. Then suddenly, without any transition, he brings the episodes of the horse race between Listnitskii and young Korshunov. And then, there is the meeting with Aksin'ia which we referred to above. So far there was no love affair.

The episode of the horse races was needed by Sholokhov to introduce Listnitskii into the novel. Listnitskii was created for the original design of the *Donshchina,* but apparently Sholokhov had decided to use him in *The Quiet Don.* A character like Listnitskii was needed in the novel to play the counterpart to the Cossacks. Remarkably, in dealing with Listnitskii on this first acquaintance, we see that there is no social or political overtone where he is concerned as we had constantly observed in the *Donshchina* fragment. Actually we learn nothing about him. From the conversation of Mit'ka Korshunov and Grigorii Melekhov we find out that his name is Listnitskii, that he is a *sotnik,* i.e. a commander over a unit of one hundred Cossacks. And then the race took place in which the *sotnik's* horse was over raced. The *sotnik* was not confused, however. On the contrary he showed tranquility and self restraint, usually not expected from a representative of landed gentry in proletarian literature.

It must be said, that the interpolation of the Listnitskii episode is masterfully done. The author does not let the reader notice his intention to introduce the character of Listnitskii. Mit'ka Korshunov and Grigorii Melekhov act in this episode as the main heroes. From the formal literary point of view this interpolation is an independent novella.

Finally in the next chapter, Chapter IX, we learn that the actual love affair has taken place, when Aksin'ia gave herself to Grigorii at the haymaking.

Of Aksin'ia's love in the next chapter, Sholokhov speaks strangely, that it was a woman's belated love. Aksin'ia should have been at that time hardly twenty years old. From her biographical data in Chapter VII we learned that she was married to Stepan Astakhov at seventeen. One year and a half after her marriage,

Stepan's mother died and Aksin'ia bore her husband a
child. The child died, not having lived even one year.
So Aksin'ia must have been about nineteen and a half or
a bit more at the outset of *The Quiet Don*. In any case,
she was not yet an old woman. As a matter of fact, her
love for Grigorii could have been her first love. Sholokhov said that she had no feeling for her husband except
pity, and that he had simply become a habit with her.
(Chapter VII.)

When her liaison with the young Grigorii became
known in the hamlet, Aksin'ia behaved defiantly. The
author said in his own words that she proudly and
loftily carried her happy but shameful head. (Chapter
X.)

This is not a very flattering compliment for the young
Aksin'ia, and since these are the author's words, they
reveal his attitude to the character he created. There is
something of a raptorial quality in her nature and in the
way she loved. Her love is not a sacrificial giving love,
but a violent and possessive one.

Several critics have pointed out time and again that
the words Sholokhov used in reference to Aksin'ia
(proudly and lofty, happy, but shameful head) are reminiscent of Tolstoi's words in *Anna Karenina,* in Part
Two, Chapter XI (her proud, happy, but now shameful
head). Though these words sound similar, there can be
no proof that Sholokhov had borrowed them from Tolstoi deliberately. He was, of course, aware that in case
of borrowing, the critics would surely point this out.
Thus, he could not have failed to see the danger that he
would be accused of imitating the great master. But
even when Tolstoi's expression "proud, happy, but

shameful head" was known to Sholokhov and he, never-theless, took it over in order to characterize his Aksin'ia, we can hardly speak of imitation or borrowing. It is not the words that acquire an independent meaning here, but rather the concepts of a "fallen" woman. And these are no doubt different in Tolstoi and Sholokhov. The difference lies, perhaps, not so much in the different attitudes of the two authors toward the subject of the "fallen" woman as in the different times and societies in which they treat the "fallen" woman. Taking this difference into consideration, it must then be said that Sholokhov presented his Aksin'ia in her own time and society, much more different from the time and society in Tolstoi's work.

There is one other expression in this chapter that is reminiscent of Tolstoi's *Anna Karenina.* I have in mind the words spoken by Pantelei Prokofievich: "with her husband alive."

Grigorii's liaison with Aksin'ia became the object of much talk in the hamlet Tatarsk. His father, Pantelei Prokofievich, was the last one to hear about his son's love affair with a married woman, though he was the first to warn Grigorii early enough, when there did not yet exist an affair. The rumors had by now reached him also. The local merchant Mokhov, probably half-jokingly, half-seriously said to Pantelei Prokofievich: "I hear that you're getting yourself a daughter-in-law, Aksin'ia Astakhova." What Pantelei Prokofeivich answered could have come from Tolstoi, but again, it is hardly probable. His reaction was: "I! With her husband alive?"

"Is it possible to take a wife from a husband who is

still living" is a theme of the novel *Anna Karenina,* as it was conceived by Tolstoi as early as the winter of 1869-70. Tolstoi, in his turn, took this expression from the Russian *byliny.* [4]

It is hardly possible that Sholokhov heard this expression as it was used by Tolstoi and then adopted it to his novel. Undoubtedly he was well acquainted with the novel *Anna Karenina.* But he could not have studied the genesis of the novel at the early time, when he was writing his own masterpiece.

Chapter X is a short chapter, but it has thus formed the beginning of the novel's actual conflict.

As Sholokhov started with his rather negative attitude toward Aksin'ia's predatory love, so he continued in this attitude. In Chapter XII we have the author's words: "Aksin'ia was raging in her belated, bitter love." We have already discussed that it could have been her first love. In any case, it could not have been a belated love. As to the fact that it was a bitter love, we have to accept the author's verdict as it is, since this is what he said about her. Sholokhov has reflected here the popular Cossack-peasant attitude toward a "forbidden" love liaison. In popular concept, such a love could not have been anything but bitter and evil.

The following words of Sholokhov probably bring him closer to Tolstoi's concept than any of those discussed above:

If Grigorii had made some show of hiding from the world his affair with this grass-widow, and if the grass-widow Aksin'ia had kept her relations with Grigorii comparatively secret, without shunning others, the world would have seen nothing unusual in it. The village would have

gossiped a little and then forgotten. But they lived together almost openly, they were bound by something greater, which had no likeness to any temporary association,
and for that reason the villagers decided it was immoral
and held their breath in peeping expectation. Stepan would
return and cut the knot. (*Part One, Chapter XII.*)

The same idea, but in different words, was also expressed by Leo Tolstoi in his *Anna Karenina.* In Tolstoi's novel the ladies of high society, who considered
Anna to be a woman of high moral caliber, rejoiced
because of her love liaison with Vronskii and waited
only for the time to come when they could openly
convey their contempt for Anna.[5]   And a bit later
Tolstoi had put almost the same thought to Vronskii:
If this would be the usual, fashionable, trivial liaison,
surely, no one would ever care. All would leave him,
Vronskii, in peace. But because the society felt that
this liaison was not the usual fleeting fancy, but a great
and deep love, the society could not forgive it.[6]

In all probability, Sholokhov knew these Tolstoi passages and used them consciously. But he did not do this
because Tolstoi used them before him. We have to
exclude the probability of imitation, or borrowing.
Sholokhov, like Tolstoi, knew that this was the attitude
of people, an attitude as equally tenacious in the high
Petersburg society as in the Cossack-peasant community
on the Don. The people prefer to approve a secret
liaison rather than an open one which defies the established norm and accepted standards. Sholokhov and
Tolstoi have presented in their novels, not a fleeting,
superficial liaison, but a deep and mutual feeling that
has fatefully bound two loving persons for life. Herein
lies their similarity. But the similarity ends here. There

is also a great difference in the scope of their treatment of the love theme and the "fallen" woman.

Even whereas Sholokhov and Tolstoi display an equal attitude to the "fallen" woman, their concepts and the scope of treatment are different. While discussing the extra-marital love affair, Tolstoi also discusses the meaning of love and family life, and even the meaning of life in general. Sholokhov limits his plot to the love affair only. He never touches the broad concept or meaning of love or marriage. Tolstoi has, in addition, much more conflict in his novel. His plot branches out in many directions. And it is this that makes his novel and the concepts treated therein more universal.

When we have said all this, there remains still one point to be mentioned here. Sholokhov could not have borrowed from Tolstoi, for the simple reason that it is plainly impossible to borrow from the great master. Tolstoi, with his authority and treatment of the "fallen" woman weighs heavily on everyone who tries to treat the same subject. It is virtually impossible to pass around Tolstoi without taking notice of the great master's attitude and treatment. This happened to Sholokhov also. He was neither influenced by Tolstoi, nor did he borrow from him. He just could not bypass this rock without having touched it, even if only slightly.

In this chapter we hear for the first time of Natal'ia Korshunova. Grigorii said to Aksin'ia that his father would like him to marry Natal'ia. That Natal'ia is a young, beautiful woman we hear from Aksin'ia herself. The author has so far said nothing of Natal'ia.

Further events unfold in the novel through a number of inserted novellas. The friendship of Stepan Astakhov with his neighbors, the Melekhovs, came to an abrupt end. To loosen the conflict of love, the author has brought in the incidents with the broken leg of Stepan's horse.

Aksin'ia goes to a fortune-teller, an old woman, to find ways and means to keep Grigorii faithful to her. And then there is the fight of the Melekhov brothers with Stepan. All these small insignificant events, though they detach the reader from the main conflict of the novel, nevertheless enrich the novel's realism. The life of the novel's characters appears fuller, more complete. The novel seems to be overloaded, but on the other hand, these trifles of life make the novel seem more alive and closer to everyday life reality. In connection with the fight of Stepan Astakhov with the Melekhov brothers and the resulting feud between them, the author made a somewhat puzzling remark:

> From this day on the feud between the Melekhovs and Stepan was tied into a tight Kalmuck knot. It was given to Grigorii to untie this knot two years later in the East Prussia, under the town of Stolypin. (*Part One, Chapter XIV.*)

What happened two years later in the fields of East Prussia was reported in Chapter IV of Part Four, as an insertion to *The Quiet Don.* But there was no untying of the Kalmuck knot. Grigorii saved the life of Stepan, his enemy. On that occasion Stepan had admitted to Grigorii that he was aiming several times to kill Grigorii, but that he missed each time. Even after Stepan was saved by Grigorii, he still could not forgive Grigorii for Aksin'ia. Nothing is said about how the knot was untied. In Chapter V of the same Part Four was reported the new feud between Stepan and Petro Melekhov, and the new Kalmuck knot. And immediately thereupon, Stepan was captured by the Germans.

Before Grigorii's wedding took place, there was what could be termed in English a bridal inspection, a custom among respectable Cossack families. This is reported in Chapter XV, following the fight of the brothers Melekhov with Stepan.

In the bridal inspection there is one passage that again is reminiscent of Tolstoi. Natal'ia was called before Grigorii so that they might see each other. It was not their first encounter. Living in the same hamlet, they, undoubtedly, had opportunity to see each other many times before. But the custom required this ceremony, and it could not be broken. When Natal'ia came out Grigorii looked at her:

> Grigorii's eyes in a minute glanced over all of her— from head to long beautiful legs. He looked over, like a horse buyer looks over a mare before buying, and thought: "fair," and met her eyes, directed toward him. Natal'ia's direct, almost embarrassed, truthful glance seemed to say: "Here I am, as I am. Judge me as you will." "Beautiful," answered Grigorii with his eyes and smile. (*Part One, Chapter XV.*)

What we have in this passage is the language of eyes and glances. Grigorii speaks to Natal'ia with his eyes and she answers him with her glance. And they seem to perfectly understand each other. The same language of eyes and glances we find in many passages of Tolstoi's *Anna Karenina* to which we have already referred to previously. It would be sufficient to point to Chapter XVIII, Part One of Tolstoi's masterpiece. The chapter describes Vronskii's and Anna's meeting at the railroad station in Moscow at that one fateful morning. It was not their first acquaintance. They had met before, as they had often encountered each other in the high society circles of St. Petersburg. But having met for the first time in Moscow in the most unusual circumstances one morning, they both experienced an unusual reaction.

Undoubtedly, there are two different languages in the passages of Tolstoi and Sholokhov, but they have in common what was described as the language of eyes and glances. Anna, like Sholokhov's Grigorii, spoke with her eyes and Vronskii understood her. These two passages are not unique for both authors. Very often both of them resort to the help of this kind of language. In Tolstoi's *Anna Karenina* especially, the language of eyes and glances holds great significance for the fateful love of Anna and Vronskii.[7]

Sholokhov certainly knew about the language of eyes and looks. He could have been impressed by the method of conveying a conversation by this kind of language, but he did not borrow it knowingly. It is simply one of those traditions of Russian classical literature which as we say, weighs heavily on everyone who attempts to approach the same subject. It is hard to bypass around certain traits and expressions of the great masters without noticing them in one way or another, positive or negative.

Grigorii seems to have accepted the new turn in his life without a conflict. He was ready to give up his passionate Aksin'ia and to take whatever may come to him. The conflict of the novel has been thus established without Grigorii's active participation. It has been established on the fact of his marriage. Sholokhov pursued this conflict with a merciless consequence. But again and again it must be stressed that the conflict of love affair was being built into a larger frame with many small and insignificant details from the Cossack life.

After the bridal inspection, the wedding should have followed. Sholokhov has, however, inserted three chapters with various novellas before the wedding took place —Aksin'ia's and Stepan's apparent reconciliation, Grigorii's and Aksin'ia's rendezvous. Grigorii called Aksin'ia for this rendezvous to tell her that they should "put an end to their love." The next novella is about the brothers Melekhov at work. Seen structurally, these novellas are only loosely connected with the main plot line, they are united actually only through common characters. Otherwise they do not belong to the content of the plot.

In connection with Grigorii's marriage, Sholokhov had to introduce the Korshunov family, whose Natal'ia will become Melekhov's daughter-in-law. This is done in Chapter XVIII. Sholokhov described Korshunov's wealth in detail. They are the richest family in the hamlet Tatarsk. While presenting the wealthiest family, Sholokhov withheld in his language any social or political overtones. There is nothing in this presentation that could indicate Korshunov's exploitation of the underprivileged Cossacks. In regard to social and political aspects of the Cossack life, the author has consequently maintained his distance and neutrality.

The bridal inspection was followed by the agreement

of marriage. This is a new novella. The object of Sholokhov's art is not to present the end, the final result of the agreement, but rather the process of the agreement. Actually, we never learn what was agreed upon. It was not important for the author to disclose the conditions of the agreement, but only steps in the movements of the negotiation. One can detect a certain irony in Sholokhov's treatment of the rough Cossack customs and traditions.

The wedding itself took the rest of Part One, with a brief insertion of a novella devoted to Aksin'ia's decision to gain Grigorii back from the happy Natal'ia (Chapter XX). The wedding is a very colorful and gay event, and there are numerous insignificant details. It is depicted very expressively and is almost incoherently panoramic, with many kaleidoscopic pictures which constantly unroll and change before the reader's eyes. And all this is disclosed from the inside, as if the reader himself were present to observe the people and the events. The author does not make any comments. He leaves the people themselves to act and speak as they please.

If the wedding is described kaleidoscopically, as if it were incoherent, in like manner is presented every chapter and every novella in each chapter, in relation to each other. Part One consists entirely of incoherent novellas, which are connected only through common heroes. The details presented by the author have no consecutiveness or succession. This seems to be the main feature of the style employed in Part One.

Sholokhov ends Part One with Grigorii's wedding. In certain respects, Part One serves as an introduction to the whole novel. Sholokhov has set here a mechanism, like the railroad switch, for the further direction and course of this eventful life.

If Part One was to a certain degree an introduction to the novel, then Part Two is the expansion of the novel. The expansion, however, does not go along new plot lines, but rather on account of new characters. In this part we encounter more new characters than in any other part. The characters are of divergent social groups, and many of them are non-Cossacks.

From the beginning of Part Two, in Chapter I, before continuing the main plot line, Sholokhov introduces new characters. We met the local merchant Mokhov previously in Part One. Now, in this part, Sholokhov has created Mokhov's genealogy. In doing so, he detaches Mohkov from the plot line. Mokhov does not fit in with the Cossack life. He stays aloof of the quiet Don. Likewise, the local hamlet intelligentsia, the student Boiarishkin and the teacher Balanda stand apart. Not forming their own plot line, they nowhere interfere with the main plot and its characters. Their role in the novel is to form a certain antithesis to the host of Cossack characters.

While introducing the merchant family, Sholokhov displays a rather strong social overtone, quite different from the previous part with the Melekhovs and the Korshunovs. This gives an impression that this chapter was created as a supplement, or a commentary, to the life of the quiet Don. In addition, while in the chapters dealing with the Cossack families the author was able to preserve his sympathetic neutrality and a certain distance without interfering, in this chapter, however, dealing with the merchant Mokhov, the author changes his position from a sympathetic but neutral observer to that of a narrator who himself takes a part in the events. The chapters dealing with the merchant Mokhov are written in the style of the author's narrative.

More characters are created by presenting the workers at the Mokhov mill. There are the representatives of the local proletariat: Valet, Davydka and Ivan Alekseevich Kotliarov. They are created to be a revolutionary nucleus in the hamlet, and as such to prepare a ground for Stockman's propaganda activity. Together with Mishka Koshevoi, a Cossack from the hamlet, they will form a group around Stockman, the main force of the Revolutionary Don. Now they and Stockman form a circle. Stockman arrived at the hamlet Tatarsk in the fall and settled there as a locksmith.

In contrast to the genealogy of the merchant Mokhov, Sholokhov reveals nothing about Stockman's person and mission. Nothing is known about his past, or his family. His mission follows, however, from his activity—to organize a revolutionary group from among the Cossacks. At the beginning, his role is only a negative one.

We first learn about Mishka Koshevoi in Stockman's circle. In Sholokhov's initial concept, Mishka Koshevoi's part was most probably very insignificant. Actually, Sholokhov gave him no role at all. He is only a silent observer. If it were not for his role at the end of the novel, we would hardly notice the character of Mishka Koshevoi, the Cossack from the hamlet Tatarsk.

Parallel with the expansion of the characters, Sholokhov also develops the main plot. The love affair between Grigorii and Aksin'ia, having subsided at the end of Part One, arose here anew with vigorous force and reached its culmination.

In connection with Grigorii's departure from home, Sholokhov took up the Listnitskiis and their estate. After the first fleeting acquaintance with the young *sotnik* Listnitskii in Part One (Chapter XIII), we now meet not only him, but also his father and their estate. Having left home, Grigorii, together with Aksin'ia, worked on the Listnitskii's estate. The life on the estate was like a dreamy idyll. Sholokhov omitted all reference in regard to social and political pitch. There was neither exploitation nor social contradiction between the master-owner and his hired people. The old Listnitskii was like a father to the people who worked for him, and a good neighbor to the Cossacks.

The fact that Sholokhov did not mention any social contradiction is insignificant, per se. But in proletarian literature, the presentation of economic exploitation and class contradictions are the main features. The omission of this fact in Sholokhov, who himself was a young representative of proletarian literature, therefore makes it a significant fact. From this point of view, the criticism which the Proletarian writers made of Sholokhov in the nineteen twenties was not quite unjustified. But on the other hand, it must be said that Sholokhov's concept was of course broader, more universal than the norm required by Proletarian literature. He did not want to and could not narrow his vision and concept of life only by the Proletarian point of view. This, together with his mastery of plot and structure makes his novel a masterpiece not only in Russian, but in world literature.

So far, the young Listnitskii is the only character, who serves as an element of contiguity with the *Donshchina* fragment.   True, others like Ivan Alekseevich Kotliarov and Valet were mentioned in Part Four, i.e. in the former *Donshchina* fragment too.   But they appear in the chapters inserted into the former *Donshchina* fragment from *The Quiet Don,* while Listnitskii, though designed for the *Donshchina,* receives his proper place as also the beginning in *The Quiet Don.*   No doubt, the original concept for Listnitskii was laid with the *Donshchina* fragment.   But while transplanting him from the *Donshchina* into *The Quiet Don,* Sholokhov has recreated him and organically united him with the new plot.

Since Listnitskii is the only character known to equally belong to the two novels, several questions arise in this connection.   In the former *Donshchina* fragment Listnitskii occupies a much more prominent part than in the new novel.   As the protagonist to Bunchuk, he was designed to play an independent role.   In *The Quiet Don,* though organically belonging to the plot, Listnitskii's role is only auxiliary.

Why then has Sholokhov only chosen Listnitskii to play a part in both concepts?   Apparently there was need of a character who would oppose Grigorii in his love affair.   Such a character would aggravate the affair and increase tension in the novel.   This character could not be a neutral Cossack, but rather someone from the opposing social camp.   Evidently, he could not be from the revolutionary camp either.   Since Sholokhov felt there was a need for such a character, what was then more simple than just to use a character created for the

Donshchina. Sholokhov took Listnitskii and, so-to-speak, re-introduced him into the new novel.

Even if it is *one* character, there is a great difference between the Listnitskii from the *Donshchina* fragment and the same Listnitskii in the parts of *The Quiet Don.* While Listnitskii in the *Donshchina* fragment is the bearer of a distinct political idea opposing the revolutionary forces, the same Listnitskii in initial parts of *The Quiet Don* is only an opponent in Grigorii's love affair. In *The Quiet Don* he is devoid of any political or social ideas and forces. True, he belongs to the gentry, is a rich land-owner and an officer-monarchist who zealously serves his Sovereign, but nowhere does he speak of his political and social affiliations. It is as if he had none. Primarily, he is only a rival to Grigorii, vying for the affections of a beautiful young woman, Aksin'ia.

The structural need for a hero, a rival in Grigorii's love affair, also explains his initial introduction and his being devoid of all the ideological factors. We already discussed how Grigorii and his friend Mit'ka Korshunov made first acquaintance with the young *sotnik* at the horse races. (See p. 80f.) Sholokhov has done this by way of a novella, inserted into the plot between the scene of partition of the meadows and Grigorii's accidental meeting with Aksin'ia. The acquaintance was presented by the author imperceptibly, without constraint. But it does not change the fact that it was an insertion.

As to the structural features, Part Two, with a few exceptions, displays the same traits as we observed in Part One. It contains a multitude of details which very often seem to have no relation to the main plot line, such as the partition of the woods for cutting (Chapter VIII) or the loss of a gander on the Listnitskii estate Iagodnoie, where Grigorii was working. Per se, details like these and many others have no meaning for either the plot or the structure. They contribute nothing. Yet it is these trifling details that make the life of the novel richer. The novel's realism appears more plastic, as was indicated above.

One of Sholokhov's characteristic features of style and structure is the use of unexpected transitions and sudden breaks in events. Thus, Chapter XVII ends with the hunt and Grigorii's accidental face-to-face encounter with Stepan Astakhov. Then the next chapter makes a sudden turn and presents events around Natal'ia and her attempted suicide. The following chapter (XIX) then again takes up the meeting of Grigorii and Stepan. By these sudden breaks and transitions, Sholokhov has created simultaneous occurrences of events. Not a word was ever said about the fact that Grigorii's encounter with Stepan at the hunt on Melekhov's field (Grigorii and Natal'ia plowed this field together) and Natal'ia's suicide occurred at the same hour. Yet a definite impression is made that it was so, that this happened at the same minute. There are many events and occurrences in the novel that happen simultaneously. This simultaneous vision of reality contributes to the wealth of the realistic life portrayed in the novel.

Here as in Part One, Sholokhov also makes rich use of novellas. We can only indicate a few of them. In Chapter V the fight of the Cossacks with the Ukrainians is obviously a novella, inserted into the description of the developing relationship of coolness between Grigorii and Natal'ia.

Chapter VII contains also a novella—story of the Cossack Brekh and his capture of a dangerous state criminal. There is also Khristonia's story about students and Karl Marx in Petersburg. These are but a few instances.

Sholokhov brings this part to an end with Grigorii's departure for military service. It was not only Grigorii who was going into the service. It was simply the fact that all men born the same year as he were being drafted. Sholokhov named several other characters going into the service. It must be noted that Mishka Koshevoi was not mentioned at all as being drafted, although he was of the same age as Grigorii. It is important to notice this, in view of Mishka's later role in the novel as opponent to Grigorii. This adds to our suggestion that Mishka was not originally designed to play any role in the novel. In any case he was not important enough to mention as being drafted. Only later, where structural need arose, when Grigorii needed an opponent, did Sholokhov give him a significant part. We will discuss this in connection with the last part of the novel.

With Grigorii's complete break with his meek Natal'ia and his home on the one side, and his wild marriage with the rapturous Aksin'ia on the other, the novel seems to come to an end. When at the end of Part Two Grigorii, having established a new family, departed for service in the Cossack army and refused all attempts at reconciliation with Natal'ia, the author's design seems to have reached its completion. It seems there was nothing more to say about the Cossack Grigorii Melekhov and his unusual love affair with the possessive Aksin'ia.

No doubt, Sholokhov had at this stage reached a new turning point in the novel. He had either to end his novel here or to take a new direction with it. There is no indication, however, that Sholokhov intended to end his novel with Grigorii's break from his wife and home. Rather, his concept was to create a novel in which the love affair would be subordinated to the broad panorama of the Cossack life. Thus, it is only natural that Part Two found its continuation. The years of peacetime served as only a beginning of the novel.

Though Grigorii's love affair came to the end with Part Two, the novel, as we assumed, could not stop at this point. Sholokhov's intention was to bring his hero beyond his love affair and to connect him with the history of his time. If Sholokhov did not have a clear design for Grigorii from the beginning of his portrayal to the end, he had, however, a firm concept of the general course of the Cossack life.

Having introduced and expanded the characters, Sholokhov continued in Part Three with the ramification and deepening of the plot line. As Part Three opens, we find the first mention of a date. It is March of 1914. So far Sholokhov noted only seasons of the year, or holidays such as Christmas or Easter. Now we have the first historical grasp. Not far removed from this date is the fateful summer of 1914 and the outbreak of the war. The time between March and the outbreak of the war is filled as usual with innumerable Sholokhovian details and trifles which made up the gist and wealth of the Cossack life.

As an incident of life in the hamlet, Sholokhov mentions Stockman's arrest (Chapter I). As a necessary trait of Proletarian literature he had to stress the rudeness of the police officers at this occasion. At the time of Stockman's arrest we hear for the first and only time of his wife. When he arrived in the hamlet, Sholokhov said Stockman was single and that he took a dwelling in the house of a widow, Lukeria.

Grigorii's service in the Cossack army is seen first from his home. Here Sholokhov reports of Natal'ia's return to the Melekhov family and of Grigorii's letters to his parents.

Since Grigorii's break from his home in the previous part it was as if the Melekhov farm has ceased to hold Sholokhov's interest. He transferred the center of his attention to Listnitskii's estate and Aksin'ia. Now, as Grigorii left the estate, Sholokhov changed his center of attention again to the Melekhov farm. It is as if Sholokhov had foreseen Grigorii's reconciliation with his parents and wife, and wanted to make his return easier.

Although Part Three focuses on the Melekhov family, the plot branches off into many directions. There are the Melekhov and the Korshunov families, Aksin'ia and her new love affair with the young Listnitskii, and there is the war with its many ramifications; and finally there is the hospital in Moscow, where Grigorii spent a few days.

The war is shown first as the Cossacks from the Don hamlet Tatarsk heard of it and later as the Cossack soldiers at the front experienced it. But it is always as seen by a simple Cossack.

The war came to the Cossacks' homes like a fast horseman riding in the dust through the Cossack fields. The Cossacks were working in their fields as they noticed a swiftly moving horseman. Actually it was not even a horseman but just a cloud of dust quickly moving through the fields.

> As they crossed the field truck, Petro glanced at his left and noticed a tiny cloud of dust moving swiftly along the distant highroad from the village. (*Part Three, Chapter III.*)

Not a word was yet uttered about the war, but as soon as the people working on their fields caught sight of the horseman, the fear of a great misfortune came upon them. The swiftly-riding horseman appeared thus as a kind of apocalyptic vision, a strong, inner, foreboding of a disaster.

The mobilization of the Cossacks was followed by the fast riding horseman. The war came not as big news, heralded by trumpets, but imperceptibly and quietly. The consequences of it were, nevertheless, no less disastrous.

Equally imperceptible but nevertheless disastrous, the war came to the Cossack soldiers. There was not even any news of the war. The beginning of the war is presented from the point of view of Grigorii and his participation in an attack. It has much in common with Nikolai Rostov's participation in the first attack against the French. Unwittingly and immediately the question of borrowings and imitation will, of course, arise. But again, it must be said that this is neither the first nor the second time that it arises. It is one of those factors which was discussed above in relation to Aksin'ia's and Grigorii's extramarital love affair. (See pp. 82ff., 88ff.)

The author's view of the war as senseless slaughter is revealed in connection with the Kriuchkov incident. Sholokhov needed this incident to disclose his own attitude toward the war. He has partially done this through Grigorii Melekhov. But apparently he felt it was not enough. He constantly preserved a certain distance and neutrality to Grigorii. Therefore, Grigorii's point of view was not necessarily that of the author.

Since the author restrained from making comments on Grigorii's point of view, he felt a stronger urge to make his remarks on the war. For this he used the historical events built around the national hero Kuz'ma Kriuchkov. He undoubtedly heard of Kriuchkov as a boy in the *gymnasias* where he studied, as every Russian has heard of him. In addition, he made use of the newspapers. Then he added his own character, Mit'ka Korshunov, and thus blended history and fiction in splendid unity. This made it possible for him to make his own comments on the war.

As we said above, one of the characteristic structural features of this part was the ramification of its plot. Actually, the plot branches off into so many sides and directions that it loses itself. There is hardly one main plot line remaining in this part, as we observed in the two previous parts.

Having presented Grigorii's first participation in the attack, Sholokhov has turned his attention to the Tatarsk Cossacks as they were drafted to the front. The villagers meet with an old Cossack, a veteran of several Russian wars with Turkey. The veteran is an old man of a particular frame of mind and morality. He knows the old human law about war which the young Cossacks never knew, and which by all means should be observed in this war. The words *human law,* in Russian *chelovech'ia pravda,* actually should mean universal, rather than human. The law of the war is thus a universal law of any war. It was: don't take other men's goods, don't do wrong to any woman, and know certain prayers.

The story of the universal law is a novella. Sholokhov probably heard it from stories and tales told by the old people among the Cossacks. It reflects the popular, folkloristic notion of wars.

Part Three contains several chapters that actually do not belong to *The Quiet Don.* One of these is Chapter XI. It represents the diary of an unknown young man, probably a student, who at twenty-one years of age volunteered for the front. It is a very long chapter and could have actually been written for the *Donshchina,* but was later adapted to *The Quiet Don.* The characters mentioned here belong, nevertheless, to *The Quiet Don:* the student Boyarishkin, Lisa Mokhova, the spoiled daughter of the Tatarsk merchant Mokhov, and also Grigorii Melekhov, as it was he who found the diary of this unknown, fallen young soldier. The purpose of this chapter is, on one hand, to disclose the corruption of young people from the upper classes in the person of Lisa Mokhova, and on the other, to point to the senselessness of war.

Chapter XIII tells of Grigorii's injury. Then the author makes a sudden break; there is a long section, an interruption lasting through six chapters, in which Sholokhov takes his readers to various other places and events. Only in Chapter XX does he again return to his account of Grigorii's injury.

In Chapter XIV of this section, he first tells of the young Listnitskii, of his patriotic feelings and his decision to volunteer for the front. Listnitskii's monarchistic feelings and his devotion to the person of the monarch remind us of Nikolai Rostov's monarchist sentiments and his devotion to the Sovereign. But there is also a difference in the method of presentation of these feelings in both authors. While Tolstoi himself did not share this affection for the monarch, he was nevertheless able to present a most genuine and fine pathos of his character; Sholokhov, on the other hand, viewed the figure of his monarchist character ironically. Listnitskii's devotion to the monarch is brought to the point of absurdity.

It must be kept in mind that Listnitskii, as the antagonist to the revolutionary Bunchuk, was created for the *Donshchina*. From the *Donshchina* fragment he was brought into *The Quiet Don*, where he underwent a transformation, being stripped of his ideological cant, as has been discussed previously.

In this part, Sholokhov had to, so to speak, prepare the apolitical Listnitskii for the role which he was designed to play in the next part, as the opponent of the revolutionary forces. No doubt, Sholokhov has written this chapter, as well as the next one, for *The Quiet Don,* but he kept in mind the role he gave Listnitskii in the *Donshchina*. Apparently, while working on Part Three, Sholokhov decided to use his former *Donshchina* fragment as a continuation of his new book, which eventually became *The Quiet Don.*

It is from this point of view also that we have to look at Bunchuk in Chapter XV. This is again a long chapter. It seems that the long chapters noted here have their significance. Usually, the chapters of *The Quiet Don* are brief and filled with many events, very often with inserted novellas. The long chapters, on the other hand, either belong to the former *Donshchina* fragment or form a kind of transition or introduction to the *Donshchina.* Their stylistic feature usually is the author's narrative. This one is a long chapter, and undoubtedly serves as a transition from *The Quiet Don* to the fragment of the former *Donshchina.*

In this chapter Bunchuk, like Listnitskii, was being adapted for the role which he was designed to play in the *Donshchina.* When Sholokhov decided to take up his former *Donshchina* manuscript and use it as a continuation of *The Quiet Don,* he had recognized that there was a need for some adaptations. This chapter was written, then, with the purpose of adjusting the two books.

Bunchuk does not yet play an important role in this part. He does not take up much space in the text either. All we learn of him is that he is a common soldier and that he would like to become a gunner. It is impossible to guess that, in the next part, he will suddenly rise to become one of the main characters.

We said that Sholokhov could not simply take his fragment from the *Donshchina* and attach it to *The Quiet Don.* There was need for certain adaptations. So he created the chapters with Bunchuk and Listnitskii. They serve as an introduction and bridge to the former *Donshchina* fragment.

Literary criticism cannot question as to why Sholokhov did this or did not do that. Literary criticism can only state that in the new novel Sholokhov confined himself to a simple adaptation of the former *Donshchina* and did not attempt a more revolutionary change. The two books, as they appear now in the second volume of *The Quiet Don*, stand parallel to each other. At no point do they run into each other. At no time does the main character of *The Quiet Don* run across the *Donshchina* and its characters. Likewise, the main character of *Donshchina*, Bunchuk, does not blend with *The Quiet Don* and its characters. Even Listnitskii, the only character who, without much strain, is connected with the two concepts, runs across the main character of *The Quiet Don* only as his rival in the love affair, but never as the bearer of a social and political force.

The above statement that the two books stand in paralleled relationship to each other needs some modification. Inasmuch as *The Quiet Don* is a much larger piece, the novel as a whole creates a definite impression that the *Donshchina* fragment is an insertion into *The Quiet Don*.

Sholokhov made many people influence Grigorii Melekhov. One of them in this part was Garanzha, Grigorii's neighbor in the Moscow eye clinic. But for some reason, Sholokhov did not want, or could not have Grigorii meet Bunchuk, possibly the only true revolutionary in the entire novel.

Grigorii has his own peculiar Cossack way of life, far removed from the Revolution. One could assume that this was probably Sholokhov's initial concept of Grigorii devised for him from the very beginning.

One cannot help but notice the author's warm attitude to his beloved Don in Chapter XVI. True, most of the time he is a neutral observer who stands and watches the life of his people at a distance, but he is not an indifferent observer. Though he does not directly involve himself in the life of his characters, he cannot hide his sympathies.

In Chapter XVI, the Melekhovs received a letter informing them of their son Grigorii's death. It is as if the invisible deceased took a dwelling in their house. A haze of sorrow covered the once gay but now sad Don. The episode is written in a different tone and style. It reveals a popular-sentimental attitude to life. The author was indifferent to the death of the unknown young student, whom we mentioned earlier. But he is not an indifferent outsider when it comes to the Melekhov family. It seems that Sholokhov himself suffers with his Cossack characters at the loss of one of their members and he strikes his readers with his suffering. The news of Grigorii's death proved, however, to be wrong. Chapter XVII reports of Petro's letter and that Grigorii was alive.

From the remainder of Part Three, Natal'ia's visit to Aksin'ia must be mentioned. (Chapters XVIII and XIX) The meek and humble Natal'ia hoped that Aksin'ia would give up Grigorii. But all she experienced was more humiliation. All the possessive and raptorial Aksin'ia could do was to further insult Natal'ia. Later, in Chapter XXII, when Aksin'ia's daughter becomes ill, she, in a wave of repentance decided for herself that God is punishing her for taunting Natal'ia. In reality, however, it was not so much God, as Sholokhov himself

who wanted to punish Aksin'ia for her mockery of
Natal'ia. Aksin'ia's daughter died. Sholokhov did not
let Aksin'ia grieve for her child in the same way as he
let the Melekhovs grieve over the loss of their son.
Neither did the author himself grieve over Aksin'ia's
loss, as he grieved over that of the Melekhovs. When the
young Listnitskii approached her, Aksin'ia gave herself
to him with all her passion. Thus Listnitskii became
Grigorii's rival for Aksin'ia's wanton beauty.

Having finished Part Three with all the necessary
adjustments, Sholokhov turned to his *Donshchina* fragment and again readjusted it to *The Quiet Don.* He had
written and interpolated a few chapters from *The Quiet
Don,* as was discussed previously. (Cf. pp. 70f., 80f.)
Seen on the whole, he let his *Donshchina* remain what
it was. Apart from a few insignificant adjustments and
interpolations, he did not make any major changes in
his original *Donshchina* concept. The *Donshchina* parts
remained a different book, a foreign body in the
structure of *The Quiet Don.*

In this way, Sholokhov had brought together Four
Parts. To continue the book, he needed a transition.
This was written as the last chapter of Part Four and the
first chapter of Part Five.

Continuing with his writing, he thus arrived at Part
Five. It would be natural to expect that Part Five
should become a synthesis of the concepts of *The Quiet
Don* and of the former *Donshchina* novel. Sholokhov
did not, however, make a synthesis. He did not bring
the two different concepts into one organic unit, but
continued the two lines, each separately from the other.

The end result was that in spite of the mutual readjustment of the two plot lines, if he had omitted the former *Donshchina* fragment, i.e. Part Four, the structure of *The Quiet Don* would not have lost anything. There would be no great break between Parts Three and Five. In fact, the opposite is true. Part Four probably adds more to the achievement of a break for the novel.

Continuing the novel with Part Five, and having inserted Part Four, Sholokhov did not overcome a gap in the structure. While the plot line of Part Three—Grigorii and the Cossacks in the hamlet Tatarsk—finds its direct continuation in Part Five, the *Donshchina* plot line—Bunchuk-Listnitskii—has disintegrated in this Part. Bunchuk, to be sure, occupies relatively much space in Part Five, but he has hardly any connection with the previous part. He is not a chief protagonist of the Revolutionary forces, but an insignificant screw, one among many others. As to Listnitskii, Bunchuk's former antagonist, he is mentioned only once in the whole of Part Five, and in a different connection—as a rival to Grigorii.

Having disintegrated the Bunchuk-Listnitskii plot line of the former *Donshchina,* Sholokhov created two new lines in addition to his earlier Grigorii plot lines.

In the structure of Part Five it is possible thus to discern three independent plot lines, or parallel centers. Here there is the same ramification of the plot that we observed in Part Three. As in Part Three, the ramification in Part Five took place at the expense of Grigorii's plot line.

The first center is the continuation of the Grigorii Melekhov line, with his participation in the Revolution and his subsequent conversion to the Counter-Revolution. The second line was created anew for this part. It presents, apart from Grigorii's participation, the revolutionary, and the counter-revolutionary Don respectively. The third line, also a new one, is built around Bunchuk and his end. Bunchuk in this part is a new creation. He has hardly any connection with the Bunchuk from the previous Part Four. All three lines interweave with each other without forming an organic unity. Grigorii, forming his own center, is connected first with the Revolution, and later with the Counter-Revolution. At the end Bunchuk's line flows together with the revolutionary line where they both find their end. These connections are, however, only superficial. Seen on the whole, the three lines run parallel. The Revolution proceeds its own way, and the Cossack life goes its own way in turn. It is the same method of the parallel presentation of various focal points that may be seen in Tolstoi's masterpiece.

The revolutionary, and respectively the counter-revolutionary line is a new one. It contains a great deal of documentary material. It came into the novel as the front line was discontinued. Possibly it was thought of by the author as a continuation of the former *Donshchina* concept. Here Sholokhov has created quite a number of the new characters—Podtëlkov, Kryvoshlykov, Lagutin, the latter having been taken from the *Donshchina*. (Cf. p. 75.)

Bunchuk, for some reason, was not made a main character and an organic part of this line. Rather, as was indicated, he formed his own line. Having first introduced the revolutionary situation on the Don. Sholokhov then devoted four chapters to Bunchuk. We remember Bunchuk from the *Donshchina,* where he played a most important role as the opponent to List-nitskii. In this part, however, Bunchuk is reduced to a second-rate character. Sholokhov devoted enough space to him, but did not give him a decisive role. He does not occupy the same prominent place in the structure as we would expect him to occupy. In the battles against the White Cossacks for the *stanitsas* Kamenskaia and Glu-bokaia in January, 1918, Bunchuk played a small and utterly insignificant role. Grigorii Melekhov, who was also fighting here on the side of the Revolution, has not only overshadowed, but has completely replaced Bun-chuk. We see Bunchuk only as Grigorii saw him. Thus, he plays not an independent, but only an auxiliary role. Sholokhov had Grigorii and Bunchuk meet each other, but did not have them come into much contact with each other. For Grigorii, Bunchuk, the fiery revolution-ary, remained only the nameless commander of a machine-gun detachment, and a skirtchaser.

After these events, Sholokhov had Bunchuk serve in the Revolutionary terror tribunal. To be sure, in this capacity Bunchuk was more revolutionary than many other good revolutionaries in the novel. Nevertheless, his role in the Revolution and in the novel was of small importance. Bunchuk never again rose to the role he played in the opening chapters of the *Donshchina* frag-ment. At the end of Part Five he dies. With Bunchuk's death the *Donshchina* line ceases completely in the novel. Listnitskii, to be sure, will appear in the subse-quent parts, but his role in the novel will never be the same as in the *Donshchina's* opening chapters. Listnit-skii will be needed by Sholokhov as an auxiliary character. He will be mentioned later in the course of our discussion.

Grigorii Melekhov, as we already noted, does not occupy a prominent role in the plot of this part either. Sholokhov mentioned him in Chapter I, when all the Tatarsk Cossacks were returning home from the collapsing front, late in the fall of 1917. Grigorii did not return home, but was the only one among the Cossacks from the hamlet to join the Bolsheviks. Chapter II then, in retrospect and in official style, and only as if by chance mentions Grigorii's past promotion to the rank of officer, his sickness and his vacation at home. After the October coup he was appointed to the rank of *sotnik* (an officer in command of one hundred men). Here began his search for the meaning of the Revolution.

> After this time his opinion underwent a considerable change, as a result of the events occurring around him and the influence of one of the officers in the regiment. (*Part Five, Chapter II.*)

This is a documentary style, different from those passages which usually deal with Grigorii. The break seems to have occurred not only in Grigorii's frame of mind, but also in the author's style. When the author, continuing with his hero, tried to adjust him to the new circumstances of life, he could not achieve a smooth transition.

Grigorii could not find his place in the new circumstances. He was not made for great passions and fateful turns of history. He left the Revolution and returned home to plow the soil and to care for his family. Sholokhov showed him how to be a true son of the Don. His tragedy was that when he left the Revolution, the Revolution could not leave him alone. The Revolution forced him to take a position.

At the time of his return home there is an apparent break in the text. According to the text (Chapter XIII), he returned home in January, 1918. Chapter II of this part reported that in the fall of 1917, after his illness, he had spent a month and a half at home. Consequently, it must have been a few weeks that Grigorii was absent from home. Chapter XIII presents his return home in January of 1918 as occurring after a very long absence. Years must have passed since he had last been home.

The gap could have occurred when Sholokhov put the manuscripts of the former *Donshchina* fragment and that of *The Quiet Don* together. The break suggests that in Chapter II Grigorii could have been the organic part of the *Donshchina,* and in Chapter XIII Sholokhov had suddenly transferred him to *The Quiet Don.* As a matter of fact, some Soviet critics have asserted that Grigorii was a firm component of the *Donshchina* concept. This would easily explain the break.

Yet, this can hardly be the case. We saw that there was practically no place for Grigorii in the *Donshchina.* The gap had occurred, rather, when Sholokhov attempted to combine the plot line of the *Donshchina* and that of *The Quiet Don.* The break in Bunchuk's and Listnitskii's lines can also be explained by this abortive attempt. He did not succeed in combining the two concepts into one organic unity. Part Five, with its three different plot lines, bears vivid witness to the author's attempt.

As Sholokhov continued with the novel, he let only Grigorii survive beyond Part Five.

Sholokhov's original design for his large novel, *Donshchina,* as we have discussed above, was to present the Cossacks and the Revolution. When Sholokhov recognized that he could not realize this design in the *Donshchina,* he started a new novel, which eventually became *The Quiet Don.* It, in turn, became a novel about the Cossacks and the Revolution and, respectively, the counter-revolution. But for this Sholokhov needed different characters and different events, which he subsequently had created anew.

The Quiet Don thus became the fulfillment of the *Donshchina* concept, but with new and different characters. All the characters created for the former *Donshchina* fragment did not survive Part Five. Only Listnitskii, who is an integral part of the both designs, will be mentioned in passing in the following part.

To continue the novel beyond Part Five, Sholokhov has taken the characters from *The Quiet Don* and then attached them to his original *Donshchina* design—which was the Cossacks and the Revolution.

The whole of Part Six, as the rest of the book, is then devoted to the theme of the Cossacks and the Revolution, and respectively, the counter-revolution. Actually, there is much more written about the counter-revolution in the novel than about the Revolution.

In Part Six the Revolution is first of all presented only as a fleeting event in the course of life at the hamlet Tatarsk. The Revolution in the Don area is seen mostly through the eyes of those Cossacks who opposed the Revolution, i.e. through the eyes of the actual participants of the counter-revolution.

With a more or less positive degree of certainty we may assume that the whole of Part Six was written from the author's personal observations and experience. He spent the years of the Civil War on the Don and could thus witness the proceeding events as they appeared to him in his boyish Cossack imagination. This must be especially true in regard to the first brief reign of the Soviets on the Don. As this reign is presented in the novel, it must have undoubtedly been a reign of terror, from the point of view of the local Cossacks.

Grigorii Melekhov, after having been pushed into the background in the course of the last two parts, in Part Six emerges again as its main character. We remember that the main plot line in *The Quiet Don* started with the love affair between Grigorii and Aksin'ia. As Sholokhov continued his portrayal of Grigorii, he brought him beyond the love intrigue and connected him with the social and political problems of his time. In Part Six, which constitutes all of Book Three, Grigorii defiles before us not in his love conflict, but in his political and social dilemma—rejection or acceptance of the Revolution. The love conflict does not play any role in this part, as the social and political conflict did not play any role in Parts One through Three.

Grigorii could not accept the Revolution. From his Cossack point of view, the Revolution was utterly incomprehensible, and an event that was foreign to him. The author did not present any reason as to why Grigorii, a simple Cossack, should or could have accepted the Revolution. To be a Red and to fight for the Reds meant as much as to betray the Don and its traditions. True, he equally questioned the cause of the Cossacks in their fight against the Reds, and did not seem to be entirely willing to accept the Cossack cause either. But the questioning of the Cossack cause arose only because he felt that it would be a lost cause. Nevertheless, he accepted the Cossack cause truly and he fought on for its behalf. The real tragedy in his case was that there was no third alternative open to him.

Part Six began with April, 1918 and the new war. At that time, the Cossacks seemed to have fresh hopes for a quick victory over the Red intruders. None of them thought that the new war would last very long, and nobody wanted to do any real fighting. But as the fight was imposed by the Reds, everybody was forced to fight for his home and for his piece of land. The struggle for existence guided Grigorii and all the Cossacks in this fight. The motive of the struggle is proper to the whole novel, but Part Six seems to be especially loaded with it.

Sholokhov brought much documentary material into his plot, as was the case with Parts Four and Five. Thus, Chapter IV reports of the Conference of the Don Government with Generals Krasnov, Bogaevskii, Alekseev, and Denikin as participants. This is all part of history. To such historic events belongs also the uprising in the *stanitsa* Veshenskaia and its variable course.

Sholokhov again took up young Listnitskii and, in this part, brought him to an end. Thus, Chapter V is devoted to Listnitskii. This chapter produces an effect of being an insertion into the body of *The Quiet Don*. The Listnitskii presented in this chapter had nothing to do with the former Listnitskii, the fighter against the Revolution. True, he was still an officer in the White Army, but he is not presented as that arch-enemy of the Revolution and the staunch monarchist that we knew in the former *Donshchina* fragment. We see him in his relationship with another officer, his friend Gorchakov and his wife Olga. Listnitskii quotes verses from Bunin's poetry and from Blok's sweet and languorous *Unknown Lady.* He is not without human charm and warm human feelings. Tired of war and killing, he is a decent human being. This is not the attitude of Proletarian literature to a representative of the gentry.

At the end, Sholokhov had Listnitskii lose his arm. As an invalid he had to retire from the service. Having married his dead friend's wife Olga, he arrived at his father's estate Iagodnoe. Upon seeing Aksin'ia's wanton beauty, Listnitskii flushed heavily and felt oppressed. He now had to send Aksin'ia away.

Here Listnitskii found his end in the novel. In Part Eight it is mentioned indirectly that he committed suicide. Nothing more is known of him. Once Listnitskii was created by the author to play a major part in the novel. But as the author had changed the concept of his novel, he also changed Listnitskii's part, from that of being a protagonist of the Revolution to the unknown end. It seems he has lost interest in Listnitskii.

In order to enhance the love intrigue, the author had Aksin'ia return to the hamlet Tatarsk, her home. In time she will be again driven toward Grigorii. This was required by the structure of the novel. Meanwhile, Aksin'ia returns to her husband who, after spending the years of the war in Germany as a prisoner of war, reappears again in the novel to play the role of husband and rival. It was for this purpose that the author had brought him from Germany. In connection with Aksin'ia's return to Stepan, the author again revealed his negative attitude toward her, as we observed in the beginning. The author called her pride a black pride and her will an evil will.[8]   A certain irony is felt in her answer to Stepan, when she promises to stay with him for good and never to leave him.

The Cossacks' fight against the Reds is shown through the eyes of the local Tatarsk Cossacks. Sholokhov seems to want to say that from the very outset his Cossacks had no chance for victory. They were tired and did not want to fight. They hoped for a swift victory. But when swift victory was not attained, the Cossacks deserted the front, and their defeat became thus inevitable.

Melekhov's family, as all other Cossacks, had to go through an agonizing decision: to stay home and wait for the Reds or to leave their homes and farms and venture out into the unknown. (Chapter XIII.) Sholokhov could not conceal his feelings that for his beloved Cossacks it was a very hard lot.

The arrival of the Red soldiers and the short-lived reign of the Soviets in the hamlet Tatarsk is described in the words of an eyewitness:

> Terrible as was this first moment of the enemy troops, the giggling Duniasha could not restrain herself. . . .
>
> . . ."Oh, Natal'ia, my dear, how they ride their horses! One man was wriggling backwards and forwards, backwards and forwards in the saddle. . .and his arms and elbows were knocking against his sides."
>
> So well did she imitate the Red Army men fidgeting in their saddles that Natal'ia, suppressing her laughter, ran to the bed and threw herself face downward on the pillow, to avoid drawing down her father-in-law's wrath upon her. (*Part Six, Chapter XVI.*)

Sholokhov could not hide the fear and trembling felt by all the Cossacks before the oncoming Reds. Nor could he hide the fact that the reign of the Soviets on the Don was a reign of terror. Equally, he could not hide the fact of the Cossacks' hostility toward the new regime. There was much chaos and confusion in the Revolution, which his Cossacks could not understand or accept.

Thus the Revolution is presented only negatively, as a destructive and disorderly force. Chapter XX, for instance, reports of Grigorii's attempt to find some meaning in the Revolution. Once, in January (it must have been the year 1919) he dropped into the office of the local revolutionary committee in order "to tell them what was boiling inside him." The only answer he received from the representatives of the new government was that he should not speak against the authority. "And don't say too much about the government because I'm village chairman, and it is not wise for me to argue with you here."[9] Thus, all Grigorii had to do was accept the new government without reservation. The Soviet authority regarded itself to be a model of the ideal where everyone knows how to behave and consequently everyone behaves exceptionally well. Those who do not know how to behave are enemies and, as such, should be annihilated.

Probably with the purpose of strengthening the revolutionary plot line and bringing some system into the chaos of the Revolution, Sholokhov brought Stockman back to his Tatarsk Cossacks. But again Sholokhov could not conceal the fact that Stockman's revolutionary zeal only further alienated the Cossacks from the Revolution.

Sholokhov said not a word about Stockman's private life, as if he had none.   When he was arrested (Part Three, Chapter I), we heard for the first and last time that his wife stayed behind in the hamlet Tatarsk.   But now, when he has returned from exile and arrived again in the hamlet Tatarsk, nothing is said about his family.

The Cossack uprising against the Revolution, as it is presented by Sholokhov, was spontaneous and was carried out unanimously.   This was experienced not only by the many enemies of the Revolution, but by Mishka Koshevoi, the local Cossack revolutionary.

Having spent all the years of the Civil War on the Don, Sholokhov was thus a witness of the Cossacks' attitude toward the Revolution and their uprising against the Red regime.   Thus, he was able to present the uprising from first-hand experience.   Its spontaneity, the indecisiveness of the Cossacks, the lack of a strict organization among the insurgents, the many plastic details like Astakhov's refusal to take a side, the liberation of the old Melekhov from arrest, the death of Petro Melekhov and the capture of the Red commissar Likhachev, his appearance, and then the initial enthusiasm of the Cossacks and their hope for swift victory over the Reds, —all these could only have been presented from personal observation.

The unknown Red commissar Likhachev was captured by Grigorii and tortured to death by the Cossack mob in the *stanitsa* Veshenskaia, as he was leading the punitive expedition against the insurgents.[10] Sholokhov has created Commissar Likhachev only to have him die a heroic death. He serves no other purpose in the novel.

The site of the uprising, the operations of the Cossack

Command, and the whole course of the uprising as well, are presented from the Cossacks' point of view and could have been taken from the Cossack press of those years. The documentary materials were imbraided with Grigorii's personal involvement in the actions, i.e. with the author's free invention.

The initial successes of the uprising were soon stalled by overwhelming forces of the Red Armies. The insurgents sharply felt the shortage of ammunition and arms. The Cossacks had only their sabres to rely on. Sholokhov had created a mood of doom for the Cossacks' endeavor. Grigorii, more than any one else, felt the mood of doom and predestination for the lost cause of his Don. Even Grigorii's personal bravery and reckless daring, as once in the German War, could not change the mood of futility and hopelessness he felt for the cause to which he had given his life. To the contrary, his personal bravery, like the massacre of the four Red sailors, had even more enhanced his own gloom and desperation as that of the cause for which he was fighting.

In spite of the Cossacks' enthusiasm and their devotion to their cause, there was nothing that could bring about their victory over the Reds. Neither the sabering of the 147 Red Army men (Chapter XLI) nor the death of the Tatarsk Communists, Stockman and Ivan Alekseevich (Chapters XLIX and LVI), could avert the shadow of destiny over the beloved Don.

Into the mood of desperation Sholokhov has brought many lyrical retreats. The spring of the Cossacks' insurrection was beautiful as no other spring had been in their lives.

> The spring of 1919 was brilliant with unusual beauty.
> The April days were fine and as translucent as glass. Over
> the inaccessible azure sweep of heaven the flocks of wild
> geese and copper-tongued cranes floated, floated, over-
> taking the clouds, flying away to the north. (*Part Six,
> Chapter, XLIII.*)

This passage, like many similar ones in this part,
served the author as a means of relieving tension. The
tensions of the plot became so loaded with explosive
material that the novel threatened to grow one-sided
and perhaps even to lose its grasp of the reality of
everyday life. Sholokhov felt a certain need for dis-
charging elements. He created this by the factor which
we termed as a lyrical retreat.

Chapter XLV reports in this vein of Grigorii's hunt
for a goose. The previous chapter was loaded with
extreme tensions. Grigorii, in a moment of delirious
attack, sabred four sailors and then fell into a state of
oblivion. He seemed to have lost control over his
actions and thoughts. The following day he, having
handed over the command of his division to one of his
regimental commanders, left the front. While riding to
Veshenskaia, he caught sight of some wild geese and
began to hunt. Structurally, the scene of hunting does
not play any role in the novel. But it was a necessary
pause, introduced to relieve the tension and probably
also to present another side of Grigorii's personality:
his human quality. He was not only a reckless soldier-
hero, but also a peaceful and thoughtful Cossack-hunter.

Continuing with the elements of the diversion, as a
means of creating a counterpart to the military side of
the novel, Sholokhov had Grigorii resume his old love

affair with Aksin'ia. Now as before, Sholokhov's attitude to Aksin'ia is very negative. The author in his words said of Aksin'ia that "she still retained her wanton and seductive charm."[11] In regard to the novel's structure, Grigorii's new love affair fulfills the same function as the author's lyrical retreats—to introduce a balance to the military and historical factors.

The new turn in Grigorii's old love affair coincided with a turn for the worse in the personal relationships of the Melekhov family and in the Cossacks' military endeavor as well. At the Cossacks' front, in spite of the temporary successes, the depressed mood continued to prevail among the Cossacks. Sholokhov seems to want to convey a thought that there was no longer a force which would prevent the Cossacks' final defeat and then their destruction. Everywhere there were seen signs of desolation in life, and of a coldness and emptiness in the people. After Grigorii had spent a night with Aksin'ia he felt more strongly than before that there would be no more peace and calm for his Cossack life.

> Well, life has taken a new turn, but my heart is still cold and empty. . . . Even Aksin'ia can't fill that emptiness now. . . . (*Part Six, Chapter LI.*)

Sholokhov finished Part Six with a note that forebode destruction. The Cossacks had been retreating under the attacks of the Reds. Grigorii, as if forgetting his duty and place, fully succumbed to his passion for Aksin'ia. He felt that he had to reward himself for those loveless years, which, as he thought, were the lost years of his life. The retreating Cossacks left the hamlet Tatarsk to the revenge of the Red soldiers. The hamlet was thus visited by Mishka Koshevoi.[12]   Seven Cossack farmsteads were set on fire by him.

All of Part Six was finished probably toward the end of 1929.   Chapters I-XII were already published in the January issue of the literary monthly *Oktiabr'* of that year.

In December of 1929, the Rostov literary journal *Na Pod'eme,* the organ of the local Association of Proletarian Writers, announced that soon it would publish the third volume of *The Quiet Don.* The novel, however, did not appear in print until late 1932, when it was published in the literary monthly *Oktiabr',* the same magazine which published the first two volumes.

What happened in the course of these three years— we know only partially.   It is known that the author had undergone several hard trials during these years. Complete information as to what did actually transpire will probably be made available only after Sholokhov's death.   As long as he is alive, there will be no access to all the documents necessary to elucidate what was involved behind the scenes of the difficult experiences which nearly destroyed his work and his personality.

In 1929, rumors were heard that young Sholokhov was not the real author of the excellent novel, but that Sholokhov presumably used a manuscript of a certain Goloushev, a White Officer, a former friend of Sholokhov's wife.[13]   The rumors were very persistent, and soon they must have reached Sholokhov himself.   The RAPP was forced to form a commission to investigate the charge.   On March 29, 1929, the commission published in *Pravda* a declaration which cleared Sholokhov of plagiarism and which stated that the aforementioned rumors had no substance.[14]

The rumors were, however, not stopped with this declaration. One year later, on April 1, 1930, Sholokhov, in an unpublished letter to Serafimovitch, still complained about the slander.[15]

The second trial occurred when there had arisen a question as to the ideological substance of his work. Proletarian literature critics chided Sholokhov for his failure to understand the cause of the Communist Revolution and for the justification of the well-to-do Cossacks and their uprising against the Communists in 1919.[16] It was apparently on this account that the proletarian journal refused the publication of the novel.

Complete scholarly research on these charges would over extend the frames of this book. We have to limit ourselves here only with a general statement. The facts of the charge became partially known in Russian and in foreign Sholokhoviana. In any event, I would not be able here to shed new light on them and, therefore, would only be repeating what became known in earlier works on Sholokhov.[17]

Sholokhov, young and optimistic as he was at that time, was not intimidated by this harsh and, as he thought, unjust criticism. He took his case again to his old friend and well-wisher Serafimovitch, and then to Gorky.

Meanwhile, waiting for a good outcome of their judgment, Sholokhov began to write a new novel. It was the first volume of *Virgin Soil Upturned.* To prove his loyalty to the proletarian cause, he at the end of 1930 applied for and was given membership in the

Communist Party, first as a candidate and, two years later, in November of 1932, as a full-fledged member.

We do not know exactly to what extent Gorky and Serafimovitch placed their authority behind Sholokhov's troubled novel, and what was happening behind the scenes in regard to its publication. But their intercession and support on behalf of the young author brought good results. The third volume of *The Quiet Don* was published, although with several cuts, in the literary monthly *Oktiabr'* in installments in January-October, 1932, simultaneously with *Virgin Soil Upturned,* which appeared in January-September, 1932 in installments of *Novyi mir.*

The last installment of *The Quiet Don* announced that the fourth and final volume of the novel would be published in 1933. This, however, did not happen until seven years later, when the whole book was finally finished.

Before the publication of the third volume of *The Quiet Don,* Sholokhov had already witnessed numerous translations of the first two volumes into foreign languages. In 1930, *The Quiet Don* was published in German, Spanish, French, Czech and Swedish translations; in 1932 it was put out in Danish and in 1934 it was translated into English and published in London and New York. At once, Sholokhov became a celebrity.

At home, however, things did not go as smoothly for him as one would expect. Even though the general response to his novels had become friendly, Sholokhov was headed for personal troubles in the struggle over collectivization. At that time he had enough courage and idealism to believe in the best intentions of his

Party in regard to the individual peasant's lot. When, in the course of collectivization, the first signs of savage catastrophe for the peasants' lot became apparent, Sholokhov did not hesitate to interfere on behalf of the hard-stricken peasants. He wrote to the local Party bureaucracy, he wrote to *Pravda,* and finally he even wrote to Stalin, asking and begging the authority to intervene and to investigate the massive excesses of the harsh and irregular methods of collectivization.

But Sholokhov did not have much success with his intercessions. Khrushchev revealed in 1963 that Stalin not only disregarded Sholokhov's letters, but even rebuked Sholokhov for not understanding the issues behind collectivization and for taking the peasants' side.

In the answer, as it is quoted by Khrushchev, Stalin, on one hand, in his way gave Sholokhov credit for reporting the distortions and atrocities of the bureaucracy, but then on the other hand, (and this was the real sense of Stalin's answer) he severely reprimanded Sholokhov for interfering in the political affairs of the state and, of course, ignored Sholokhov's deep concern for justice and fairness in the administration's dealings with peasants.[18]

Sholokhov's interference testifies to the unusual boldness and enthusiasm of the young author. It was not yet the end, however, of his personal troubles. A greater trial awaited him.

Sholokhov seemed to have been tireless in those years, where the well-being of his Cossacks was at stake. He interfered on their behalf whenever he could. A certain Plotkin, one of the Twenty-five Thousanders who were sent by the Party to carry out the collectivi-

zation of agriculture, and who, like Sholokhov's Davydov from *Virgin Soil Upturned,* had become chairman
of one of the Kollectiv farms and whom Sholokhov
befriended, in his unpublished memoirs tells of the
following incident: "Coming one day to Sholokhov, I
met him on the porch. Laughing, he pointed to the
door and said: 'Look, guests have tore away the door-
handle!'" By guests, Sholokhov meant those numerous
people who came to him with their various complaints
and worries. Many people came to him: peasants,
clerks, loyal Communists, and non-Communists, men
and women. Everyone wanted Sholokhov's advice, help,
or had a complaint against an unlawful action of the
authorities. Sholokhov never refused to help. Whenever he could, he gave his advice, called, or wrote.[19] In
December, 1933, Sholokhov wrote to the same Plotkin:
"Prosperous life did not succeed this year. It will not
succeed in the future either. Maybe in two or three
years hence."[20] The famous "prosperous life" here is
used ironically, as a parody on Stalin's known slogan,
coined in early 1933, in which Stalin declared that life
in the country was becoming more prosperous and
happier with every coming year.

Because of all this, Sholokhov's literary work had, of
course, to suffer during that period, and was much
delayed. Sholokhov himself declared that he would
finish Volume Four of *The Quiet Don* toward the end
of 1934. In the plans of the State Publishing House for
the year 1937, *The Quiet Don* and *Virgin Soil Upturned*
were accepted as facts. But only in 1938 was Part Seven
published in the monthly, *The New World.* The whole
novel was not finished until 1940, and then *Virgin Soil*

Upturned was not completed until twenty years later.

In 1937 the stormy clouds gathered over his personal life, as they did over life in the whole country. A group of local Party functionaries in Veshenskaia was arrested and accused of aiding the enemies. Sholokhov had known the arrested well for many years, and was friendly with them. Among them was a certain Lugovoi, secretary of the Party Committee in Sholokhov's home *stanitsa* Veshenskaia. Sholokhov had not even the slightest doubt as to Lugovoi's integrity and sincerity. He could not understand the charge. Iakimenko, the only Sholokhovist who has so far revealed this dark story, tells it, apparently, from Lugovoi's own words.

Sholokhov took upon himself the fight for Lugovoi's release. He succeeded in getting a rendezvous with Lugovoi in the presence of the infamous Ezhov, the People's Commissar of the Internal Security in those years, (the notorious N.K.V.D.). As a result of this interference, Lugovoi and his group were released and the fantastic charge was apparently dropped and forgotten. It was not yet the end, however, of Sholokhov's personal trials, nor of those of his country in those troublesome years.

The next trial, probably the hardest and the most cunning of all of Sholokhov's troubles, is again so far only reported by Iakimenko. And again it is narrated apparently from the oral report of a certain Pogorelov, who played a key role in this trial. Iakimenko does not give any source for his report, but indicated clearly that he knew and met Pogorelov in person.[21]

Pogorelov took an active part in the Civil War as a *Chekist* (member of a special commission to fight coun-

ter-revolutionary activities—1917-1922) and was decor-
ated with the Red Banner for his services. In the years
of Stalin's purges, he worked for the Party bureaucracy.
Then suddenly he was acussed of sympathies to the
enemies of the people and was expelled from the Party.
He was not yet arrested, but, of course, he expected
that this would happen any time.

Once he was called by the Chairman of the Rostov
Provincial Secret Police and was given a special assignment. The assignment seemingly came from Stalin and
Ezhov, the Chief of the Secret Police. Pogorelov
answered that he was ready to fulfill any assignment
from Stalin. The assignment was devised to the effect
that Pogorelov was given a chance to prove his loyalty
to the Party.

Stalin's special assignment consisted of the following:
the Soviet intelligence service had obtained positive
evidence that the famous Soviet author Sholokhov, together with friends such as Lugovoi and others, were
preparing an uprising of the Cossacks against the Soviet
Government. Pogorelov's assignment was to find more
connections in the conspiracy. He was told that Sholokhov had involved many people in his conspiracy and
that he even had connections abroad. For this purpose
Pogorelov had to gain Sholokhov's confidence, and by
talking to Sholokhov against the Soviet Government to
try to find Sholokhov's confidants and agents.

As Iakimenko told the story, Pogorelov could not
refuse this special assignment without endangering his
own safety. He also had to give a written promise that
in case he revealed his assignment to anyone, he would
be shot without an investigation or trial.

Pogorelov did not believe "the positive evidences" revealed to him by the Chief of the Provincial Secret Police. He did not have any doubts as to Sholokhov's innocence. He knew that this was a provocation, which meant that for some reason Sholokhov was already counted as one of the enemies of the people, and as such he would be liquidated. But he accepted the assignment in order to save Sholokhov.

Pogorelov, risking his life, managed to inform Sholokhov of the provocation against his life. In turn, Sholokhov managed to bring the case to Stalin's attention. A special session of the Party's highest power cremium, the Politburo, devoted to the investigation of this special assignment, took place in Moscow soon after. Sholokhov, Pogorelov and Lugovoi were present at the meeting together with the Rostov Provincial Secret Police Administration. Stalin asked who gave the assignment. The Chief of the Rostov Provincial Secret Police answered that he coordinated this assignment with Ezhov. But Ezhov denied that he ever knew of this affair and stated that he never gave any instructions in regard to Sholokhov and his conspiracy.

At this meeting Stalin assured Sholokhov that he could work peacefully, and that the personal safety of his life would be guaranteed.

This is a story told by the Sholokhovist Iakimenko.[22] There are many platitudinous assertions and open questions in it. First of all, Iakimenko does not reveal any written sources for his most unusual information, aside from those narrated to him apparently by Pogorelov himself. There are also no exact dates. On the whole, however, the story belongs to those more plausible. It is evident that at this time no complete investigation of the whole affair is possible in the Soviet Union. Iakimenko, finishing and publishing his book at the crescent of the so-called Second Thaw period, could reveal only partially and in only the most general terms the dramatic mystery of those years. This is what we are allowed to know at this time.

In any event, under such circumstances, Sholokhov could not think of finishing his started works. In addition to the personal disturbances, there were also difficulties of ideological order with the censorship. He must have had more than enough of these difficulties. On May 10, 1936, *Sotsialisticheskii Vestnik* in New York, the journal of the Russian Mensheviks in exile, informed its readers that the manuscript of the second volume of *Virgin Soil Upturned* was returned to Sholokhov for substantial changes.[23]

However that may be, Part Seven of *The Quiet Don* was published only in 1938, and Part Eight two years later, in 1940.

Part Seven is a direct continuation of the previous Part Six and is actually the end of the long novel. The author continues without interruption in the same vein of presentation as he did in the previous parts. It must have been written long before it was published.

There are again, as we observed in the previous part, two focal points which are constantly interchanged. At one end there is the Cossack uprising with Grigorii in its background. The second is the Melekhov family in the background of the general ravage of Cossack life through the long, devastating war. Sholokhov created a picture where life showed an incessant propensity to ebb, to decrease in its quality and quantity. At one time the life of the Cossacks had been full of lighthearted gaiety, where untroubled peace prevailed. The Cossack took pride in their wealth and the abundance of their labor's fruits. But now, everywhere there were seen signs of neglect and ruin. This neglect and ruin saw Grigorii in the Listnitskii's estate Iagodnoe, where he used to work in his youthful years. Surrounded by all the fury of the raging war, Sholokhov nevertheless had enough time for his Grigorii to pause for a moment and see the signs of desolation and devastation.[24] The Cossack life was moving not toward a new and joyous beginning, but was rolling faster and faster down hill, to an unknown and a terrible catastrophe.

The signs of desolation and ruin were seen not only in the Cossacks' way of life outwardly, but also inwardly in their families. The strong ties in the Melekhov family were breaking. There was destruction, swift and unexpected of all centuries-established relationships.

On the fronts of the Cossack uprising there were enough successful operations. Chapter III reports of 800 captured Red Army soldiers sabred by the enraged Cossacks. Chapter XV reports again of 200 captured Reds. In the spring of 1920 the Cossack insurgent divisions were enforced by the regular White Army. The new hope for a swift victory over the Reds began to flicker again among the Cossacks. On the other hand, the weariness and unwillingness to fight beyond their own home grounds and their Cossack fields prevailed among the Cossacks and brought the temporary successes to naught. The temporary successes of the Cossacks' sabres did not change the mood of doom and desperation which began in the previous chapter.

Grigorii as if in his subconscious vacillation between the possessive Aksin'ia and his meek Natal'ia very vividly reflected the mood of the Cossacks in their struggle for their own way of life against the Red intruders.

Yet in spite of this life, doomed to pass, Sholokhov was able to present a picture of struggles, the outcome of which was yet unknown. There were no foreboding symbols or signs in the text which would point to the end of the old life and the beginning of the new one, or which would indicate the senseless end of the struggle. There is nothing in the novel that might give even the slightest inkling to the effect of how it might end. Sholokhov is a hard realist, and such he remained consequently to the end.

Part Eight, the last part, serves as an epilogue to the long novel.

In the previous part Sholokhov had either lost, or brought to an abrupt end many of his characters. Bunchuk, Stockman, Kotliarov and many, many others were killed in the long struggle. The others, like Listnitskii, Mit'ka Korshunov, Stepan Astakhov, were lost on the long étape, or left behind somewhere. Their fate remained unknown. Sholokhov seemed to have no interest in their end. It was only in Grigorii's Odyssey that the author did not lose interest. Sholokhov wanted to bring him to a certain end.

Apparently, Sholokhov neither had nor did he see the end of his concept as he set out to write the novel. This came to him in the process of the work, as he continued his novel. This is evident from the treatment of the *Donshchina* fragment. At the beginning Sholokhov did not intend to make Mishka Koshevoi Grigorii's antagonist. But in Part Eight it became obvious that Grigorii needed an antithesis to his ill-fated life. Sholokhov, as we mentioned previously, had lost all his characters who could play an opposing role to Grigorii, merely maintaining the novel's balance. Only Mishka could fulfill this role. Mishka combined in his person two lines necessary for what we termed as the novel's ideological balance. He represented the new life and at the same time he was a successor to the old traditions of the Cossacks' life.

Sholokhov felt that only a man such as Mishka could restore and continue the traditions of the ruined Melekhov house. Thus, it was necessary first, to have him settle in the Melekhov home and second, to make him related to the Melekhov family, to be accepted into the family. This was achieved by means of Mishka's marriage to Duniasha, the Melekhov's youngest daughter.

Having settled in the Melekhov family, Mishka seemed to have resumed his old Cossack way of life.

> From the day when Koshevoi installed himself in the Melekhov home, everything on the farm took a new turn; . . . Mishka proved to be a zealous farmer. Despite his fever he worked without downing tools for a moment. (*Part Eight, Chapter III.*)

But Sholokhov could not leave Mishka as he was—a good, laborious Cossack, guardian of the Cossacks' old tradition. There arose a structural need for an antagonist to Grigorii. Grigorii had to be counterbalanced by someone who, as a Soviet man, would oppose him. What was more natural than to give this role to Mishka?

Sholokhov thus not only made Mishka a relative to the Melekhovs, but also upgraded his role in the novel. From a small and insignificant character, as we knew Mishka from the beginning, Sholokhov transformed him into the role of the protagonist to Grigorii. Thus, Mishka became a representative of the new life in the country, and at once himself emerged a new man, with all the best qualities of a Stalinist Party functionary.

The five initial chapters in this part are devoted to life in the old hamlet Tatarsk. Sholokhov succeeded in presenting the Cossacks' way of life, but he did not succeed in creating a new life. Life in the hamlet Tatarsk continued in the old vein, except that it was now much poorer and sadder.

In the conditions in which Sholokhov was finishing his novel, he could not do otherwise but condemn his beloved hero. In Chapter IV Sholokhov inserted a novella incident with a certain Kirill Gromov, a Cossack from the hamlet Tatarsk. This incident was needed not only to serve as a warning to Grigorii, but actually to condemn him.

Kirill Gromov, an insignificant character not previously mentioned in the novel, returned now to his native hamlet after having served in the First Cavalry Army. In the Cossack uprising, Kirill Gromov served under Mamontov and was distinguished by his irreconcilable and bitter attitude to the Soviets. Now, being discharged from the Red Army, he turned into a bandit.

It is as if by this novella Sholokhov wanted to say that there can be no confidence in a man such as Gromov. He will always remain an enemy to the Soviet Government. In part, Gromov's career was parallel to that of Grigorii's, except that Grigorii's alleged past crime against the Soviets was possibly greater than that of Gromov's. If Gromov cannot be changed into a new Soviet man, how then can Grigorii be trusted? He must be punished for his participation in the Cossack uprising.

After a prolonged absence of Grigorii from the pages of the novel, Sholokhov felt the need to reintroduce him. This was done via a novella of *Zovutka*. After the defeat of the White Armies, Grigorii disappeared from the novel. As we said above, Sholokhov turned to life in the hamlet Tatarsk, but nothing was heard of Grigorii. It is as if he had become a stranger. Now, in Chapter VI of the last part, we meet him again as he was returning home, after having been discharged from the service. As a demobilized Red commander, he was assigned a wagon and horses for his transportation. In one village not far from his native hamlet, for lack of horses he was given a pair of bullocks and a young widow for a driver. It is in the conversation between Grigorii and this unknown young widow, *Zovutka*, "call-me-what-you-like," that Grigorii was, as we said, as if reintroduced to his readers. First, we learn of his moral features, and, second, that he remained the same Grigorii that we knew from the beginning.

Here Sholokhov also revealed Grigorii's plans for his life, and his thoughts. It looked as though Sholokhov was preparing his hero for a quiet end and a happy life. Grigorii was longing to peacefully labor on his Cossack soil.

Sholokhov did not cast any signs foreshadowing the course that life in his novel might take in the future. He employed no symbol to try to divine what awaits his hero—happiness, or disaster. Sholokhov seemed to have refuted all the literary means and devices which could indicate which step his hero should choose, to take precautionary measures in his ill-fated life. Sholokhov remained an implacable factual statist of life.

Let us illustrate this by the novella of Aksin'ia's death. Grigorii, having reunited with Aksin'ia, seemed to have achieved that inward harmony which had evaded him his entire life. There was nothing in him, or in the nature around him that could portend the oncoming catastrophe. But when catastrophe ensues, it always has accompanying signs. At Aksin'ia's death and especially at her burial all the elements of nature, as accompanying symbols of the catastrophe, were not only mourning with Grigorii but were actually participating in his grief. There was "the brilliant morning light" and "the smoky haze" rising from the east and "above the black sky and the blindingly glittering, black disk of the sun."[25] All this was blended together as if it were an ill-omened sign over Grigorii's life. But actually it could no longer be an omen, inasmuch as at this moment, everything he hoped for was shattered and doomed.

Likewise, the end of the book does not give any positive sign—optimistic, or pessimistic, happy or unhappy—as to the future course of the Cossack life in the hamlet Tatarsk, or for Grigorii's own posterity. True, the author stated that Grigorii "stood at the gate of his own house and held his son in his arms."[26] Some critics regard this ending as a sure symbol of optimism in regard to the future course of the Cossack life.

The accompanying signs of this alleged optimistic ending however, do not give much reason for optimism.

While Grigorii was holding his son, "the only little thing that life left to him," Sholokhov also stated that this was "the only thing that bound Grigorii a little longer with the earth and with the wide world under the cold sun."[27]

Sholokhov gave indeed no reason for any optimistic hope in a world hostile to his beloved Cossack hero.

Sholokhov left many open questions, which he either could not, or did not want to answer. But it should be stressed once more that the charm of the novel lies exactly in the openness of its problems.

NOTES AND REFERENCES

1. Cf. V. Vasil'iev, *Tikhii Don.* Kandidatskaia dissertatsiia, Alma-Ata, 1948. Quoted in L. Iakimenko, *Sholokhov,* p. 339.

2. Cf. V. V. Gura, *Zhizn'i tvorchestvo, M. A. Sholokhova,* Moscow, 1960. Also literature there.

3. Zhdanov, *Trorcheskaia istoria Anny Kareninoi,* Moscow, 1957.

4. See about this N. N. Gusev, *Lev Nikolaevich Tolstoi Materialy s 1870 po 1881 god.,* Moscow, 1963, p. 5. See also my article "*Anna Karenina* Seen as an Expression of Schopenhauer's *Wille zum Leben*" in: *Proceedings of the Pacific Northwest Conference on Foreign Languages,* vol. XXI, University of Victoria, 1970, pp. 271-279.

5. Cf. *Anna Karenina,* Part Two, Chapter XVIII.

6. *Ibid.,* Part Two, Chapter XXI.

7. Cf. Eikhenbaum, *Lev Tolstoi, semidesiatye gody,* Leningrad 1960, p. 189ff.

8. Part Six, Chapter VII.

9. *Ibid.,* Part Six, Chapter XX.

10. *Ibid.,* Part Six, Chapter XXXI.

11. *Ibid.,* Part Six, Chapter L.

12. *Ibid.,* Part Six, Chapter LXV.

13. Iakimenko, *op. cit.*

14. Cf. Gura, Abramov, *Sholokhov, op. cit.,* p. 174.

15. *Ibid.,* p. 176.

16. *Ibid.,* p. 19.

17. Gura, Abramov, *Sholokhov, op. cit.,* pp. 6-28; Iakimenko, *op. cit.,* p. 130ff.; Stewart, *op. cit.,* pp. 163-174.

18. Iakimenko, *op. cit.,* pp. 140ff.

19. Quoted in Iakimenko, *op. cit.,* p. 142, without giving a source. This is why we have to presume that Plotkin's memoirs are not yet published.

20. *Ibid.,* p. 143.

21. *Ibid.,* pp. 146ff.

22. *Ibid.,* pp. 146-150.

23. Cf. Vera Aleksandrova, *Literatura i zhizn , Ocherki Sovetskogo obshchestvennogo razvitia,* New York, 1969, Under Sponsorship of the Russian Institute of Columbia University, p. 199.

24. Part Seven, Chapter VI.

25. *Ibid.,* Part Eight, Chapter XVII.

26. *Ibid.*

27. *Ibid.*

VISION OF LIFE

Recalling his plan for the novel *Donshchina,* Sholokhov said that he wanted to write about the people among whom he was born and whom he knew.[1] *The Quiet Don* appears to be such a book. It is a book about his people, the Cossacks, about their peaceful life, their wartime life, and their attitudes to the new Soviet system which was born in the Civil War following the Revolution. It is a book about the farming Cossack world at its most disturbed moment of its history.

But *The Quiet Don* is not only a book about the people as a whole, not only about the so-called general and typical in life, but also about the individual, personal, and particular. If it had been only a book about the people, then it would not have been a work of art but merely a textbook of sociology, anthropology, or ethnography, which depicted the way of life and the structure of the Cossack province in the years 1912-1922, immediately before and after the First World War. The book could have been masterfully written, using rich material about the little-known life of the Don Cossacks, but it would have been deprived of all the qualities of great art.

Sholokhov selected one hero, singling him out and choosing a number of critical junctures in his personal life. He imparted to him a literary form, as if dressing him in clothes through linguistic means. Above all, he provided him with the author's most personal loving care. His hero appeared not only against the background of his people, but together with his people at one of the most crucial moments of their social life and history.

Social life, as far as it consists of the aggregate of many personal lives, is always reflected in a personal life. Such events as war or revolution cannot help but be reflected in the personal lives of numerous people. The Melekhov family, appearing on the personal level, serves at the same time as a symbol of the Cossack host on the quiet Don. Therefore, all events in the family reflect not only a local mood, but acquire a universal significance. The spirit of the novel is not limited by local color, but acquires national and even international character.

The two levels of the novel, personal and social, are not separated in the artistic creation as independent parts. They constantly interweave to such a degree that it becomes impossible to speak of one without mentioning the other.

Nevertheless, in order to better understand Sholokhov's individual character of Grigorii Melekhov we must try to separate him from the background against which he appeared. Also, in speaking about the background, i.e. about the social level of the novel, we are aware that we cannot avoid touching upon the individual characters as well.

In interpreting Sholokhov's work, we will very often rely on his words. We will carefully watch and listen for the written and spoken word in order to avoid as much as possible the inescapable—one's own interpretation—reading into or adding on to the author's own concept.

Tolstoi spoke of the focus of an artistic work. The main thing in an artistic work was for him the disposition of the parts around the focus.[2]   He said this apropos of *Anna Karenina.* Later Tolstoi repeated this thought, expressing it even more simply and clearly. Speaking about the main features of a large poetic creation, he said that such a main feature is the focus around which the characters, personalities, and events develop.[3]

One probably understands Tolstoi's focus to be the center, that place of a poetic work from which everything spoken about flows, the center in which and through which every part is reflected and interpreted. Certain parts of the work may develop independently (which happened often in Tolstoi), but their significance must depend only on the center, on the focus in which they are reflected.

Such a focus in Sholokhov's novel is the life of a Cossack family the Melekhovs. In the Melekhov family is reflected the whole life of the unquiet and stormy Don, the whole Cossack host and not just one cell of it, one family, or one social strata. From the Melekhov family, the threads lead out into many directions, connecting the family with the life outside.

The Cossacks of the Don with their way of life thus serve as the broad background for the novel. But the author took his observing vantage point in the center of the novel, i.e. in the Melekhov family. From here he surveyed all the events which he described, not only in the family but also the events of the whole Don.

We will let Sholokhov himself tell about the life which he has registered from his central position where he stood and from which he observed everything that happened in his work.   Here is a passage taken from Part Two, Chapter III of *The Quiet Don.*

> The village, grown fat on the harvest, having stretched over the Don like a beaded snake across the road, pulsed under September's chilly heat. In every farm, surrounded by wattle fences, under the roof of every farm house, bitter-sweet life was rolling on cyclically, separate from the others; Grandfather Grishaka, growing cold suffered from toothache; Sergei Platonovich, stroking his forked beard in his palms, wept alone and ground his teeth, crushed with shame; Stepan nursed hate toward Grishka in his soul, and nighttimes, in his sleep, tore at the rag blanket with iron fingers; Natal'ia, running into the shed, fell to the ground, shaking, huddling into a ball, weeping over her lost happiness; Khristonia, who had drunk away his heifer at the fair, was tortured by conscience; Grishka sighed, distressed with unappeasable misgivings and recurring pain; Aksin'ia, caressing her husband, poured out her undying hatred for him with her tears.

This rather long passage reflects the author's vision of life.   These are the author's words as narrator.   The author himself, not one of his heroes, said how he understands and sees the life which he is describing.   This is not a result of his observation, but rather the process of observation itself.   The author does not generalize upon that which he has observed in life, but rather unrolls a whole picture of life in all its pettiness and insignificant details.   The important is here interwoven with the insignificant and even meaningless.   Properly speaking there is nothing in this fragment of major or secondary importance. Or, more strictly speaking, one will neither recognize nor distinguish here what is the main thing and what is not. The fact that Grandfather Grishaka had a toothache here seems as important as the dissatisfaction and indecision of the main character Grigorii, or the langorous passion of Aksin'ia. All this is presented equally.

Lost somewhere on the shores of the Don River and "fattened on the harvest" lies the Cossack hamlet Tatarsk, in which the heroes of Sholokhov's *Quiet Don* live. Among them, the author has placed the Melekhov family as the center of his attention. Although having selected the Melekhov family as the means of presenting the entire quiet Don, the author did not restrict his field of vision to one family only. He did not look at the Cossack life exclusively through the Melekhov family. All his characters came forth in the novel independently, not always reflected in the Melekhov family. Every one of his characters builds his own circle of life and leads his own life independently. Sholokhov has no auxiliary figures, serving only for the greater relief of the main characters. All characters are depicted equally in conspicuous relief, and all exist for themselves and in themselves.

The author looked more intently at the Melekhov family and presented it in greater detail. But the lives of the other characters are filled with the same details, only in lesser quantity. The description of details and the small things of life is one of the characteristic methods of Sholokhov's realism. Through his interest in the small things of life which make up the novel, he enriched his characters and the novel. Many of the trifles of life distributed on the pages of the novel might have been dispensed with. And who knows, without them the novel might have been shorter and structured more tightly. But on the other hand, the many small incidents of life in one way or another constitute the richness of Sholokhov's realism and his characters. Sholokhov's little things of life have no function other than to fill out the picture. Without them, the life of *The Quiet Don* might not have been so complete.

It must be said that the above quoted passage is related to the autumn of 1912, to that peaceful, almost idyllic, Sholokhovian, Cossack-peasant way of life. It is not difficult to deduce the year from the novel. Sholokhov began his peaceful narration about the Cossack way of life with that memorable morning when old Melekhov woke up his younger son Grishka, and they set out to the Don for fishing. (Before this, the author in one chapter had related the history of the Melekhov family.) Old Melekhov wanted to talk seriously with his son about his relationship with the young, married, neighbor woman, Aksin'ia. Then the Cossacks of the hamlet left for the summer military camp. Towards autumn they returned. During that same autumn Grigorii was married off. In winter he went away from home. During the summer of the second year he worked on the Listnitskii estate, and in the winter went away to military service. The following summer, the third in the book, the German War broke out. This was the momentous summer of 1914. Two summers before that was the year 1912. Our fragment is related to the autumn after the first summer. But the year does not play a special role here. It is important only because it was at peacetime.

The author sees life in all its diversity, without beginning or end, the small things and large things, the unimportant and important. All the reality of life is perceived and interpreted through the author's subjective attitudes and views. That which may seem to be absolutely objective, in reality, is only the objectivity of a personal, i.e. subjective attitude of the author, thus his subjective vision of life.

It is indisputable that social stratifications existed and had to exist among the Cossacks, as they existed everywhere. But social stratifications do not primarily interest the author. His interest lies in the richness of every character's personal life. Every character has his own sadnesses, his own personal grievances. A peculiar and special life flows in every home. There is no idyll in Sholokhov. On the contrary, there is sharp tension in life. In each home there is a unique and very personal bitterness, each unlike any other.

It is to Sholokhov's merit that he did not narrow life down to only its social contradictions and contrasts, and that he did not limit his vision by societal frames. *The Quiet Don* bears witness to the fact that Social Realism's standards of the exclusively social approach and social evaluation of literature is not always applicable or possible. Sholokhov does not express any social interests and does not force any conclusions. He focuses his light and attention equally on every side: the poor and rich, the wrong and right. Possibly, he did not even know who was right and who was wrong in the life he described. He, apparently, knew that it is not his business to judge.

The Cossack way of life with its small troubles and passions had been formed throughout the centuries. The truth of this life was bitter and hard, but it was simple and acceptable to every Cossack from the time of their childhood. And because it was known, everyone submitted to it naturally. Anyway, no one rose in protest against that simple truth.

The goal of their life was to work and gain prosperity. Much later, in the seventh part of the novel, when Grigorii returned home after the death of his wife, his father said to him: "This damned life made us a little poor now. We also used to be well-to-do people."[4] To be a wealthy landowner was the pride of the Cossack. Not without regret did old Melekhov recall the past. Labor was the joyful, willfully obligatory destiny of every Cossack. The Cossacks did not know any other truth of life. The Melekhovs labored as did the rich Cossack family, the Korshunovs, and the poor Koshevois. Of course there was resentment and bitterness between the rich and poor. But the author did not impart to any of the characters a feeling of unquestionable rightness about a possible new truth of life or new social relationship among the Cossacks.

Sholokhov perceived and depicted the apparently indestructible order, which had been built up through the centuries. He spoke calmly about the labor of the poor and the rich, without class resentment.

Besides labor, the lot of the Cossack's life was to serve in the Tsar's army. Service was another hard, inescapable duty among the many other hardships of

life, but it brought respect and honor. Pantelei Prokofe-
vich wrote to his son Grigorii in the army: "Serve like
you're supposed to. Service for the Tsar won't go to
waste."[5] Service had its firm place in the age-old,
established, bitter-sweet order of life. Although the
Cossacks bore the service as a heavy obligation, none of
them ever thought of changing this order of life.

Events in the obscure Tatarsk hamlet are interwoven
with each other simultaneously, yet independently from
each other. As Natal'ia threw herself onto the scythe,
attempting an evil suicide, Grigorii met Stepan in the
field. As the pre-Passover churchbells were sounding
service, ice was breaking and floating along the Don
River.

The Sholokhovian serene life flows like a mighty
river in its established order in the village Tatarsk, as it
does everywhere. It never stands still and calm. Only
on the surface does it appear to be calm, eventless,
almost dead like the steppe in winter. In reality the
Sholokhovian life is very alive. Under the surface there
are passions and storms. There is a bitter struggle for
existence, between death and life. This is the struggle
for a place in life. It is essentially the same vision which
was observed in Sholokhov's early works.

A description of life as it appeared on the surface as
well as its hidden potential can best be illustrated by
taking a passage directly from Sholokhov's text. The
following passage describes the life of the Don area early
in 1918. Nevertheless, it is the same life which opened
the first pages of *The Quiet Don.* The author's vision
of life could not radically change in so short a time.

An easterly wind raged over the steppe. The snow had levelled out all the hollows and depressions. Neither road nor tracks were visible. In all directions stretched the bare, white, wind-swept plain. The steppe was dead.

But beneath the snow the steppe was still alive. Where the ploughed land lay in frozen waves of silver snow, where the long, deep swell of furrowed earth had heaved since autumn, there, gripping the soil with greedy, living roots, lay the winter rye under the frosts. . .waiting for spring, for the sun, in order to rise, to break through the fine, diamond-studded snowy crust, and to spring up a vigorous green in May. And it would rise in its time. . . .

All the Don Region was living a secret crushed existence. (*Part Six, Chapter XIX.*)

In this manner Sholokhov presented life. It was calm, but only on the surface. It was rising again and again in its deadly struggle for survival. It seems that Sholokhov did not know life without struggle and violence, as demonstrated by his early Don stories, as well as by the novel, *The Quiet Don.* The parts of his book where there is no struggle or violence, or where the outcome of the bitter struggle could be anticipated, appear to be dull and flat. However, this seldom occurs in Sholokhov's work. Seen on the whole, *The Quiet Don* is permeated with violence and struggle, which serve as leitmotif throughout the whole novel.

It was impossible to foresee which direction the violent life would take, and which end would be met.

When swept out of its normal channel, life scatters into many streams. It is difficult to foresee which it will take in its treacherous and winding course. Where today it trickles, like a rivulet over sandbanks, so shallow that the shoals are visible, tomorrow it will flow rich and full. (*Part Three, Chapter XVIII.*)

There is something irrational and illogical in the Sholo-khovian life. It is so in society as well as in the life of every individual character presented in the novel. There are certain elements in the Sholokhovian life which nobody can foresee or control. It is as though the author himself did not know where the life and characters that he had created and presented so masterfully in the novel would take and lead him.

Later, during the war and the Revolution, when the long-established order of life was about to be destroyed and was apparently departing forever, the author gave his feelings about the Don through a story told by one of his characters. This character, Minaev, is by himself an insignificant figure in the novel. He is notable perhaps only because he was a supporter of the new order of life which was bursting upon the quiet Don in the whirlwind of the Revolution. But his story about the Cossack's relationship to the Don is remarkable because Sholokhov has timed it to January 1918, at that moment when life on the quiet Don had visibly taken a turn off somewhere into the unknown.

They were nearing Novocherkassk. Having taken a look on the map at the Don broadening away from the town, Minaev began to relate quietly:

"It used to be once, when the Cossacks had finished their service in the Ataman's regiment, they were outfitted for leave at home. They were carrying trunks, their property, horses. The echelon would move, and then above Voronezh, where they have to cross the Don for the first time, the engineer, who was driving the train, would give a slow pace, couldn't be any slower—he already knew what's up. Just as the train comes on the bridge—My friends!—what goes on there! The Cossacks just go wild: 'Don! . . . our Don! Quiet Don! Dear Father, bread-giver! Hura-a-a-ah!'— and through the windows they then throw, from the bridge directly into the water, through the iron railing, military caps, old cloaks, trousers, pillow cases, shirts, different things. They give presents to the Don, returning from the service. It happened, you look on the water, you see blue Ataman's caps are floating, like swans or flowers. Such a custom had been since long ago." (*Part Five, Chapter X.*)

This was narrated when the representatives of the revolutionary Don went to Novocherkassk for a conference with the Cossack government which was defending the independence of the Don. This was a turning point in the life of the Don. For the time being, the life of the Cossacks was at a crossroads, as if thinking about where to step next. It was uncertain at that time whom the quiet Don would follow, and who would possess it. For this reason, this disclosure by the author through the story of the simple Cossack about the customary, old quiet time with which the novel began sounds so touching. In this story is reflected that quiet, serene Don, which "nips at your heart," as Sholokhov admitted in another passage through the words of the elder Melekhov to his son Grigorii. Here one feels the joy and longing for the Don. It is as if Sholokhov wanted to say that this is how it used to be in the old days. Continuing the author's thought, we could add further the words of an anonymous ancient author—"but now great misfortune has occurred, a

sickness to Rus' and the Don."[6]   The quiet Don was
bursting and foaming.

But we have gone ahead.   We have to return to the
past, to the beginning.

Just before the war broke in and threatened to disturb the serene and peaceful Sholokhovian life, the
author once more confirmed and intensified the old
established order of life:

> Life in the village went along in its customary, in-
> violable order: Cossacks who had served out their time
> returned home, on weekdays the dull labor imperceptibly
> consumed time, on Sundays from morning on, the village
> poured into the church in family droves; the Cossacks
> went in uniforms and holiday trousers; the women, tightly
> bound in decorated blouses with gathered sleeves, swept
> the dust with their long, rustling hems of their skirts.
> (*Part Three, Chapter I.*)

Then came the war: the peaceful life was disturbed,
but it did not break out of the established and sanctified
shores.   If the war had disturbed the way of life, then it
was only that side of life that was concerned with petty
passions and the daily anxiety of Sholokhov's characters.
Everyone continued to live by his own worries and the
worries of near relatives.   War was a hard experience,
which everyone had to try to live through somehow.
The Melekhov family received news of Grigorii's death.
It fell with terrible grief on every member of the family.
Everyone suffered in his own way.   Rejected by Grigorii, Natal'ia for the second time attempted an evil
death by suicide.   She was restrained only by force.
"A whole week she spent in dull oblivion and returned
to the world of realities much changed, quiet, gnawed

by black infirmity. . . the deceased invisibly took shelter in the Melekhov home, and the living sniffed its mouldering, disintegrating odor."[7]

The following is Sholokhov's description of the father's suffering:

> After receiving the news of Grigorii's death, Pantelei Prokofievich suddenly sank. He was growing old from day to day before the eyes of his family. A hard end was overtaking him inevitably; his memory weakened and his reason was disturbed. He went about the farm stooped, iron-hued; the feverish, oily gleam of his eyes betrayed his soul's distress. (*Part Three, Chapter XVI.*)

The death of the main heroes could have been used as a sufficiently important event meant to emphasize the poignancy of the moment and to imbue the novel with more critical moments. But there is nothing of this kind in Sholokhov's realism. It is as if he wanted to say that life goes on in the same way.

Many times in the course of the long novel, the Melekhovs will receive news of death and react intensely to the death around them until the whole family will be eventually ruined by the long war and the Revolution.

The mood conveyed in the above quoted fragment is barely noticeable. Sholokhov seems to want to convey how life receded and declined. But because his whole novel is imbued with this mood of decline, this fragment seems to be only an additional insignificant event, a barely noticeable link. Sholokhov presents this mood many times in later incidents. Again and again he will repeat that the quality of life was constantly declining.

This time the news turned out to be false. The older

son Petro informed them two weeks later that "our Grigorii almost gave his soul to God, but right now, thanks the God, is alive and well."[8]   But even here with the arrival of joyous news, "through the strokes of the crumpled letter, soaked with rain, bitter sadness breathed palpably."[9]

The war was reflected in the Cossacks' life in such a way that life lost something. This was directly stated by the author himself, as a commentary to the Cossack life on the Don. There was no longer the fullness of the previous, prosperous life.

> In those years life declined—like full water on the Don. The boring days languished and, alternating, passed imperceptibly in continual pettiness, meaningless work, small needs, small joys, and continual great worry for those who were in the war. (*Part Four, Chapter V.*)

The author continued his narration about the declining life with news about the Melekhov brothers, Petro and Grigorii, the new enmity between Petro and Stepan Astakhov, the Melekhovs' neighbor, and then the capturing of the wounded Stepan. This is still basically the same life and the author uses the same method of conveying it through the eyes of an observer. But the reader cannot help but feel a different attitude to life— life has grown poorer. It is no longer turbulent, full-watered, like the widely flooded spring Don. The spring waters receded, and the river had quieted down.

Sholokhov had to touch on the war, too. Since he led his Cossacks from the quiet hamlet Tatarsk, lost on the banks of the Don River, to the front of the German War, he could not leave the war outside his field of vision. He presented and described in length several war scenes in which his main hero participated. These pictures are presented through the eyes of the main hero as he actively participated, and also through the author's eyes as a witness. It is as though Sholokhov is not entirely sure of Grigorii and his feelings, and where his hero was. He described the first collision of the German and Russian mounted patrols, including the historical figure Kuz'ma Kriuchkov, a glorious and well-known Cossack in his time. In Sholokhov's descriptions of war there is, if one may express it this way, nothing military. "Gone wild from fear, the Cossacks and Germans struck and slashed at whatever fell in their way: at backs, hands, horses, weapons."[10]

This is taken from the author's narration. It seems he is a participant in this skirmish. But while taking part, he was able to preserve his impartiality in conveying what he was seeing.

A little later, however, having described how a legend was made and how Cossack Kuz'ma Kriuchkov was glorified out of a small event, the author did not withhold his commentary on the skirmish which he had been able to describe so neutrally:

> In reality, it was like this: people who had not yet gotten the knack of killing people similar to themselves met on the field of death. In the mortal terror which embraced them they collided against each other, inflicted blind blows, maimed each other and their horses, and, being scared by a shot which had killed one of them, they had run away morally crippled. (*Part Three, Chapter IX.*)

There is a certain Tolstoian note in Sholokhov's attitude toward war. War appears here, as everywhere in *The Quiet Don,* not as heroism or an occasion to exhibit heroism, but as an incomprehensible, cruel exhibition of mortal terror and passion. If Sholokhov had remained faithful to this attitude toward war in all his later works, describing war as a place where man exhibits himself in all his animal fear, he would undoubtedly have been considered a great humanist of contemporary time. But the later Sholokhov replaced this attitude with a romantic heroism and thus replaced the early Sholokhov.

The war had to come to an end somehow for the heroes of *The Quiet Don.* There would no longer be the need to be afraid and to grieve for the deaths of the young people. This was the way that the end of the war was felt and thought of on the Don and in the village Tatarsk.

In reality, however, it did not happen this way. The war never really ended. Peaceful, serene times never again resumed for the heroes of the novel. After the war came the Revolution. Then came the Civil War, cruel and incomprehensible to Sholokhov's peace-loving characters.

The Revolution remained outside the focus in descriptions of the lives and the characters of *The Quiet Don.* Faithful to the point of view which he had initially taken, Sholokhov described to his readers only those events which immediately concerned the Cossacks from their own point of view. Only rumors arrived to the Cossacks about the Revolution:

In the first days of November, contradictory rumors

> about the coup in Petrograd began to penetrate the Cos-
> sacks. . . .The Cossacks guardedly quieted down, many were
> glad, expecting the termination of the war. (*Part Four,
> Chapter XXI.*)

The Revolution held something of the unknown for the
Cossacks. They did not know what it would bring. But
among the Cossacks was felt the foreboding of something bad and disturbing. The very fact that the
Revolution appeared on the Don in the form of "contradictory rumors" was enough to show that the Revolution heralded disturbance.

But before the Revolution had entirely engulfed the
Cossack world and their way of life, Sholokhov presented the return of the Cossacks from the German War.
Perhaps the first visible appearance of the Revolution
on the Don came with the Cossacks who had returned
from the front. They brought the first news of the
Revolution.

The end of the far-off war came to the Don Cossacks
in the three-fold aspect of life. There were three visions:
joy of the returned warriors and their families, grief
over the fallen Cossack-warriors, and finally the wailing
of the orphaned.

At first the Cossacks could rejoice at the end of the
war: "The farmsteads to which the Cossacks returned as
masters and expected guests were filled with joy."[11]
But Sholokhov's joy always lives next to sadness and
grief, in accordance with his vision of life. And this is
always the way things are in Sholokhov.

> Many Cossacks were missing. They had been lost on the
> fields of Galicia, Bukovina, East Prussia, Pre-Carpathia,

Rumania. They fell there as corpses and were rotting under a gunfire requiem. And now high hills of brotherly graves were overgrown with weed, smothered with rain, and wrapped with drifting snow. (*Part Five, Chapter I.*)

Melancholy and longing as in old Cossack songs and legends are soaring over the neglected, forgotten graves in this text. But the forgotten Cossack graves in strange lands, among foreign people is not the whole vision of life. There remained the third aspect, the relatives of those killed at war. Their lives were filled with sorrow and longing. Sholokhov also included them in his vision of life, as he saw them wailing and sobbing.

The wife of Prokhor Shamil beat her head against the hard ground, gnawed at the earthen floor with her teeth, seeing how Martin Shamil, the newly returned brother of her deceased husband, caressed his pregnant wife, fussed over the children, and passed out presents to them. She knocked and crawled, writhing, on the floor; and nearby, like a herd of sheep, crowded the children. They wailed, looking at their mother with eyes wide with fear.

Tear, dear one, at the collar of your last shirt! Tear at your hair, thin from a joyless, hard life, bite your gnawed lips till the blood comes, wring your hands grown ugly from work, and beat yourself against the ground by the threshold of the empty hut! Your hut has no master, you have no husband, your children haven't a father; and remember that no one will caress you or your orphans, no one will save you from back-breaking work and poverty, no one will press your head to his breast at night when you fall, worn out by weariness, and no one will say to you like he once used to say: "Don't worry, Anis'ka! We'll live it through." You will not have another husband be-

cause work, need, and children have withered you and made
you plain.   Your sniffling, half-naked children will not
have a father; you yourself will have to plow, harrow,
panting from the back-breaking strain; you yourself will
have to throw down from the mower, throw into the cart,
lift on the pitchfork the heavy bundles of wheat and feel
how something tears beneath your belly, and then you'll
be writhing, covered with blankets, and will issue blood.

Looking through the old underwear of Aleksei Beshniak,
his mother sobbed, shed bitter, niggardly tears, sniffed; but
only the last shirt, brought back by Mishka Koshevoi, has
in its folds the scent of the son's sweat, and, dropping her
head to it, the old woman rocked, lamented grievously,
and patterned the stained, coarse, dirty shirt with her tears.

The families of Manitskov, Afon'ka Ozerov, Evlantii,
Kalinin, Likhovidov, Ermakov, and other Cossacks were
orphaned.

Only for Stepan Astakhov did no one wail—there was no
one to wail.   His forgotten home was empty, half-ruined,
and gloomy, even in the summer. Aksin'ia lived at Iagodnyi;
little was heard of her as before, and she never dropped in
on the village.   She had no interest, it seemed. (*Part Five,
Chapter I.*)

The wailing of the ones left behind has again the
character of an old folk song.   It is the lamentation for
the dead which had lived in the Russian lands from
ancient times, and was handed on from generation to
generation.   Here, one hears the lamentation of the
widow at the bitter fate which has befallen her, the
sobbing of the children, and the wailing of the mother.
Sholokhov has presented this in moderation.   His lamentations never degenerate into tearful sentimentality or
lachrymosity.   Nowhere does he fall into a cheap, false

tone of sympathy. It is as if he had come as an observer, saw and heard what was going on in each home, stood and listened for a while, then had written it down, and gone on further, neither interfering nor giving comfort. These are not the words of the wailers; they are the author's descriptions. He wrote them down.

There are many elements of folk songs in this long passage of lamentation that could have been taken directly from folklore and worked into the literary text. The many repetitions, like the fourfold use of "no one will," and the use of repetitive imperatives—tear, bite, wring and beat and others—sound like a refrain of the lamentation. The reiteration of certain words creates a definite rhythmic tone of this section's prose. Further, the enhanced emotionality also belongs to the treasury of folklore.

The author serves here not as an indifferent observer, but rather as a sympathizer and direct participant in the people's misfortune. His direct discourse in this and many other passages makes it hard to delimit the author's thoughts from the words of wailers. These words could have been written only by an author who loved his characters.

This passage is not the only one in the novel which is impregnated with direct mood and motifs of folklore. We shall point out other sections in their respective places.

There was personal tragedy, personal sadness. But no matter what grief was suffered, life did not stop on the Don. Together with the end of the war came the Revolution. But for the time being the Revolution raged on somewhere far away.

> About the war, which was about to start boiling close to
> the capital city of the Don Province, people knew only by
> hearsay; hazily examining the political tendencies which
> had risen, people waited for further events and listened.
>
> Until January they lived quietly in the hamlet Tatarsk.
> The Cossacks who had returned from the fronts rested
> beside their wives, ate their fill, and could not guess that
> lurking at the thresholds of their huts were more bitter
> woes and burdens than those which they had to bear dur-
> ing the just endured war. (*Part Five, Chapter I.*)

At the beginning of the Revolution, life still continued according to the established ancient order. But the
calm on the Don was now deceptive. There was still no
bitterness among the Cossacks. Grigorii Melekhov returned from the Red Guard Regiment. Valet also
arrived at Tatarsk village from the Red Guard. Among
the Cossacks of Tatarsk village there existed a revolutionary committee. In January, 1918, the former
Tatarsk front line Cossacks chose delegates to the Congress of the Veterans. But this did not disturb the way
of life built up through the centuries. The bitterness
among the Cossacks came later. It was brought in by
the Revolution.

Only later, when the local revolutionary in the hamlet
Tatarsk, Ivan Alekseevich Kotliarov, hurled at Grigorii
Melekhov, "You became a stranger. You are an enemy
to the Soviet power. Don't stand across our way,"[12]
the bitterness arose. It was a new language, the language
of the Revolution, heretofore unknown among the Cossack. But in 1917, at the dawn of the Revolution, the
alienation was not yet heard among the Cossacks.

The Cossacks did not want to fight again, and did not

expect the front to pass across their homes and families for many years hereafter. It did not occur to them to think that the Revolution would be so cruel. It is as if Sholokhov used the above quoted text to warn them about future adversities and additional bitter misfortunes.

Somewhere far away from Tatarsk, passions were already raging. A revolutionary tribunal had been set in action, passing down harsh judgments and revenge upon seized White Guards.[13] At night there were executions of numerous enemies of the Revolution outside the city walls.[14]

The Revolution seized the power in order to use it unchecked. More than that, the Revolution considered itself to be the sole legal power in and over the country. Having taken high principles for its program, the Revolution exhibited extreme intolerance; for the sake of a better future it began the annihilation of its many opponents. On the fronts of the beginning Civil War there were senseless executions of prisoners.

In time, the senseless, wild passions also reached the village of Tatarsk and the home of the Melekhov family. As in the German War, Sholokhov did not limit his observations in the exploding Civil War to just the Tatarsk villagers. He led his Cossacks from their native farms to where the struggle was going on and where passions were raging.

The Cossacks did not tolerate the Revolution and rose against the new government which had forcefully burst upon their way of life. It was in this uprising that a great division occurred on the Don. In the uprising the Cossack paths crossed and their passions flared. The

Revolution attracted, however, only an insignificant minority of the Cossacks from the Tatarsk village.[15]

The stormy events which were played out among the Cossacks, Sholokhov described decades later. These turbulent events ended with a victory for the Revolution. Nevertheless, Sholokhov succeeded in watching the events of that disturbed time in such a manner that he was able to describe them without treating the situation as one with a foregone conclusion, as is now required by Socialist Realism, but as if the outcome were still undetermined. In this, perhaps, lies the whole attraction of his works.

Later, in the novel *Virgin Soil Upturned,* Sholokhov, describing the events of collectivization on the Don, presented them from the predetermined point of view demanded by Socialist Realism. Because of this, Sholokhov's work lost much of the tension which is necessary for art. The first three volumes of *The Quiet Don* were written in the years when Socialist Realism had not yet been proclaimed to be the sole standard of Soviet literature. Sholokhov was able to execute his own concept without constraint. This freedom is exhibited first of all in his descriptions of the Civil War in which Sholokhov was able to preserve his particular Cossack point of view about the Cossack participation in the Revolution and the Civil War. Sholokhov looked at the mood of the Cossack host and remained an impartial observer. He did not interfere in the events and did not interpret their meaning. He remained detached, as he had been at the beginning of the novel.

There are presented in the novel two Cossack uprisings against the Revolution. The first one occurred against the Podtëlkov Soviet government early in 1918. It ended with the Cossacks' defeat and the occupation of the Don Cossacks by the Red armies. Following the defeat, the Soviet power was established in the hamlet Tatarsk—but not for long. Early in 1919, the Cossacks again rose against the Soviets.

Our object here is not to pursue the history of the revolutionary events among the Cossacks in the hamlet Tatarsk as they are reflected in Sholokhov's masterpiece, but solely to display the author's point of view as it was revealed through his Cossack characters. Faithful to this objective, we cannot discuss here the variable success of the Cossacks' fight against the Revolution in chronological order of the novel, but rather must concentrate our attention on the Cossacks' attitude toward the Revolution, dealing thus with the two uprisings as a unit.

The Cossacks' attitude toward the revolutionary Soviet authority on the Don area was revealed by the author again through the Cossacks themselves.

> . . .Dreary days had arrived. Something was in the offing. A sombre rumor crawled from the upper reaches of the Don, down its tributaries. . .men said it was not the front that was to be feared, but the extraordinary commissions and tribunals. It was said that any day they would arrive in the Cossack districts, that they had already appeared in Migulinskaia and Kazanskaia and were holding brief and illegal trials of the Cossacks who had served with the Whites. . . .The court procedure was terrifyingly simple: an accusation, a couple of questions, sentence—and then machine-gun death. It was said that already in Kazanskaia and Shumilinskaia many a Cossack corpse was lying neglected in the brushwood. (*Part Six, Chapter XIX.*)

This is the Cossacks' vision of the Revolution. The author remained neutral. In no way did he try to convince his Cossack characters that the rumors could be false. He did not present the Revolutionary side of the story but confined his descriptions only to the Cossacks' opinion. Doing so, he remained aloof from the Revolution.

Sholokhov's Cossacks could not stand the terror of the Revolution and rose against it. Having risen against the Revolution, the Cossacks advanced the slogan "For the Soviets, but against the Communists." For a writer who was describing events from the point of view of a victorious Revolution, this slogan must have seemed counter-revolutionary. However, Sholokhov was able to restrain himself from commenting on the possible meaning of the slogan. For the heroes of *The Quiet Don,* "For the Soviets, but against the Communists" signified the striving of the Cossacks toward self-government by their own chosen power—without revolutionary tribunals and without foreign professional revolutionaries, such as newcomers like Stockman and Bunchuk. The Cossacks rose against the powers that arrived on the Don with violence and murder. Their own local Soviets, like Ivan Alekseevich Kotliarov or Mishka Koshevoi did not represent force or violence. Ivan Alekseevich Kotliarov, like the Cossacks from Tatarsk and other Cossacks on the outskirts of Petrograd who were witnessing the agitator Bunchuk's outraged murder of the officer Kalmykov, did not understand and could not approve of the fury of the Revolution brought about by professional revolutionaries. (See page 75.) The local Soviets were but subordinate instruments to the organized and strongly cohesive groups of revolutionary professionals. The Revolution imposed its will upon the local Soviets in the form of the revolutionary tribunals. It was this that the Cossacks rose up against.

With the exception of two men from the hamlet Tatarsk, all of the Cossacks rose in the struggle against the Communists. Sholokhov left no doubt that support for the uprising was almost unanimous and that the Cossacks rebelled for the defense of their way of life, their farms. The only exceptions were two local functionaries of the new Soviet authority: Ivan Alekseevich and Mishka Koshevoi.

The goal of the Cossacks in their struggle for the Don against the Communists was expressed by Grigorii Melekhov as a struggle for survival.

> . . .For a piece of bread, for a strip of land, for the right to live, people had always fought, and would fight as long as the sun shines on them, as long as the warm blood flows in their veins. One has to fight the one who wants to take away your life, the right to life; one has to fight strongly, not wavering—as if against the wall. The white heat of hate and strength will come with the fight. One must only not bridle his feelings, one must give them room, as if to madness—and that is all.
>
> The paths of the Cossack host crossed with the paths of landless peasants of Rus' and with the paths of the factory people. We have to fight with them to the death. We have to wrest away from under their feet the fertile Don earth, washed with the Cossack blood. We have to drive them like the Tatars from the boundaries of our province. We have to shake Moscow and impose upon her a shameful peace! You can't pass on a narrow path; somebody has to push somebody. We tried once. They have

let the Red regiments on to the Cossack lands and they
have tested it once. It is enough. And now—to the
sword. (*Part Six, Chapter XXVIII.*)

These were Grigorii's thoughts at the beginning of the
struggle, as well as the thoughts of all the Cossacks
whom he led to the struggle. In this passage, Sholokhov
views life as he viewed it throughout the novel—as the
struggle for existence. It was undoubtedly easier for
the author to observe life in all its fullness and variety
on a stormy turning point, like this one was, than in a
peaceful, calm of life. The truth of life—the struggle for
existence—is more fully revealed here.

It was not only easier to observe life on a turning
point, but, as a matter of fact, the observation itself
became more meaningful. Grigorii's thoughts as revealed
in this passage seem to implement the struggle for self-
preservation more than any other passage in the novel.
The phrase "Self-preservation" should not necessarily
be understood in the biological sense of natural selection
and the adaptation of the fittest, but rather as an idea
of the preservation of the Cossacks' entity of life, in
its ethnical and social unity. Grigorii did not fight
alone for his life; he fought with the Cossack society
for a cause common to all.

The struggle for the survival of the Cossacks' way
of life was thus one of the most poignant issues of the
Revolution, as it was revealed throughout the novel.
But in turn, the Revolution was only one of the many
expressions of the struggle for life. In this struggle there
was no mercy. The Revolution had burst violently upon
the Cossack way of life. Violence was in its very nature.
It strove to impose its own violent order upon the

Cossacks. To this end, the Revolution established the terror methodically and systematically. The Revolutionary tribunals, organs of terror, executed the victims in order to frighten and intimidate the people. The Revolutionary terror thus fed the Cossack uprising. The Cossacks had to protect themselves in order not to fall victim to this terror. Their uprising in the novel had a defensive character. In defending themselves, they could not refrain from their own terror. This was the tragedy of their struggle. However, they did not create their own tribunals to be used as instruments of terror. As the need arose, they created military-field courts for the execution of captured Red warriors. An occasional military-field tribunal was created, such as for the execution of Podtëlkov and his expedition. Though this court was created out of vengeance more than for a trial, it had the appearance of the people's will. The trial of Podtëlkov served as a kind of revenge against a traitor to the Don.

Commissar Likhachev, captured in the field, was also brought before such a tribunal.[16] It must be reemphasized that in *The Quiet Don* such tribunals were created by the Cossacks for reprisal and not as instruments of systematic terror. More often, in the course of the furious Civil War, the Cossacks themselves took revenge on captured warriors without tribunals or military-field courts. In this case the reprisal became an elemental, unplanned, cruel, folk court of the crowd. Ivan Alekseevich Kotliarov was killed in this manner in his native village Tatarsk at the hands of his neighbors. This was unpremeditated, savage mob law, a primitive form of revenge. This mob law was not organized by any one person, but was solely directed by the uncontrolled sentiments of an embittered crowd. Reprisals, expressed in cruelty to war prisoners by both sides, were brutal, but they were not systematic reigns of terror as was the one established by the Revolution.

Sholokhov withheld his commentary on the uprising. To the Cossacks who rose up against the Revolution, their struggle was just. But the author is not a judge; he is only a chronicler, reflecting the course of the struggle. He does not interfere on anyone's side or with anyone's truth. If, nevertheless, the justification of the Cossack struggle has found its reflection in *The Quiet Don,* it is only because the author placed himself in a position amidst the Cossacks. He observed the Revolution from the Cossacks' point of view.

Before the struggle came to an end, Sholokhov revealed again and again through descriptions of the once strong Melekhov family how life was constantly declining. Once it had been a strong, firmly welded family, abiding in harmony and existing by rules and regulations sanctified by long traditions. The work was carried on by all jointly. All members of the family shared with each other their joys and sorrows. Everyone unconditionally obeyed the head of the family. Pantelei Prokofievich was an all-powerful master. Now, through the Revolution and the Civil struggle, the once strong order in the family had become weak and was gradually being destroyed, until the whole family was ruined.

In one year the Melekhov family had been reduced to half its members. Pantelei Prokofievich was right, when he remarked one day that death became fond of their home. Hardly had they had time to bury Natal'ia when once more the scent of incense and cornflowers filled the Melekhov's spacious best room. Some ten days after Grigorii had departed to the front, Daria drowned herself in the Don river. (*Part Seven, Chapter XXI.*)

Life was decreasing not only in the Melekhov family. In several beautiful descriptions of oncoming autumn, Sholokhov gave his readers an understanding that autumn, no matter how beautiful and lively it might seem, meant the maturing and then slow withering of fruits and of life itself. People in the Tatarsk hamlet might not have thought of death, but death itself constantly reminded them of its silent but unfailing presence.

Three new dead Cossacks were brought into the hamlet from the front. Two of them, Anikushka and Khristonia, were the Melekhovs' neighbors, and the third was a seventeen-year-old youngster from the far end of the hamlet. This visibly disturbed Pantelei Prokofievich. To calm himself, he went to the woods to seek a means of forgetting the life and death around him. The stern, silent beauty of the forest had a soothing effect on him. But, even in the forest, he could not stay away from the ever-present and omnipotent death:

> While in the forest he heard the bell tolling and felt impelled to take off his cap and cross himself. But then he grew annoyed with the priest: was there any sense of ringing the bell so long? He could have tolled the bell and had done with it; but it went on ringing for a whole hour. And what good came of all that ringing? It only wrenched people's hearts and made them think of death more than they needed. And as it was, in the autumn everything reminded you of death: the falling leaves, and the geese flying and crying through the azure sky, and the drooping, withered grass. (*Part Seven, Chapter XXIV.*)

Here again, as in many previous passages, the author's own thoughts mingled with that of his hero so that it is impossible to delimit and differentiate between the thoughts of the author and his hero. The author is not an impartial observer but a participant.

Before we reach the conclusion of the passionate struggle, let us point briefly to one other passage describing the retreat of the Cossacks from their native hamlet, Tatarsk. In the variable course of the struggle against the Reds, when fate once more favored the forces of the oncoming Revolution, the Cossacks had to flee from their homes and soil, leaving behind all that was dear to them. Again, the author is not a dispassionate outsider. He takes his place amid the retreating Cossacks, his friends. He understands their grief and their sorrow, and wants to comfort them as much as he can. But, on the other hand, he knows that he can offer no real comfort to his beloved Cossacks. A hard, implacable lot had befallen them, and no amount of cheap comfort could be of help to them.

> Who can foresee where he will meet his death? Who can guess the end of the human road? Hard it was for the horses as they plodded away from the village. Hard it was for the Cossacks to tear sorrow for their dear ones from their chilled hearts. And as they traveled that road, many remembered their homes, and many heavy thoughts were pondered. And maybe tears as salt or blood slipped over the saddle down from the stirrup to the hoofgnawed road. And not even the yellow-red flower of parting will grow there in Spring. (*Part Six, Chapter XIII.*)

This passage contains the motif of a folk song about a Cossack parting from his home to the far-off unknown and hostile world. No solace awaits the Cossack outside his home. Not even a yellow-red flower will grow where his tears have fallen.

After long struggle the war on the Don came to an end. The Cossacks had to give up their struggle. They were defeated. All the passions and storms seemed to have quieted down. The Cossacks, having no other alternative, had to accept their lot as the only possible way for their new way of life. It seemed that life should now return to the Don as it had been in earlier years: full-watered, joyous and prosperous. However, there was no return to the past way of life. Life was no longer the same; the life which Sholokhov had presented in the beginning as vigorous and enjoyably lovely was gone forever. Life declined below its previous quality. "Not joyous was the life in that fall in the hamlet Tatarsk."[17] This was stated by the author after many Cossacks had returned home from various fronts of the Civil War—some from the Red Army, some from the Whites, and some from the evacuation or, as the Cossacks who were fleeing the Red Army called it, the retreat.

Here, Sholokhov has preserved the vision of life which he had drawn once before, at the end of the German War in 1917: as before, joy and grief appear together, next to each other. "This was in those days in Tatarsk: joy, entering one home, was bringing the implacable grief into the other."[18] There is no pure happiness for Sholokhov's heroes as there is no one-sided grief. But Sholokhov did not delve deeply into a psychological analysis of joy and sorrow. He seemed satisfied with a surface observation. He observed detail, but it is always an external detail.

One detailed feature of his vision of life concerns labor. The Cossacks had to work, as they always worked. Those Cossacks who returned to their farmsteads after the Civil War, immediately began to restore their ruined farms.

> Next morning the master, clean-shaven, looking much younger, rose before dawn, went round the farm, and noted the jobs which needed to be attended to at once. Immediately after breakfast he set to work. Merrily the plane hissed or the axe tapped somewhere under the eaves of a shed, in the cool, as though announcing that capable, masculine hands, greedy for work, had come home to that yard. (*Part Eight, Chapter II.*)

This is the author's observation. By this, he seems to want to say that the labor related to a peaceful life, as they had known it in the past should now be reinstated among the Cossacks.

After the many years of hefty storms and senseless killing, the life on the Don now seemed to return to the beaten track. But it only seemed so on the surface. In reality, peace would never come to the characters of *The Quiet Don.* Sholokhov did not leave any doubts that his Don Cossacks had not yet given up their hopes of returning the old customary way of life. They were not yet willing to accept their lot of being defeated. This attitude was experienced by the local representative of the Soviet power, Mishka Koshevoi. He knew the reality of the Cossack life in his native hamlet Tatarsk.

> But he was especially disturbed by the attitude of the villagers; certain of them openly saying that the Soviet Government would be ended by winter, that Wrangel had

advanced from Tarvia and together with Makhno was already close to Rostov, and that the Allies had landed a
great expeditionary force in Novorossiisk. (*Part Eight,
Chapter IV.*)

These are the author's words expressing Koshevoi's point
of view. Koshevoi, the new man, a Communist, heard
these rumors. The author has chosen not a counter-
revolutionary, an enemy of the Soviets, but a new Soviet
man to experience the Cossacks' hopes for the end of
the Soviet power. Sholokhov did not leave any doubts
that the hopes among the population for the end of the
new power were connected with discontent over life
under the Soviets.

The novel had to come to an end, but not the life.
The Sholokhovian life, as we stressed many times, is
without any hidden meaning, or any symbolic signs.
It is open, like an open book, that has neither beginning
nor end. It had to go on and on. It is as if the life
created by Sholokhov has not only rights to exist, but
also an obligation to itself to continue to live. No grief
is strong enough to bow this life down to the ground
or to break it.

Before we close the discussion of Sholokhov's vision
of reality of the Cossacks' life, we have to pause for a
moment for a brief reflection on Sholokhov's vision of
death. Sholokhov's theme in his novel was life, not
death. But he could not ignore death, because it plays
a role as the reverse side of life.

One of the most insignificant characters of the novel
is Valet, a hired man in the merchant Mokhov's mill at
the Cossack hamlet Tatarsk. Though very insignificant
as a character, Valet is very significant for gaining an

understanding of Sholokhov's vision of life and death. In this sense it should be stressed once more that there are no important and unimportant characters in the novel. The fact that an important aspect of Sholokhov's vision is revealed through one unimportant character attests that for Sholokhov everything is of equal importance.

Except for the death of this insignificant character Valet, there would be no need to mention him at all. His life would attract no one's attention. Even the fact that Valet once per chance was found among the soldiers of the Revolution would not be cause enough to include him in these pages. Before the war, it was mentioned in passing that Valet worked in Mokhov's mill. After the war and Revolution, Valet appeared again at the Tatarsk hamlet. Here is how Sholokhov speaks about him in those stern years of the Revolution, when Valet returned to the hamlet Tatarsk:

> The Cossacks asked him where he had been since he was demobilized, but Valet gave evasive answers, avoiding the dangerous questions. To Ivan Alekseevich and Mishka Koshevoi he admitted that he had spent four months in a Red Guard detachment in the Ukraine, had been captured by the Ukrainian national troops, had escaped and joined the Red Army close to Rostov, and had now given himself furlough to get a rest and re-equip himself. (*Part Five, Chapter XXII.*)

The character Valet, who writes for himself the furlough, i.e. simply deserts from the Red Guard detachment and comes to his native village, could not be created by Sholokhov as a conscious fighter of the Revolution. His life was like the life of millions of other people, neither remarkable nor distinguished. He was killed by the Cossacks because during the Cossack uprising he tried to break through to the Reds.

Such was his end. With this, Valet could be left. But the author seems to want to say more. He wants to say that a shot in the back is not yet the end. He speaks of Valet's grave. *The Quiet Don* is a book of blood and death. Sholokhov could not possibly include descriptions of the graves of all those who had been killed. But about the graves which are mentioned, he writes with a specific sadness and affection. He has nothing to say about the life beyond the grave. In the description of the graves, however, a certain reverence to the mystery of death cannot be missed. Valet is no more. But at his grave life continues. Life, cruel and violent as it is, nevertheless speaks clearly that no life can ever be forgotten. This is what Sholokhov said about Valet's grave:

> Within two weeks the little mound was overgrown with burdock and wormwood; wild oats were dancing on it, grape was yellowing gaily at the side, clover was raising its head, and the air was scented with thyme, spurge and honeydew.
>
> Soon afterwards an old man drove out from the village, dug a little hole at the head of the grave, and set up a little shrine on a freshly cut oaken pole. The sorrowful features of the Virgin glowed softly under the little gable and on the base below her was painted an inscription in old Slavonic:
>> In the years of strife and trouble,
>> Brothers, judge not thy brother.
> The old man rode away and the little shrine remained

in the steppe to sadden the eyes of passing travellers with its eternally mournful aspect, and to stir in their hearts a strange and sad longing.

Later on, in May, two bustards fought around the shrine. They beat out a little bare patch in the blue wormwood, crushing the green flush of ripening quitch grass, fighting for the hen, for the right to life, for love and fertility. And again after a little while, under a mound, right by the shrine, in the shaggy shelter of the old wormwood a hen bustard laid nine speckled, smoky-blue eggs and sat on them, warming them with her body, and shielding them with her glossy wings. (*Part Five, Chapter XXXII.*)

Such is the vision of life and death in Sholokhov. Life is a hard struggle, a violent struggle in the society of people as it is in the world of animals. In every struggle there are victims. The weak fall and the strong survive. But life never stops. Those who do not survive and have to depart from life, they bequeath to those who remain a continuation of life and struggle. And life, too, stormy and uneven, is a constant reminder of those who once lived, but have departed from this life. It is as if Sholokhov would like to say that there is no end in death per se.

NOTES AND REFERENCES

1. I. Eksler, "How *The Quiet Don* Was Created," *Izvestia*, June 12, 1940, n. 134, cited in Gura, Abramov, *op. cit.*, p. 170.

2. L. Tolstoi, Letter to Fet, Sept. 5, 1878. Jubilee Edition, vol. 62, p. 441.

3. See Jubilee Edition, vol. 34, p. 520.

4. Part Seven, Chapter XVII.
5. Part Three, Chapter I.
6. From the Thirteenth Century *Lamentation on the Ruin of Rus'* by an unknown author. Cf. *Medieval Russia's Epics, Chronicles, and Tales* edited by Serge A. Zenkovsky, H. Dutton Paperback, 1963, p. 174.
7. Part Three, Chapter XVI.
8. Part Three, Chapter XVII.
9. *Ibid.*
10. Part Three, Chapter VIII.
11. Part Five, Chapter I.
12. Part Six, Chapter XX.
13. Part Five, Chapter XIX.
14. Part Five, Chapter XX.
15. Part Six, Chapter XXIV.
16. Part Six, Chapter XXXI.
17. Part Eight, Chapter V.
18. Part Eight, Chapter II.

THE MAIN HERO

The Quiet Don displays abundant multiformity and colorfulness of characters. Their lives are rooted and formed somewhere far and deep, as if in an abyss. They disappear into a mystery, elusive, indefinite. The diversity and multiformity of the heroes creates a richness in the life brought into existence by the author and brings an attractiveness to his work. Sholokhov's people combine situations in which a hard, hating love, which repulses, coexists with a light, burning hate, which attracts. Unrestrained, savage violence can suddenly be transformed into similarly unrestrained, uncontrolled happiness. Cruelty exists next to warmhearted affection, and boundless humility and submission coexist with uncontrolled protest. Reckless daring can be changed instantaneously into meekness, and violence can be transformed into tenderness. Shyness stands next to easy familiarity and impudence. Incorruptible honesty is transformed into petty, unprincipaled knavery, and naivete slips into shyness. The people's crudity in their language and their morals coexists with solicitous softness and weakness. In addition, vile deeds stand next to nobility. But above all there is the author's consistency in presenting the mercilessness of life and fate itself, without pity or compassion towards the great or small. The author united all these contrasts and diversity into one whole and emerged into a world that was strange, but so close and appealing in its vivid details. It is as if the author wanted to say: "Here, look at your life, what you are suited for, and what you yourselves have done. But I am not here for anything. I am only an outsider." Such is the world of Sholokhov and his hero.

The main hero of this novel is Grigorii Melekhov. If Sholokhov had entitled his novel by his hero's name, it would probably have been as appropriate as the present title, *The Quiet Don.* If Sholokhov did not entitle his novel with the name of his hero, it is probably because his novel was conceived and created on a wider and deeper level than the fate of one character. But at the same time the novel has its limitations in one family and one man.

The main hero rose on the foreground of the turbulent, restless stormy Don. Grigorii Melekhov, with a few exceptions in Parts Four and Five, appears on all the pages of the novel, from beginning to end. Grigorii reflects the whole radiant, turbulent Don. Because of this, Sholokhov entitled his novel not with the name of his hero, but with the name of the entire Don. It is as though Grigorii appears as a personification of all the Cossacks and their way of life. Having depicted in Grigorii the common features of the Don, inherent to all the Cossacks, Sholokhov also endowed him with deeply individualized features. In Grigorii, Sholokhov united everything typical and common, yet kept separate those deeply personal qualities inherent to Grigorii alone, making him an unusual, uncommon Cossack. He is not a blurry average man of the Don. He has his own fate and character that is uncommon to any other man. His personal characteristics separate and lift Grigorii from his surroundings.

The author said very little about his hero in his narration. Sholokhov as an author and witness to his hero's life is sparing in the characterization of the hero. He does not talk about his hero's inner world, his emotional experiences, and his thoughts and worries. Rather, he lets Grigorii speak for himself. We learn about Grigorii not in the author's narration but in the actions of life itself, directly as Grigorii lives it. It is as if the author created his hero and then said, "think what you want about him yourself, condemn or justify him. It is not my business. He himself will tell you about his life." Only in two places, toward the end of the novel, did the author step away from his non-interference in Grigorii's life, and directly censured him. We will speak of this later, when we reach the end of Grigorii's life. Now, let us start with how Grigorii appears before us.

We come upon Grigorii in the first pages of the novel as a full-grown village lad. The author did not devote one line to his hero's past. Only through seemingly accidental strokes in all four volumes did he scatter small, separate sketches about his hero's childhood and past. But these separately scattered touches barely convey anything important and essential for an understanding of Grigorii's character and his inner world. All of him is before us in his present state and actions, not in his thoughts or past. The author was very sparing in using his author's right to tell all he knew about his hero. It is as if the author wants to let the reader himself see the hero in life and then judge the hero's actions and deeds for himself. Sholokhov knows economy of place and time. Thus, it is only at the beginning of the fourth volume that we, as if by chance, find out from a conversation over-heard between Grigorii and Kopylov, his fellow Cossack-officer, that Grigorii had finished parish school.[1]

Likewise as if per chance, in the third volume, we find out from Grigorii's mother complaints that Grigorii was affectionate and tender in childhood.[2]   Later we will find out still another detail from Grigorii's childhood, that Grigorii was left-handed. In itself this detail would not be significant. Therefore, the author did not consider it important enough to mention it specifically, as if not to take up time and space. He disclosed it in a place where it was most appropriate: to show Grigorii's skill or even invulnerability in attacks. Here, this small detail turns out to be very important in the life of Sholokhov's hero. That he was able to handle his left hand as he did his right was to his great advantage during attacks. Hardly any more is told about Grigorii's past in the novel.

At first we see him as a country lad, a Cossack like many other Cossacks, in close relation with a married woman. But the author never devoted a line to reveal how his hero had fallen in love with the neighbor woman Aksin'ia. Their relation is disclosed in the subsequent unrolling of events. Aksin'ia's husband Stepan Astakhov was with the other village Cossacks in summer training camp. In the affair between Grigorii and Aksin'ia nothing serious was seen at first. This was a chance affair like many others in the village among soldiers' wives. When, shortly before Stepan's return from the camp, Aksin'ia begins to worry, she asked Grigorii what she is to do. Grigorii answered calmly and recklessly, as if the matter did not concern him, "How do I know?" When Aksin'ia tried to persuade him to go away with her somewhere to a city, this seemed impossible to him. He is a village lad and cannot leave the soil.

"You are a fool, Aksin'ia, a fool. You talk much, but there's nothing to hear from you. Well, where would I go from farming? And then again, I must go to service this year. This won't do, what you say. I won't budge from the soil for anywhere. Here is the steppe, there is much air to breathe here. And the city? Last winter I went with father to the station. I almost got lost. The steam engines roared, the air there was heavy from burning coal. How the people live there, I don't know, maybe they're used to those fumes." Grigorii spat and spoke again. "I won't go anywhere from this village." (*Part One, Chapter XII.*)

Grigorii is a Cossack and can live only on the soil. A different life, a different environment, a different truth from that inherited from his forefathers is unthinkable for him. But in this rude Cossack with uncommon intelligence and character, yet similar to all other Cossacks, there is his own life. He was not suited to a protest and to an independent life, but this does not mean that he did not have his own life. Certainly, he was inconsistent, and often did not know what he needed or what he wanted. He appears as such to the end of the novel. Not succeeding in choosing his own route, he always bowed to circumstances, such as when he did not dare to take responsibility for Aksin'ia. When circumstances forced him to break with Aksin'ia, he did this easily. He accepted marriage to Natal'ia

Korshunova as a duty, because circumstances had forced him to do so. Such a marriage was common for Cossacks like Grigorii.

The Cossack, Grigorii Melekhov, would have lived peacefully in his family, and life with his wife would have been quiet in dutiful affection toward her, if again, circumstances had not forced him away from his family and wife. Circumstances are always higher than Grigorii's personal decisions. But if it were not for these circumstances, we would not have this remarkable novel about the Cossack, Grigorii Melekhov, who has grown very close to us. First, an accidental meeting with Aksin'ia at a winter woodcutting in the forest played a part in Grigorii's fate. Aksin'ia firmly resolved "to take Grigorii away from the happy Natal'ia who knew neither loving joy or suffering."[3] She never passed an opportunity to draw him to herself. The meeting, accidental for Grigorii, again brought him closer to Aksin'ia. Then his father's threat played a decisive role in Grigorii's break with Natal'ia and with his parents' house. Actually this was not only a threat: the father Melekhov literally threw his son out of the house.[4]

As we have already noted, the author did not narrate about Grigorii's love for Aksin'ia in his own or even his hero's words. Only once did the author, as if by chance, say that Grigorii was thinking about Aksin'ia. This was during the taking of the oath, on the eve before that memorable evening when his father had thrown him out of the house.[5] Thus, his departure from home and his new closeness with Aksin'ia was forced on Grigorii.

Again life would have flowed peacefully for the average Cossack Grigorii Melekhov with its small happinesses and tribulations. This uncommon and yet so average Cossack would have been lost in his cold egotism and indifference to the grief of other people, such as his mistress' husband, Stepan Astakhov, or his own wife, driven in desperation to attempt suicide. He would have no dealings with anyone. With his mistress Aksin'ia he behaved crudely, cynically. Grigorii felt nothing toward the daughter born to him by Aksin'ia "except sometimes hostility for those moments lived through when he had carried Aksin'ia from the steppe when she was writhing in childbirth."[6]

But circumstances again changed Grigorii and his life: military service and then the war. Once in military service, Grigorii was ready to raise himself above his peers, fellow Cossacks in service. This was when he saw that the Cossacks of his detachment were raping a Polish serving girl, Frania. Out of indignation he shouted that he was ready to make a protest, but the Cossacks threatened him, and he became silent.

Sholokhov did not raise his hero above circumstances. Not having created a self-willed, integrated hero who used the circumstances of life for his own goals, Sholokhov remained probably truer to the Cossack way of life. He did not fabricate his hero, did not create him as a man of firm, strong spirit, but took him from everyday life and molded him from common clay. He provided him with trivial ordinary details, which, though they are present in everybody, made Grigorii unique among his own kind. By means of details, the life of Sholokhov's hero is made rich. Through the use of many details, the author enriched his heroes. Accidental circumstances pushed Grigorii his whole life. And only they made an outstanding Cossack out of him, as he rushed restlessly around. Yet, the reader feels that just this man is much like every other man.

What Grigorii thought about Aksin'ia, his forgotten wife Natal'ia, of his parents while in the service—the author hid from his readers. Maybe the author wanted to emphasize by this means that his hero lived only for those things immediately before him, for those things directly experienced. The things remote from his sight, hearing, and thought did not concern him.

His first participation in military action is marked by fear. "Hazelike, fear flooded his cowed eyes."[7] These are the author's words about his hero when he heard the first shots. The author did not want to hide his hero's human weaknesses. Again and again Grigorii appears before us in an unidealized light.

Grigorii lived through his first cavalry attack in a kind of unconscious stupor. Rushing forward on his horse with other Cossacks, Grigorii felt that "that organ in the middle of his breast which until the attack had busily pumped blood, now turned into wood, and Grigorii felt nothing besides the noise in his ears and pain in the fingers of his left hand."[8] In addition the author added: "Thought, castrated by fear, tangled together a heavy paralyzed ball in his head."[9] This is not a conscious, individual participation in war, but more like submission to mass fear and the inevitable. Man is transformed here into a small particle, carried along by a strong current. He does not have the strength to stop or resist the current. He can only surrender to the current and be carried along without thought, will, or resistance, or even thinking what might happen to him in the next minute.

The first two victims sabered by Grigorii, strange Austrian soldiers, were killed more by unconscious reflex than by conscious heroism. And afterwards, in conversation with his brother Petro, whom he has met along the road, Grigorii complained:

> My conscience is killing me. I stuck one with a pike by Leshnev (a Prussian town, M.K.). In the heat of the moment. . .couldn't have been otherwise. But why did I cut him down? I killed a man, and now I suffer in my soul because of him, the skunk. I dream of him, scoundrel, in the nights. But am I to blame? (*Part Three, Chapter X.*)

Cossack that he is, Grigorii was not able to understand why he had to kill strange people. But somehow he felt that because he was assigned to a company which he could not leave, he had to do what had to be done. Such is the way of life in the war. It is a way different from the Cossack village way which Grigorii had known since childhood, but he knows that he cannot change it. And so, he submits.

In the act that brought him his first decoration and the rank of cavalier, there was nothing heroic. Sholokhov presented the heroism as the most ordinary act, which any man in the same circumstances could have done. In the novel it appears to be dutiful heroism. While saving his own life, Grigorii saved the life of a wounded colonel, taking him onto his shoulder and bringing him to his own unit. He did this unconsciously, as he had sabered the Austrian. In Sholokhov it appears that the wounded Russian officer saved by Grigorii displayed more heroism than Grigorii. At first the officer did not want to give himself up alive into the hands of an enemy, taking Grigorii at first for a German. And afterwards he urged Grigorii to toss him aside to die. This sounds more like selfless heroism.

After this Sholokhov puts his hero into a hospital and brings him together with a certain Garanzha, who speaks against the war. Garanzha's anti-war speeches could not have fallen on more receptive soil than Grigorii was at that time. Tired, dirty, wounded, but now on a clean bed, the war seemed like a nightmare that he did not want to accept. Garanzha was against war, and so was Grigorii. Grigorii was not able to argue with Garanzha. He could not help but feel the truth in Garanzha's cruel words.

But it would have been very strange if Sholokhov had made his hero into a conscious pacifist, a fighter against the war. This would not have been within the strength of a Cossack who accepted his life as Grigorii did. This would have been an improbable act and Sholokhov did well, having avoided it.

Upon his arrival in his native village after the hospital, two external circumstances acted upon Grigorii and determined his life. The first was his forced parting from Aksin'ia. Having found that Aksin'ia had gone to young Listnitskii, the master's son, for whom she was working, Grigorii obediently returned home to his family and wife, who, after an attempt at suicide, had waited faithfully and meekly for him in the Melekhov household. The second circumstance was the honor and respect which surrounded him, the first St. George cavalier in the village.

> Grigorii arrived from the front one man, and went away another. His own life, Cossack traditions, imbibed with his mother's milk, prevailed over universal human truth. (*Part Four, Chapter IV.*)

Here, "universal human truth" must be understood as intuitive, rather than the consciously reasoned out arguments of Garanzha's words against the war, which Grigorii had agreed with.

Sholokhov fell silent about the inner life of his hero at this time. But it can be assumed that for Grigorii this must have been a most happy period. The amazed, respectful attitude of the surrounding people could only flatter the young Cossack.

> The old men talked on the village square with him as with an equal. They took off their hats in greeting him with bows. Girls and old women looked with unconcealed fascination at the dashing, almost stooping figure in a cloak with a cross pinned on a striped ribbon. He saw that Pantelei Prokofievich was clearly proud of him, walking alongside with him to the church or the parade ground. (*Part Four, Chapter IV.*)

There was nothing to disturb Grigorii. In the family there was peace. In the service there was respect. What more did the Cossack need? But Sholokhov did not speak about what was probably the happiest time of his hero's life. Not having spoken, he seemingly left his readers to judge and think about his hero. Exactly this possibility—to let his readers judge and think about his hero, his non-interference and naturalness, his leaving things unsaid—this constitutes the full charm and fascination of the novel. It is as if the author himself did not know exactly what he had to say about Grigorii.

Aksin'ia, his love, departed into his memories, and her image faded. But this is only for the time being. He would return to her when the very ground under his feet would tremble.

The author spoke only cursorily about Grigorii's next few years in the war. The author used his own words in summarizing events. Grigorii seemed to go into the second plan of the novel. Other events and other people occupied the author: Bunchuk, Listnitskii, Cossacks in Petrograd, all events in which our hero was not placed. This is the part of the novel which originally was intended to serve as the beginning of *Donshchina.* The author remembered Grigorii as if only in passing while speaking in his own words about the rich episodes of the war.

In May, 1915, Grigorii, taking part in an unmounted attack, knocked a tall German lieutenant from his feet with leveled rifle, and took three German soldiers prisoners."[10]   Then in July, 1915, there was an episode recorded by the author, factually but cursorily; Grigorii "recaptured a Cossack battery taken by the Austrians, went to the rear of the enemy and turned the Austrian's attack into a retreat. . . .He also took a fat Austrian officer prisoner."[11]   Also presented cursorily is Grigorii's memory of the meeting with Stepan Astakhov. Examples of this go on and on and on. His heroic courage seems to have no end. The author dwells only on the service record of his hero, noting only his main deeds.

We cannot help but feel that the author does this in order to pride himself in the young Cossack whom he has chosen as his hero. The author thinks about his hero with love. In this love there is also compassion for the hard lot of the Cossack in the war, and that the war had ravaged Grigorii's heart. The author's attitude to his warrior-hero reflects the folk songs about the Cossack warriors.

> Had time scattered not a few of these days along the fields of recent and past battles? Grigorii strongly guarded his Cossack honor and always was seizing chances to show his reckless courage, to take risks, to do all possible mad adventures, like going to the Austrian rear in civilian dress, or taking outposts without bloodshed, or doing fancy riding. He felt that the pain for men which had oppressed him in the first days of the war had gone forever. His heart had coarsened, grown hard, like a salt marsh in a drought. As the salt marsh does not absorb water, so Grigorii's heart did not absorb pity anymore. With cold contempt he played with others' and his own lives; for this he became reputed for courage—he won four St. George crosses and four medals. At the rare parades he stood by the regimental banner, seasoned with the powder smoke of many battles. But he knew also that he couldn't laugh anymore, like before, that his eyes had sunk, his cheek bones stuck out sharply, and that it was difficult, kissing his child, to look openly into its clear eyes: Grigorii knew what price he had paid for his full belt of crosses and medals. (*Part Four, Chapter IV.*)

This passage reads like an old Cossack folk song about an ancient Cossack warrior. All elements of a Cossack folk song are present here: the warrior's honor, his reckless courage and pride, his hard temper and sorrows, together with his many decorations and awards. People who created and sang those Cossack songs must have loved their warrior-heroes. Thus it is with Sholokhov too. He loves his Cossack hero and takes pride in him.

We see Grigorii in a fully detailed picture only at the end of 1917, after the coup in Petrograd, and at a turning point in his life. All that has happened to him in the war, the author states only briefly, factually.

> Melekhov, Grigorii, in January, 1917, was promoted for distinction in battle to cornet (a junior officer in the Cossack army, M.K.), appointed to the second reserve regiment as a platoon leader.
>
> In September, after contacting an infection of the lungs he received leave, lived at home for a month and a half, recovered from his illness, was passed by the district medical commission, and again was sent to his regiment. After the October coup he received promotion to commander of a Hundred. (Hundred—a unit in the Cossack army with one hundred men, M.K.) (*Part Four, Chapter IV.*)

After the October Revolution Grigorii, unlike other Cossacks returning from the front, did not return home to his own Tatarsk hamlet. In the troubled times he continued to serve, trying to find some kind of sense of life. At first he fell under the influence of the Cossack autonomists. Having emerged after the February Revolution, they stood for the full autonomy of the Don region from Russia, for the restoration of that order which had existed among the Cossacks before their subordination to the autocracy. Grigorii personally could hardly find his way through the labyrinth of politics. It seemed to him that independence of the Don would secure the ancient, Cossack way of life which had been shaken in the Revolution. The old order of Cossack life seemed to be that unshakable truth which Grigorii was seeking. But only for a short time did he keep his balance on his Cossack consciousness.

In November, 1917, Grigorii accidentally met another Cossack, "who had played not a small role in the history of the revolution on the Don."[12] These author's words serve as an introduction to a new turn in Grigorii's life and mood. This Cossack was Fëdor Podtëlkov, who was drawn to the Bol'sheviks and the Revolution.

The author did not say exactly what attracted Grigorii in the Revolution. Was it the idea of Revolution which impressed Grigorii? This could hardly be. Nowhere did the author present the idea of Revolution in Grigorii's life. Podtëlkov, like the Cossack autonomists, was saying that the Cossacks had to rule their land themselves. To Grigorii's simple question, in which for him lay the whole point of life, "Who shall govern us?" Podtëlkov answered even more simply: "We ourselves shall."[13] This was exactly what the autonomists said. The only difference is that Podtëlkov wanted to be ruled without the generals. The idea seemed to appeal to Grigorii.

Thus, the October Revolution was conceived by Grigorii in its relation to the question of the Cossack autonomy: the Cossacks had to rule their lands and lives by themselves. This seemed to be Grigorii's idea of the Revolution. But Grigorii did not stay on the side of the Revolution for long. And it was the Revolution itself that pushed him away. A peaceful Cossack accustomed to peaceful work, he was unable to understand the senseless cruelty of the Revolution. This is the way the author presented Grigorii's encounter with the Revolution. It is as if the author wanted to excuse his hero's defection from the Revolution. In no way did he want to reproach his hero.

There was one scene that played a decisive role in Grigorii's decision to turn away from the Revolution. Let us dwell on this important scene in more detail. Grigorii, commanding two hundred Cossacks, participated in a military operation to capture a White detachment under the command of a certain Chernetsov. Being wounded in that battle, Grigorii had to witness Podtëlkov's merciless execution of the captured Chernetsov and his soldiers, who, like Grigorii himself, were fighting for the Don's independence, only on a different side. A certain Golubov, who had taken Chernetsov and his detachment prisoner, informed Podtëlkov through Grigorii that he would take Chernetsov and his men on bail. On this account a major disagreement took place between Podtëlkov and Grigorii. Grigorii wanted to prevent Podtëlkov from needless killing, but Podtëlkov rudely refused Grigorii's intercession. At the end of their conversation Grigorii made a hostile movement toward Podtëlkov.

> Grigorii, at the first moment when the execution began, tore himself away from the machine gun. Not letting his eyes from Podtëlkov, limping swiftly, he hobbled up to him. Minaev seized him from behind. Twisting his arms, almost breaking them, he took away the pistol; gazing with darkened eyes into Grigorii's eyes, panting, he asked:
> "And what did you think?" (*Part Five, Chapter XII.*)

The author said nothing about the inner state of his hero and his mood at this time. His action could have been unintentional, a subconscious expression of protest, but could also have been an intentional burst to hinder cruel and senseless violence. The author seems to have left something unsaid. As Grigorii observed the execution, it follows from the text that he made a movement toward Podtëlkov. Did he want to prevent the murders? The author did not say this. In any case Grigorii's action was intercepted. Did Grigorii himself want to deal with Podtëlkov? He knew that Podtëlkov was executing the prisoners without authorization, only on his own responsibility.

Afterwards, thinking about the violence which he had seen, Grigorii was unable to forgive or forget the unwarranted killing of Chernetsov and his men. The author seemed again to defend his Cossack hero.

After this Grigorii left the Reds. Thus, his departure was forced upon him by external circumstances. The scene he had witnessed repulsed him from the Revolution. His protest against the Revolution, which had burst violently upon the Cossack way of life, at first was passive though spontaneous. He returned to his native hamlet, tired, beaten by all scenes and experiences of the long years of war. He strove with his entire soul toward a peaceful life. Now as before and as it will be later at the end of the book, his only goal and thought was to peacefully plow the fields.

Weariness contracted in the war broke him. He wanted to turn away from the whole world, incomprehensible, hostile, and seething with hate. There behind him everything was confusing, contradictory. The right path had been found with difficulty; as on a swampy road the soil shifted beneath his feet, the path divided, and there was no certainty which was the right step to take. . . .But when he imagined how towards spring he would ready the plows, bullock carts, mangers of plaited willow; and when the

earth would disrobe and dry out,—he would drive out into
the steppe; gripping the plow with hands longing for work
he would walk behind the plow, feeling its living pulsation
and jerking; imagining how he would breathe the sweet
scent of young grass and black earth turned over by the
ploughshare, not yet having lost the sweet aroma of snow
dampness—his soul warmed.

He longed to round up the cattle, toss the hay, to
breathe the withered scent of the clover, the couch grass,
the spicy odor of dung. He wanted nothing so much as
peace and quiet. Grigorii guarded a shy gladness in his stern
eyes when he glanced around at the horses, his father's
broad back, covered with a sheepskin coat. Everything
reminded him of his previous half-forgotten life: the smell
of sheep from his father's coat, the domestic look of the
ungroomed horses, a rooster in the village, crowing from a
shed. Sweet, thick, like spirits seemed life to him in this
backwater. (*Part Five, Chapter XIII.*)

As we noticed the author's love and care for his
hero in the passage where Sholokhov glorified Grigorii's
reckless prowess, so in this long passage, too, we observe
the author's same loving attitude to his hero. It seems
as if Sholokhov wished his hero much luck and well-
being in his peaceful labor on the Cossack's rich soil.

The end of the turmoil and bloodshed was, however,
not yet in sight. This was only the beginning of all
troubles and bloodshed. The Revolution was not to
leave the Cossacks in peace.

Among the villagers and his family, Grigorii, until
the war, had in no way been distinguished from other
Cossacks. He seemed born to this kind of life, to work
peacefully and take pleasure in family life.

Sholokhov is not depicting an idyll of the Melekhov

family and of the Cossack village. He is far from presenting happiness and bliss without darkness or adversity. Life in Sholokhov's world is stern, with crude and often cynical relationships among people. Very often the cruelty does not know mercy for the weak. But this life went along on its own, as if a natural path, as established long ago. It was not difficult to understand this life if one took part in it. No one interfered with the free flow of this life, and no one tried to regulate or counterbalance it with another way of life. Life in Sholokhov's novel maintains itself and accounts to no one.

Grigorii felt sure of himself in such a life. Domestic cares surrounded him, and he began to look after them and care for them. At this place the author reveals Grigorii's new attitude toward his wife, moving from cold indifference to tender concern and pride for her.

> Grigorii put his hand on the wide, working back of his wife, and, for the first time, thought: "A good-looking woman, it hits you in the eye. . . .How did she live without me? Probably the other Cossacks looked at her." (*Part Five, Chapter XIII.*)

Concern and the apparently light, loving jealousy of a husband for the faithful, meek wife are heard in these author's words.

Again, the life of the Tatarsk Cossacks would have flowed as in ancient times, and Grigorii would have been lost in his own farmstead. But in the distance from the Tatarsk hamlet and the Melekhov farm, the life-and-death struggle was already in progress. Two worlds were caught up in the struggle for survival. The old world, with its cruel, but deeply indigenous and well-known truth of life was trusted by Grigorii and all the other Cossacks. The new world, which had burst in with the whirlwind of Revolution, seemed to the Cossacks an invasion of the poor peasants of Russia against the rich Cossack lands. The new world was incomprehensible and evil for the Cossacks. They had to preserve and to defend the old world against this invasion from the outside.

At the moment of Grigorii's return to his native village sometime in January, 1918, there was an interregnum, or rather a period of self-government or no government at all in the hamlet Tatarsk. Neither the Reds nor the Whites showed any authority: nobody knew and nobody worried about power. From the events which developed later, in the spring of 1918, when the Cossacks rose in defense of the Don against the Revolution, we learn that a revolutionary committee had existed on the Don before that time. But the author said not a word about its function.

Rather, in the village the old order prevailed. There was no bitterness in the hamlet toward the Cossacks who sympathized with the Revolution. The front line Cossacks sent a delegation to the Congress of Veteran Cossacks. The congress proclaimed the authority of the Military-Revolutionary Committee on the Don. In reality, however, the authority of the Revolution among the Cossacks was more in name than in fact. There were Red Cossacks in the village, too. Grigorii himself had returned from service with the Reds. None of the Cossacks ever reproached him or others who had served with the Reds. The Cossacks knew only one fact: they did not want war. They wanted to live peacefully as their forefathers had done.

In the spring of 1918, before the arrival of the Volunteer Army on the Don, the question rose for Grigorii whether he would leave the village to join the Reds. But he flatly refused to leave the hamlet. He did not want to be for or against the Reds. The village Cossacks wanted to make Grigorii their company commander to lead them against the Reds. But for Grigorii this was not an honor. Not wasting words about Grigorii's feelings, the author briefly but clearly said that Grigorii felt "persecuted" because of this honor.[14] The Cossacks finally chose Grigorii's brother Petro as their commander. When volunteers were sought, Grigorii stayed at home.

Sholokhov left no doubt that the Don uprising for the protection of the Cossack lands against the invasion of Russian peasants was unanimous. Only two men from the Tatarsk village went to the Reds: Valet and Mishka Koshevoi. But Valet, a worker from the merchant Mokhov's mill, was not a Cossack. When the Cossacks caught them both, they shot Valet, the non-Cossack, but sent Mishka, the Cossack, to herd the village horses.

When the mobilization of the Cossacks began, Grigorii could not stand aloof this time. He had to go and fight along with other Cossacks. Here he met Podtëlkov again, but this time under different circumstances— at the execution of Podtëlkov and his expedition. Grigorii did not fail to reproach Podtëlkov again for his unjustified shooting of the officer prisoners.

The author did not dwell on Grigorii's mood when he,

choking with anger, reminded Podtëlkov of the scene of the shooting. Only as if in passing do we find out that Grigorii was very upset.[15] That scene of the shooting had cut deeply into Grigorii's memory.

And so Grigorii is again on the move, at war. Wishing to escape and avoid reckless cruelty, he is forced to be not only a witness but a participant in the extreme cruelty of the Civil War. His thoughts, however, remain hidden. Not even those close to him understood what Grigorii lived by during those days. For his brother, Grigorii was a riddle. Here is what Petro said to Grigorii:

"Look how they've divided the people, the skunks! It's like they passed through with a plow: one—to one side; another—to the other, like under a plowshare. The devil's life, and a terrible time! One man can't divine the other. Take us, for instance," he abruptly interrupted the conversation. "You are my blood brother, but I won't understand you, God help me! I feel you are somehow going away from me. Am I speaking the truth?" And he answered himself: "The truth. You are all mixed up. I'm afraid you'll desert to the Reds. You, Grishka, haven't found yourself yet."

"And have you found yourselves?" asked Grigorii, looking how beyond the invisible line of the Khoper river and beyond the chalky mountains the sun was setting, and the clouds were floating away in burning black puffs.

"I have. I have fallen into my own furrow. You won't push me away from it! I, Grishka, won't waver around like you."

"Oh?" Grigorii squeezed out a bitter smile.

"I won't." Petro angrily twisted his mustache, blinked frequently, as if blinded. "You couldn't tug me to the Reds with a lasso. The Cossacks are against them, and so am I. I don't want and won't argue. There's no reason for me to go with them. It's not along my way."

"Quit this talk," asked Grigorii wearily. (*Part Six, Chapter II.*)

To Petro's insistent question whether he wouldn't desert to the Reds, Grigorii answers listlessly, unwillingly, "Hardly. . .I don't know."[16]

Grigorii indeed did not find himself in the turbulent life. He was born for the village life, to walk behind a plow, but life churned up around him like a stormy sea, tossing him and blindly playing with him. And how could he, a simple Cossack, find his own place in the complicated relationships of national passions and an incomprehensible struggle if life everywhere seemed to be stronger than himself.

After the memorable conversation with Petro, "heavy melancholy settled upon Grigorii."[17] He participated in the war with the Reds, and did his duty as he had in the German War: valiantly, but not knowing why. He commanded the village Cossack company. He was curious about the unknown Reds, as once he had been curious about the unknown Germans. This curiosity was mixed with respect for the incomprehensible behavior and simplicity of the Red soldiers. But his curiosity, respect, and pity were overshadowed by hate and anger towards the Reds, because with their invasion they had torn him from the earth and had forced him to fight again. He regarded it as his duty to fight for the Don and his free Cossack life and land.

And gradually Grigorii became filled with spite against the Bolsheviks. They intruded into his life as enemies, took

him away from the earth. He saw that the same feeling
had taken hold of the remaining Cossacks. It seemed to all
of them that it was the Bolshevik's fault, pressing in on the
Cossack region, that this war was going on. And, looking
at the unreaped waves of wheat, at the unharvested wheat
lying beneath the hooves of the horses, and at the empty
threshing floors, every one of them remembered his own
plot of land over which their women wheezed at back-
breaking labor, and every one hardened his heart and
turned brutal. In battle Grigorii felt that his enemies—
Tambov, Riazan, Saratov peasants—were moved by that
same jealous feeling towards the earth. "We fight for it,
like for a beloved woman," thought Grigorii. (*Part Six,
Chapter IX.*)

Such is the Cossack vision of life. One must fight for
the land. There appeared in the Cossacks a bitterness
toward the Reds that had not existed before. The laws
of war were cruel, and one had to submit to them.
Grigorii had once attempted to avoid the cruel ways of
war, but immediately felt that in his involuntary participation in the war, the pity for the enemy would be
turned against himself.

Plundering did not appeal to Grigorii . . .he took only
forage and food for his horse, vaguely avoiding touching
things not his own, and regarding plundering with loathing.
Especially repulsive in his eyes was the plundering of his
own Cossacks. He ruled his squadron severely. If his
Cossacks took, they did so secretively, in rare instances.
He did not order them to kill or strip prisoners. With his
extreme mildness he invoked displeasure among the Cossacks and of the regimental commander. He was ordered
to headquarters for an explanation. (*Part Six, Chapter IX.*)

In this fratricidal war, as in the German War, the author treats his hero solicitously, with caring love, as if he wants to protect him. Besides German bullets and sabres, Grigorii had been fired at three times by Stepan Astakhov.[18] But he remained whole and unhurt. The author created him for a more cruel, and perhaps even more senseless ending than death on the battlefield from a stray bullet. We have here the same attitude of the author's loving care to his hero in this war.

> Grigorii's star still burned with a quiet, flickering gleam. Evidently the time had not yet matured for it to break away and fly, lighting up the sky with its cold streaking flame. Three horses had been killed under Grigorii since autumn, his cloak had been shot through in five places. Death was playing with the Cossack, fanning him with a black wing. Once a bullet went through the copper head of his sword; the sword fell to his horse's foot as if bitten through.
>
> "Someone is strongly praying for you, Grigorii," said Mit'ka Korshunov, and was surprised by Grigorii's joyless smile." (*Part Six, Chapter X.*)

Here again, as in many other places, one feels the popular, folkloristic attitudes toward the brave Cossack. Only in popular songs are such favorite heroes sung, who know neither fear nor trembling on the field of battle. The death is playing with them. But fate is not indifferent to such heroes. Fate is preparing them for a different end. As in the folk songs, Sholokhov's hero is woven out of human material. He is not entirely heroic, nor is he entirely without courage; all he is, is an ordinary human, with all manners of weaknesses and ailments.

A terrible ailment gnaws at Grigorii. The Cossack fearless on the field of battle does not see the end of the fighting. At the beginning of the war in 1918, he had hoped for swift victory and the return to the peaceful Cossack farms. Like the other Cossacks, Grigorii did not choose to fight. War had been imposed upon him. The Cossacks had to drive the Bolsheviks from the native fields, secure the Cossack peaceful work, and then live for themselves.

But towards the autumn of 1918, the hopes for a swift victory were vanishing. Therefore, though the goal had not been attained, there seemed to be no more sense in fighting. At this time Grigorii was seized by fatalism. Briefly, in his typical style, the author presents Grigorii's inner world. "There's no way to go," he thought. Once, he "fell asleep with an irksome feeling of something left undecided."[19]

The outcome, as has happened many times before, came to Grigorii as if on its own accord—without the hero's participation. He decided to leave all this muddle and go home, where human relations are simple and where he thought he could find the lost peace and quiet. Grigorii seemed to run away from life in order to find himself and his peace. But life with its storms followed him everywhere.

It is remarkable that his decision to leave the regiment without a leave of absence came to him almost unconsciously, without the active participation of his will and thoughts. Sholokhov did not make Grigorii torment himself about the solution to a difficult question. The solution simply came about of its own accord because there was no other way out. Grigorii did not resist the hopeless situation but gave himself up to the currents. Although the author said that Grigorii left his regiment without leave "full of joyous resolution,"[20] this joyous resolution came to him when there was already no other way out, when the decision had seemingly made itself. "Joyous resolution" is here only the surrendering of one's self to the mighty currents. Life again turned out to be stronger than Grigorii.

But Grigorii did not find the peace, the hope which had driven him back to his native village. The front came to his village, too. And with the front, the Red soldiers arrived. Grigorii did not escape from the Reds, even though he had a chance to do so. Something stronger than his personal wishes and decisions seemed to guide him. He submitted to an entirely unknown inclination and did not go away from the Reds: perhaps this was not so much fear for his own life as fear for the life of his kin, which seized him at home. During the very first night which the Red Army men spent in the Melekhov home, Grigorii did not sleep. He "knew irrevocably that he was ready in spirit to undergo any trial and humiliation, if only to preserve his own and the lives of his kin."[21]

In remaining under the Reds, Grigorii almost lost his own life. The Revolution seemed to give everyone the right to create his own courts and justice. And so, the Red soldiers undertook vengeance upon Grigorii because he had been an officer: "They've arranged to kill you. Someone has denounced you as an officer. Run away," whispered a neighbor girl to Grigorii at a party.[22] And our hero ran away.

Thus the Soviet authority was established in the

village at the end of 1918. The author disclosed at this time that Grigorii, as he was earlier, was at heart neither for the Whites nor the Reds. Grigorii did not see the difference between the generals and the Soviets. He fought not for the generals, but for himself, as he candidly revealed to the Soviet power's village representative, Ivan Alekseevich Kotliarov.

"Generals" here, as many times later, signified the structure of tsarist Russia which had gone forever in the Revolution. Grigorii did not want its return. He fought for himself, in order that no one would tell him, Cossack Grigorii Melekhov, how he is to live—neither the generals nor the Revolution. And he knew only too well that his trade was to plow the land. Such was his simple truth of life, the only truth for him. But that winter of 1918 Grigorii seemed to have recognized that this old truth of him was shaking under his feet. "There is more than one truth in life. Evidently the one who conquers, can gobble him up. And I was seeking a foolish truth," thought Grigorii, in his simple Cossack thinking.[23] Here he felt, that he was lost in the complicated life.

The Revolution again did not find support among the Cossacks. With its unjustified, blind violence and executions, it incurred the anger and hate of the Cossacks. They could not bear the fear of executions, and in the early spring of 1919 they rose up again.

Grigorii did not need to decide this time whom he should side with. The Soviet power was for him a bloody power; it was necessary to dispose of it. For the time being he did not think about the future form of government for the Don. One will decide that question after the Soviets have been driven off. One thing, however, was clear to Sholokhov's hero from the very beginning: he did not wish to return to the generals' authority. He wanted to fight for his own interests, for himself, "for a piece of bread, for a plot of land,"[24] for those things which are essential for the Cossacks' life.

Thus ended Grigorii's search for the sense, or truth, of his Cossack life. In no way could it end otherwise. His search was bound to end with the fight against the Red intruders, who violently burst into his Cossack way of life.

On the occasion of Grigorii's resolution to fight the Reds, Sholokhov had dropped the following remark:

> . . .he (Grigorii, M.K.) had weighed and decided every-thing. It was as though those days of search for the truth, those hesitations, those transitions and painful inward strug-gles had never been. . . .What had there been to think about?. . .Life seemed absurdly, wisely simple." (*Part Six, Chapter XXVIII.*)

These are the author's words. The expression "search for the truth" refers probably to those days at the dawn of the Revolution when Grigorii tried to join the revolutionary forces and fight for his native Don. He failed then. But now, when Grigorii turned violently against the Revolution, Sholokhov seems as though he would like his reader to accept a proposition which he, the author has taken for granted, that Grigorii's search for the sense of his Cossack life could not have ended otherwise, but with the full and unconditional accep-tance of the Soviet authority on the Don and the un-reserved surrender of his will to the unknown forces of the Revolution. This seems to be what this passage would like to convey.

If Sholokhov indeed had created his Grigorii as one who willingly accepted the truth of the Revolution, he would undoubtedly have sinned against the reality of the Cossack's life. The novel creates on the whole a more realistic impression with Grigorii as he was, i.e. fighting the intruders, as the Reds were perceived by the Cossacks.

At the beginning of the uprising, as in the struggle which had flared up a year earlier, there was hope for a swift victory and the end to the war, "to shake up Moscow and to impose upon her a shameful peace!"[25] Grigorii and all the other Cossacks were enthusiastic in the struggle. True, sometimes it seemed to him that the Cossacks were fighting against not Rus' but as the rich against the poor. But these thoughts did not help him define his own position. He only knew that he had to fight against the Reds because they were stepping on his throat. Knowing that he did not want to fight for the generals, he did not see another way out. Knowing that he was being forced to fight the Reds, he was not able to decide whether he belonged to the rich or the poor.

It is to Sholokhov's credit here, as many times elsewhere, that he did not reveal everything about his hero but left much unsaid. Because of this, Grigorii appears not as a hero of the stereotyped image, not as an abstract scheme, not as an ideal to be imitated, but as a man like the reader himself, who often does not give account to himself or know where his place in life should be.

Sholokhov again left no doubt in the novel that the uprising was unanimously supported by the Cossacks. He let only two characters go to the Reds: Mishka

Koshevoi (for the second time) and Ivan Alekseevich Kotliarov. All other Cossacks in the novel rose against the Soviet power.

In this uprising Grigorii lost his older brother, Petro. He was killed by Mishka Koshevoi, one of the Cossacks from Tatarsk, and one who had even paid court to Grigorii's sister. Grigorii took his brother's death heavily.

Toward night, when Petro's death became known, Grigorii went away from home to the neighbors. "He was driven away by the women's lamentations for the dead."[26] Thinking about Petro, he did not sleep the whole night. "Greedily smoking a cigarette, and as if afraid to remain eye to eye with his thoughts and with grief for Petro, he again hurriedly snatched at his tobacco pouch."[27] He fragmentarily remembered how in childhood he and Petro had hunted turkeys in the steppe. Here again are memories, tears, and the quiet smile at unbidden memories, and in addition, the weeping of the mother and Daria, Petro's widow. Sholokhov knows how much he can dwell on tears and pity, without falling into a one-sided description with false, cheap sentimentality. In Sholokhov everything is within measure.

Even in these scenes he leaves Grigorii as he always was in life, somewhat crude and cynical. "There was anger in Grigorii's eyes. 'Get away, Dashka!' not understanding himself, he yelled wildly, and without thinking, shoved Daria in the breast."[28]

Folkloristic motives penetrate the description of grief:

> Grigorii was sitting on the bench opposite his brother. Rolling a cigar, he looked at Petro's face, yellow along the edges, at his hands, with bluish, round nails. The great

chill of estrangement already separated him from his brother. Petro now was not kin, but a passing guest whose time was to depart now. Now he was lying, indifferently pressing his cheek to the earthen floor, as if waiting for something, with a calm, secret halfsmile frozen beneath the wheat-colored mustache. And tomorrow his wife and mother would take him on a last journey. (*Part Six, Chapter XXXIV.*)

This is the tone of a folk song about death. Expressions like "great cold of estrangement" *(velikii kholod otchuzhdeniia),* "passing guest" *(nedolgii gost'),* or "last journey" *(posledniaia putina)* are peculiar to the folk understanding of the deceased, who is here and yet is no more here. Or expressions such as "of one blood" *(odnokrovnik),* "icy hands" *(ledianye ruki),* "naked body" *(nagota tela),* or "from where they do not return for a visit" *(ot kuda ne vozvrashchaiutsia na pobyvku)* all might have been sung in a folk song in lamentation for a killed Cossack.

It has already been observed that in Sholokhov there is a kind of folk respect for the mystery of death. In this respect for death there is felt a respect for life too. There is so much blood, death, and cruelty in the novel that it seems that life and death lose their meaning for the hero, so that he is no longer able to think about either the living or the dead. Sholokhov's hero, however, does know in measure about the deceased: "'It would have been better if you had died somewhere in Prussia than here, before your mother's eyes!' Grigorii mentally said to his brother with a reproach."[29]

Petro's death at the hands of the Reds filled Grigorii with thirst for vengeance, and gave him strength for the struggle. "'That's the first payment to them for Petro,' he thought, having given up some Red war prisoners to execution."[30] But reckless cruelty was not natural to him. Where he could, he released prisoners. This is Grigorii: full of contradictions and unresolved problems. Again and again he rises before us in this way, entirely human, close to our own doubts and moods about unresolved and insoluble problems.

Grigorii had experienced a plenitude of power when he was made commander of ten thousand Cossacks.

> Grigorii keenly felt a proud joy: he had never before commanded such a mass of people. But along with the proud joy, alarm, an acerbic bitterness stirred heavily within him: would he be able to lead as he was supposed to? Did he have enough intelligence to direct thousands of Cossacks? Not a squadron, but a division was under his command. And could he, an uneducated Cossack, wield authority over thousands of lives and carry the deadly responsibility for their lives? "And the main thing again, against whom do I lead? Against the people. . .who is right here?" (*Part Six, Chapter XXXVII.*)

Even at the height of his power, doubts and anxiety did not leave him alone.

During this war, out of the many attacks in which Grigorii participated and led his Cossack division, Sholokhov chose and described in detail one scene. This is a characteristic feature of the second half of *The Quiet Don,* this isolating and dwelling upon one out of many events. In this scene the author disclosed a new feature of Grigorii's character, existing in him since childhood, but preserved by the author until it became necessary to disclose it. I refer to the fact that Grigorii was ambidextrous. This was his advantage in cavalry attacks, where it was necessary to wield the sabre. Here is how Sholokhov presented one of the numerous attacks in which Grigorii participated.

> . . .He would guide his horse toward a chosen opponent, approaching from the left, as everyone usually did, in order to slash with his right hand; the one who had to collide with Grigorii would aim similarly. And then, when there remained some twenty meters to the opponent, who was already leaning out almost on his side, bringing down his sword, Grigorii with a sudden but smooth turn would come down from the right, switching his sword to his left hand. The discouraged opponent would change position; it would be awkward for him to slash from right to left, across his horse's head; he would lose confidence, death would breathe him in the face. Grigorii would bring down a drawn out, cutting blow, terrible in its force. (*Part Six, Chapter XXXVII.*)

In this scene is revealed, on one hand, the unusual manner of Sholokhov's hero, and on the other, the unusual attitude of the author to his hero. We have already spoken of how the author had guarded his hero with love and care. This is especially evident in this scene. It is as if the author wished the hero success. To be left-handed was, in the popular concept, connected with a bodily defect, a deprivation. Grigorii's father had been cruel to him about this. His friends on the street would abuse him for this. But for Grigorii this deprivation had turned into an advantage.

In this passage as in many others, many a reader would feel the author's sympathy for his hero. Yet, in spite of this apparent sympathy, the author kept a certain distance from his hero, not interfering in the hero's affairs. Sholokhov let the reader himself judge and interpret the hero through his hero's own actions and the events around him. The author withheld his own comments upon the actions and events connected with his hero. It is nothing so much as the distance between the author and his hero that makes the hero and the whole novel so attractive. It is as if the author created his hero not for his own enjoyment but the reader's.

The attack itself is described in the same way as were attacks in the German War. In the attack the hero practically undergoes an internal change. Reason, composure, and calculation deserted him. Only an animal instinct and a kind of stupor commanded his will.[31]

After the attack the normal feeling and pulsation of life again returned to the hero. Again he saw the sun which lighted up the world, heard the birds in the air, and sniffed the scent from the fields. Life returned to him, "unfaded, not grown old from the recently spilled blood, but even more alluring with a miserly deceptive joy."[32]

Here, at the height of his authority, when Grigorii more than ever needed full presence of mind and self-control, both these qualities left him. It is as if he were oversaturated with life, grown accustomed to everything; and now indifference took hold of him. Grigorii recalls his life. He had experienced everything in life: the love of peasant women and of young girls who lost their maidenly bloom, trod the steppes on fine horses, rejoiced in fatherhood, killed people, and had faced death himself. "'Can life show me anything new?' thought

Grigorii to himself. 'Nothing new. I can die now. It's not scary. . . . No great loss!'"[33]

At the height of his authority, when it seemed that he more than anyone should have been feeling confident, he lost the ground from under his feet. The strength and vengeance with which he had been filled after his brother's death lasted only for a short time. And went the fury went, the strength left, too. Confronted with the reproach of his wife, he did not try to justify himself:

> I dirtied myself with so much people's blood that there's no pity for anyone left in me. Children! I almost don't care for them, and I have no thoughts about myself. The war took everything out of me. I'm frightening to myself. Look into my soul, and there is blackness, like in an empty well. (*Part Six, Chapter XLVI.*)

The author placed these words in the mouth of his hero not to justify or condemn him, but perhaps to make it understood that it was not the hero's fault. Cruel, senseless war took away much personal responsibility from the hero. And now "cold, dull indifference" seized him.[34]

At this time of dull indifference, when it seemed that he had lost everything and there was nothing more to lose, he took up again with Aksin'ia. The old love had not died. To Grigorii this was his first love.

This renewed liaison with Aksin'ia came about again as before, as if unaware, without the participation of his will or thought. The earth trembled under Grigorii's feet, and secret underground forces pushed him towards Aksin'ia. After Aksin'ia had gone away from the Listnitskii's and after she had returned to her husband in the village, she had lived next to Grigorii. Grigorii used to meet with her. But the author said nothing about Grigorii's thoughts toward Aksin'ia. We see him as a good husband and solicitous father. But now, at a time of inner confusion, when Grigorii did not know where to turn, and apparently did not feel himself capable of self-control, he did not resist when his path crossed with Aksin'ia's. This happened as though without his conscious participation and decision. He is pushed into this step by the circumstances of time and by his inner devastation. This time Grigorii felt, however, that even Aksin'ia would not succeed in filling his emptiness: "...in his heart is everything cool and empty, as before," thought Grigorii.[35]

In addition, even more adversity was added to his personal distress and devastation when Grigorii was again forced to fight for the generals and under the command of the generals, whom he detested so much. The rebellion was raised under the slogan "For the Soviets, but against the Communists." The Cossacks hoped to establish an authority on the Don independent of Moscow, of the Reds and of the Whites. The Cossacks wanted neither the generals nor the Communists. But in the course of the uprising it became evident that the quiet Don, pressed between the Reds and the Whites, could not stand between these two large blocs. It was necessary to choose between the two. The choice was not difficult. Although the truth of the Whites and their order of life was not to the Cossacks' liking, it was known and was nearer to their own way of life than the alien truth of the Communists, with their incomprehen-

sible system of life. For Grigorii this change of orienta-
tion turned out to be hard. His fear and the Cossack-
peasant contempt toward the generals created a reputation even among his fellow Cossacks as being an
"incomplete bol'shevik."[36]   At one occasion Grigorii
was called by the chief of staff of his sans-culotte
division as something of resemblance to a bol'shevik.[37]
Among the officers he felt awkward.

> I got the officer's rank in the German War. I merited it
> with my blood! But when I happen to be among the
> officers' society, for me it's like coming out of a hut in a
> frost in only your drawers. I feel such a cold coming from
> the officers, that I can feel it on my back. (*Part Seven,
> Chapter X.*)

Grigorii complained to the chief of his staff. The feeling
of belonging to the peasant-Cossack strata with its
steppe elements never deserted him. Himself regarding
the gentry class with a "feeling of deep repulsion,"[38]
he felt that the gentry had the same attitude toward
him.   In a conversation with a general in the White
Volunteer's Army, Fitskhalaurov, Grigorii understood
what a large world separated him from the officers.
For them he is a "White crow." "They are all educated,
but I finished parish school only with difficulty.   To
them I am foreign from head to heels."[39]   After the
merging of the insurrectionary forces with the Regular
White Volunteer Army, Grigorii felt the difference of
worlds and alienation from the officers and generals
even more: "They don't want to understand that everything old has collapsed."[40] Grigorii understood that the
old world had gone forever.   But at the same time,

the new world, appearing in the form of the Revolution, was not acceptable to him. He could not reconcile himself with the Bolsheviks. Sometimes, to be sure, he threatened that if he went to the Reds, he would gain more importance than he had with the Whites.[41] However, this was not really a threat or wish to go over to the Reds, but only a contemplation about his place in life, only an empty, joking game. He simply would like to have enjoyed more importance. He understood the full value of his service to the Whites, and wanted recognition for his service, the type of recognition he thought Budennyi, the "former cavalry sergeant," enjoyed among the Reds.[42]

Besides all this, the appearance of the English officers in the White army sickened him. He was a true Cossack, son of his fields. There lived in him a kind of elemental, Russian-peasant, popular mistrust toward foreign, unbelieving infidels, were they Mongols, Turks, or other foreigners.

His indifference and disgust toward the gentry finally led to an avoidance of direct participation in a battle. This was neither cowardice, nor fear of death or great losses. He spared neither himself nor the lives of the Cossacks entrusted to him. But after a conversation with General Fitskhalaurov, everything seemed to be useless. He would prefer to walk alongside a pair of oxen and plow the earth peacefully than to fight for the generals. Unfortunately for him he saw that this was impossible. The old way of life was crumbling everywhere and was passing forever, and the new was not acceptable to him. And there was no third way for him to go. This was not only his own tragedy, but the tragedy of the time that there was no third way. "There was no middle way: one or the other will crush us."[43] Sholokhov said this with the words of his hero himself. They may be applied, however, not only in regard to Grigorii, with his personal life, but also in regard to the whole Cossack Don and even all of Russia and the rest of the world, wherever people are placed in situations like that of Grigorii. Having left these words with Grigorii, Sholokhov preserved again and again his distance and neutrality in regard to his hero.

In regard to Sholokhov's image of Grigorii, one might apply Eugene Ionesco's words that a work of art is always a search and discovery of the new and unknown. The author has only to ask, but never to answer. Only a primitive, one-track mind knows all the answers to all the problems. In a true work of art, every reader must find his own answers. One simple answer for any question just does not exist. And this is so with Sholokhov's Grigorii. He is a riddle posed by the author without an answer. It is because of this that he is close to us, and many can find in Grigorii something similar to their own searches.

Grigorii was not in the least disturbed after the merging with the White Volunteers that he was demoted from the rank of division commander to leader of a squadron. He did not take this as humiliation or offence. On the contrary he seemingly took up his new assignment gladly. Not the ups and downs of his personal life, but the whole sense of his life bothered him. He was at a crossroad, and this tortured him.

Yet another personal misfortune was added to his doubts—the death of his wife. The meek, silent Natal'ia and the children, too, apparently were the last bulwarks supporting Grigorii. With Natal'ia gone, Grigorii went on a decline. With the departure of Natal'ia there was no obstacle to an affair with Aksin'ia.

Did he love his humble wife Natal'ia? It seems he had been accustomed to her. There was a time in the beginning when he had left her. But afterwards he felt pride for his dear wife. In any case he loved the children which Natal'ia had borne him. And because of them he was ready to sacrifice himself. The author did not conceal the fact that Grigorii wept at Natal'ia's death.

Having received at his unit a telegram about his wife's death and one month's leave, Grigorii immediately set home with his orderly Prokhor, a Cossack from Tatarsk. Rushing along the road, Grigorii, in order to distract himself from heavy thoughts, talked a great deal with his faithful companion about the past German War. During these stories "Prokhor by chance glanced at Grigorii and saw how down his swarthy cheeks the tears were flowing abundantly."[44] These tears might not necessarily have been about Natal'ia. They were timed by the author, however, to Natal'ia's death.

Speaking about Grigorii's family and his relations towards his wife and children, we cannot avoid pointing out a certain parallel to Tolstoi's Levin. Perhaps the parallel is only superficial, almost unconsciously taken from Tolstoi's understanding of the family, but it suggests itself. Love for Levin had its basis only on the family principle. After Kitty's refusal, Levin began to think about the family. Marriage became for him the main affair of his life, on which his happiness depended. His happiness was not in love, but in marriage itself, in wedlock. First and foremost he imagined the family, and only afterwards the woman who would give him the family. Thus, for Levin marriage came first, then the family, then love for his wife.[45]

This is how it came out for Grigorii, too. His marriage had been compulsory, because of arrangements made by his father. He had not felt any love for his wife. Only when he was forced to return to his family after an unhappy extra-marital affair, and when children were born to him, was his love for the children transferred to the woman, his wife, who had given him the family.

Undoubtedly, this is a parallel conception in Tolstoi and Sholokhov as well. But nothing indicates that Sholokhov borrowed the conception for his hero from Tolstoi. This is simply one of those general notions about love and the family which since long have been rooted in the folk consciousness. In Tolstoi this popular understanding appeared to be more premeditated and conditioned by his intellectualism, while in Sholokhov it appeared in its elemental form, without being thought through. There is also a large difference between Levin and Grigorii in their understanding of the family. The disciplined mentality of Levin did not allow him to think of extra-marital love, while Grigorii was ready to surrender to a vulgar, elemental attraction, unconditioned by rational thought.

However things may have been, Grigorii had reconciled himself to Natal'ia and had been a good father. Her death fell heavily on him. He was tortured by the fact that he felt guilty before Natal'ia. He knew that she had loved him, had always forgiven him, and had once more forgiven him before her death. During the first days at home he was imbued with respect toward her memory.

> Grigorii suffered not only because he had loved her in his own way and had been used to her for six years lived through together, but also because he felt guilty for her death. . . .
> There had been a time when Grigorii had felt nothing for his wife besides cold indifference and even hostility, but in the last years he had begun to treat her differently, and the basic reason for this change, which occurred in his attitude toward Natal'ia was the children. . . .
> After the break with Aksin'ia, Grigorii never thought seriously that he would separate from his wife; never, even when taking up with Aksin'ia again, did he think that she could sometime replace the mother of his children. (*Part Seven, Chapter XVIII.*)

After Natal'ia's death, the denouement in Grigorii's life came quickly. Natal'ia had served in the novel as a symbol of regulation in Grigorii's life. With her quiet, unnoticeable presence she seemed to have protected him. When she was gone, everything at once crashed down in the Melekhov family. The whole world, strong and steady with its own order, had now come to an end. Disintegration began not only in the Melekhov family and in Grigorii's life, but on the front as well. Grigorii did not stay long on the front. Towards the autumn of 1919 the front was dispersed. Everything in life trembled.

There remained for Grigorii only memories about his swiftly departed years of "his strangely and disorderly formed life."[46] He felt that after Natal'ia's death no sorrow could shake him anymore. He had buried

his father on the way, while escaping from the Reds.
It was the fourth death in the Melekhov family in one
year. And it was still not the end. Sholokhov pitilessly
forced Grigorii to witness the cruel and senseless death
of his father from typhus in January, 1920 somewhere
on the black Stavropole land, far from the quiet Don
and the beloved steppe.

Grigorii, leaning forward, looked at his father. Illness
had changed the features of the familiar face, had made
it strangely different, foreign. The pale, pinched, cheeks
of Pantelei Prokof'evich were overgrown with grey bristles,
the mustaches hung low above the sagging mouth, the eyes
were half closed, and the bluish whites of the eyes had
lost their sparkling liveliness and glitter. The sagging lower
jaw was tied around with a red embroidered handkerchief,
and against the background of the red material, the grey,
curly hairs of his beard seemed even more silvery, whiter.
Grigorii went down on his knees in order, for the last
time, to look over attentively and memorize his father's
face, and involuntarily shuddered from fear and disgust:
on the grey, waxen face of Pantelei Prokof'evich, filling
the cavities of his eyes and the wrinkles of his cheeks
lice were crawling. They covered his face with a living,
moving shroud, swarmed in his beard, swarmed on his
brows, lay in a grey layer on the high-standing collar of
the blue overcoat. (*Part Seven, Chapter XXVII.*)

Sholokhov's realism does not spare the hero or the
reader from the worst that could happen in life. The
author, without hesitation but also without bitterness,
throws on us all the horror and senseless cruelty of the
daily violent life.

At the end of the seventh part, when the White movement had collapsed, Sholokhov remained faithful in his attitude toward his hero. In the novel we would seek in vain the author's explanations as to why Grigorii did not leave for Georgia, where his comrades had gone, early in the spring of 1920 when his attempt to embark on a steamer in Novorossi'sk had failed. Instead, he remained under the Reds. Again here, as many times before, the author hid the thoughts and calculations of his hero. For Grigorii, too, this came about as it had many times earlier, instinctively, involuntarily. Once more he was thrown involuntarily into the abyss by forces of the aroused elements. In any case, Grigorii did not have to decide when he remained under the Reds, in the same way that he did not have to decide upon his participation in the Cossack rebellion against the Revolution. Both these events were thrown upon him by the momentum of time. All he had to do was to accept what was placed before him. It is as if the author wanted to say by this that any resistance to the almighty powers, which shook the society, would be in vain. Resistance could only crush his hero. All that the hero could do was to humbly surrender to the strong current of irrepressible forces. Only this passive surrender saved him from destruction. It is as if he had understood his fate and that of Russia and surrendered to its will.

On this note the seventh part of the novel ends. The eighth part serves as an epilogue to the novel and to Grigorii's stormy life. Between the end of the seventh and the beginning of the eighth lies a large interval of time: Grigorii's service in the Red Army, where he

participated in the war against the Poles. Chronologically
in the novel, this interval falls between March, 1920,
and the autumn of that same year. For Grigorii this is
a major turn, and an entirely new beginning of another
life. But the author preferred to conceal this life. Maybe
the author did not report on his hero's service because
it was not Grigorii's service. He served in the Red Army
by necessity. By means of it he wanted to earn forgive-
ness for his sins for having served the Whites.

Anyway we find out about Grigorii's service in the
Red Army only indirectly from various separate, isolated
comments and recollections of other characters and
from Grigorii's own later remarks. The first news about
Grigorii's service in the Red Army came from Prokhor
Zykov. He brought the news to the Tatarsk village that
Grigorii is commanding a squadron in Budennyi's cavalry,[47] and that Budennyi himself had thanked Grigorii
for his bravery. By happenstance we also find out from
Grigorii's own recollections later that while serving in
the Red Army he had been closely watched. But the
author discloses nothing about Grigorii himself and his
service. We see Grigorii in full length only after his
demobilization from the army, when he was returning
home.

The novel is nearing its end, and so is the stormy life
of its hero. What do we find out about the hero in the
end? How will the author conclude the unusual life of
the Cossack whom he has created? At the end the auth-
or imparted several thoughts to his hero which may
serve as keys to the questions posed by us, and by the
hero himself. Here is what the hero thought: "He had
finished fighting. It was enough for him. He was going

home at last, in order to take up work, to live with his children and Aksin'ia."[48]   These are the hero's own thoughts. Before this the author himself said the same about Grigorii: "It was pleasant for him to think about the past, about peaceful life, about work, about everything which didn't concern war."[49] He did not want to think about the seven years of war. When chance memories of war pursued him, "he experienced a melancholy inward distress, and a vague irritation."[50]   Thus the author himself unequivocally expressed the wish of his hero.

What does the hero think about the new authority against which he had fought bitterly, but which he had later been forced to defend? The same Prokhor Zykov brought to Tatarsk village words spoken by Grigorii himself, that he would serve in the Red Army until he had redeemed his past sins.[51] We might ask ourselves how much service was necessary in order to redeem the past sins? But because the Soviet government cannot forgive anyone for anything, and because Grigorii could not know about this, and the author could not write it out in full, this question is only rhetorical.

In any case it seems that Grigorii has reconciled himself with the present. He cannot help but understand, as the author himself can not, that any struggle with the authorities now could be unequal, and therefore reckless. In any case Grigorii had decided to settle at home and to devote his life to peaceful labor. Any struggle would not be to his liking now. If he were left in peace, then he, too, would leave everyone and everything in peace. This is a brief summary from the novel of the inner world of the hero after his return home from the last war.

Later on, when the hero is about to settle in his native village, the author has revealed a bit more about the hero's attitude toward the new government through the hero's own words. In a conversation with Mishka Koshevoi, Grigorii said that he was fed up with the Revolution and counter-revolution. He only wanted peace. He would not go against the authority.[52] Grigorii did not see where his guilt might lie before the authority. Once he had gone against the authority because everyone around him had gone. He had killed because they had wanted to kill him. And if he had not killed, he himself would doubtless have been killed long ago. When Mishka Koshevoi reproached him, saying that Grigorii "had sabred a lot of our fighters,"[53] Grigorii answered calmly that he, Koshevoi, had killed Grigorii's brother Petro, but he, Grigorii, did not remind him of that now, because, "if we would remember everything, we'd have to live like wolves."[54]

Whose side is the author on here? In the conversation between Mishka and Grigorii the author so far remained neutral. A bit later he will change his neutrality. The reader himself cannot help but feel the rightness of Grigorii's words, that if one were to remember everything, there would never be peace among people. But the representative of the new government, Mishka Koshevoi, probably wanted exactly this, that people would live like wolves. The new government in the person of Mishka could not forgive Grigorii for his part in the uprising.

At this point the author himself was not able to retain his constant neutrality any longer in relation to the hero whom he had created. He condemned Grigorii

with his own author's verdict. He did this quite deli-
cately, but peremptorily.

> Well, everything took place as it had to take place. And
> why did they have to regard him, Grigorii, in a different
> way? Why did he think that his brief, honorable service in
> the Red Army would cover up all his past sins? And, per-
> haps, Mikhail was right when he said that not everything
> is forgiven, and that the old debts must be paid in full?
> (*Part Eight, Chapter VI.*)

These are the author's words. The author might have
put them into the mouth of Mishka Koshevoi, and then
they would have been the subjective opinion of one
of the characters, which would not necessarily coincide
with the author's opinion. But here the author leaves
no doubt what he himself was thinking about the hero.
With his own author's opinion he wanted to forestall
the opinion of the reader and to influence him. The
author seemed to want his hero to change his opinion
about his innocence before the new power. On the
second day after Grigorii's return and that memorable
conversation with Mishka, life appeared to Grigorii in
a different light, not as simple and clear as it had
seemed to him only a day before.

> . . .All of life seemed not so simple as it had seemed to
> him not long ago. With stupid, childish naivete he had
> assumed that it was enough to return home, change his
> cloak for a homespun coat, and everything would go as
> designated; no one would say a word to him, no one
> would reproach him, everything would order itself, and he
> would live and live well as a peaceful corngrower and ex-
> emplary family man. No, it really didn't appear that
> simple. (*Part Eight, Chapter VII.*)

It must be pointed out that from the text it is not clear whether these are Grigorii's or the author's words. The words are timed to the morning after Grigorii's return. Grigorii went to see the graves of Natal'ia and his mother. His thoughts were directed toward the dead, that four of the Melekhov family lay here together, but his father alone was on strange soil. "It's boring for him there among strangers."[55] Then he began to think about his children, about their "un-childishness," their strangeness. And then comes this paragraph where he thinks about how his life appeared now differently than he had imagined.

Are these thoughts the author's or Grigorii's? If they are the author's then Sholokhov probably wanted to say that Grigorii had erred in thinking about a calm life, that he had to bear punishment for his past struggle against the Revolution, and that in the end this would be solely a justified retribution for his guilt. But if they are Grigorii's then they could mean that it was not easy for Grigorii to find his place in the new relations among the Cossacks after the Revolution, and that there indeed was no place for him in the new society.

If the latter assumption is correct, then we do not see in the novel where the difficulty in Grigorii's adaptation to the new conditions might lie. We saw how the author earlier spoke out unequivocally about the wishes of his hero's peaceful life. Striving toward a peaceful life, he did not want to think about any fight against the government.

If, however, the first assumption is correct, then it must be said that these words are the author's second direct comment upon his hero. Hitherto the author was able to preserve his neutrality towards his hero's actions and kept a certain distance from the hero. But now coming forth with his author's judgment, he has created a distinct impression that he did not trust his hero to the end. The author guided his hero through all the four books of the novel without an attempt to judge the hero with his author's words, but here at the end he was not able to remain faithful to this objectivity. He had to pronounce his opinion.

It probably does not matter which assumption is correct. In both these cases the author had to come up with some kind of personal opinion about his beloved hero. The time during which Sholokhov wrote this last part of the novel was the decisive factor here for the change in his attitude toward his hero. He wrote the eighth and last part of the book at the end of the 1930's. The situation in the country was different than when he first started on *The Quiet Don.* Sholokhov could not help feeling the changes around him. Terror reigned in the country. The security organs searched not only for the present but also for the past activity of every citizen in the country. Even the slightest offence to the authority done in the past had to be disclosed and punished. Every enemy discovered by the organs of the secret police had to bear stern, but justified, punishment. In such circumstances Grigorii, too, could not remain unpunished for his past participation in the uprising. Correspondingly, the author could not remain neutral. So, he was compelled to destroy his neutrality and state his opinion about the guilt of his hero. Sholokhov did this very carefully, but quite clearly. He could not leave Grigorii neutral. Some kind of new turn in

Grigorii's life was necessary which finally would kill him. And thus, Grigorii, against his wishes, was pushed into the open arms of a band.

From the novel it follows clearly that Mishka Koshevoi is the cause of Grigorii's ruin. Grigorii felt the open hostility on the part of Mishka, and being warned about his arrest, had to run and hide. The escape of arrest was defensive for Grigorii. He did not find the band, but the band literally found him.

Even long before Grigorii's return to the village, Mishka Koshevoi in conversation with his wife had unequivocally affirmed that Grigorii would have to answer before the Soviet law for his service with the Whites. We have already seen that on the other hand Grigorii was returning home with quite different thoughts and hopes. If the author did not create him to be a new Soviet man (and this is one of the author's merits), then in any case Grigorii is made to be reconciled with the new authority. He had had no enmity toward the authority or its personal representative in the village, Mishka Koshevoi, his former bosom friend, now related to the Melekhovs by marriage. Once he had taken revenge on Mishka for the murder of his brother Petro. Pantelei Prokof'evich while still alive had forbidden his daughter to consider Mishka's marriage proposal. This was understandable, for Mishka was a murderer in the eyes of the Melekhov family and of the whole Tatarsk village as well. Grigorii had known this, and in his turn, as if in confirmation of his father's interdiction, had also forbidden his sister to think about Mishka. But now, in the autumn of 1920, neither old grudges, nor revenge, nor a father's ban possessed meaning any longer. What is more, Duniasha had married Mishka Koshevoi while her mother was still alive. And so Grigorii now was fully prepared to make his peace. Mishka was for Grigorii more than the local authority. Mishka entered the Melekhov family as a brother-in-law to Grigorii.

But Mishka in his turn did not forget and did not want to forget the past. Already at the first meeting Grigorii had noticed that his, Grigorii's, return was not to Mishka's liking. Mishka right then had declared that Grigorii was not a reliable man, that he did not trust him, and that Grigorii was dangerous. All Grigorii's assertions that he wouldn't go against the authority did not mollify Mishka. Mishka was afraid that in the event of a new uprising of the Cossacks against the authority, Grigorii would join the uprising.

Fear for the authority, fear of an uprising were thus Mishka's sole motives for distrusting the reconciled Grigorii. And he threatened Grigorii that he would immediately take himself up for the reckoning.

In the conversation between Grigorii and Mishka, the Soviet power as a system remained aside. Only Mishka, its insignificant local representative, took part. If the author had confronted Grigorii with evidence and a court, it would have been a different matter. The authority itself would have taken part in the decision on Grigorii's fate. But as it is presented in the novel, the whole burden and consequences for Grigorii's fate seemed to be placed on Mishka alone.

We might ask in what proportion did Mishka represent the interests of the Soviet power and in what his personal interests and concerns for his own safety. When

Mishka Koshevoi threatened Grigorii with reprisal, was he following the interests and laws of the Soviet Government, or only his own fear of a potential enemy? Under present conditions this is only an academic question. It is impossible to answer it practically. In the conditions under which this last part of the novel was written, the interests of the authority were identified with the interests of every small bureaucrat, and conversely, every insignificant bureaucrat had the right to equate his own personal interests with those of the whole system. Therefore, from the point of view of what was going on in the country, when Sholokhov was finishing his novel, Sholokhov was right, as also Mishka Koshevoi was right. But we must once again emphasize that formally Sholokhov left the authority outside the events of his novel. He could not end his novel with the idyll about which Grigorii had dreamed (peaceful labor on the fields) and with which Tolstoi had finished his great novel. For Tolstoi this came naturally. For Sholokhov any idyll would have sounded false, not in accord with the epoch. There was no idyll in a country of the Revolution, and there could be none. Grigorii's life had to end in a tragedy.

And it ended more than tragically. It ended senselessly. The author forced his hero to drink the bitter cup of life to the bottom. We have no right to ask why the author led his hero thus, and not differently. The author is willful in the fates of his heroes, and can lead them in defiance of all logic and rationales in life. But all the same, because Grigorii's life uncontrollably moved downhill, the question raises itself as to why Grigorii ended his life so senselessly. There arise dozens of "logical" answers which neither we, nor the author can accept. Thinking in human terms, Grigorii did not have to move downwards so fast. He might have gone away from the village when he felt alarm upon his return. Aksin'ia had thought about this even earlier. Fomin had advised him to go away and sit out the alarm somewhere else. But Grigorii, notwithstanding his own inward voice, remained in the village under Koshevoi's eyes, until Duniasha warned him about the arrest.

Grigorii fell into a band unwillingly when he had nowhere to go after his escape from arrest. He knew and had seen from the outset how the affairs of a band would end. The hope lived in him that he would leave the band, take his Aksin'ia, and together they would escape somewhere to the Kuban. But when Aksin'ia died, his last hope disappeared with her, and when there was nothing more to hope for, Grigorii for some reason did not give up to the authorities, but remained with the band to drink the bitter cup of life to the bottom. Here, too, Sholokhov is faithful to the course he had once taken and did not reveal the secrets by which Grigorii lived during that time.

The ending of the novel is tragic. To be sure, critics point out the optimism of Sholokhov's ending.

> Well, that little thing about which he had dreamed during sleepless nights had come true. He was standing at the gate of his family house, holding his son in his hands.
>
> This was all which remained from him in life, which still joined him with the earth and with this whole, enormous world, glittering under the cold sun. (*Part Eight, Chapter XVIII.*)

It was said that with this gesture Sholokhov seemed

to point out the succession and continuity of life through the younger generation. But for the hero himself there is no hope for a place in life. His previous return home after his demobilization from the Red Army was different. Then he could begin a new life. But the life again pushed him into the unforeseen, as it had pushed him many times earlier. This time the unforeseen turned out to be the ruin and non-existence of the hero.

In conclusion to Grigorii's portrait, it must be said that for the benefit of literary criticism it is unimportant whether Sholokhov had drawn Grigorii from a living prototype, or invented him as his own concept. We have to say, however, that Grigorii is not a real, historical person, but a literary character created by Sholokhov in accordance with his concept of reality. What is important then, is only the author's attitude to his hero, inasmuch as Grigorii reflects the hosts of Don Cossacks, and the author's attitude to the Cossacks as well. In this section we believe to have shown that Sholokhov loved his hero, he cared for him. Yet, at the same time Sholokhov was able to preserve the artist's distance to his hero and to a large extent the author's neutrality. It is as if Sholokhov wanted to say: I only watched this man, whom I called Grigorii. I observed his doing and his behavior and tried, as much as I could, not to interfere with his personal life. If Sholokhov could not sustain his neutrality and the distance to his hero to the end, it might be explained, as we saw, by the current of the time in which he was finishing his great work.

About the author's method of presentation we have to stress once more what was already said in the text of this section, that Grigorii is drawn in a human and earthy manner. If *humanum errare est,* then Grigorii is all the human and *nihil humanum alienum ei est.* Stockman, Bunchuk, Koshevoi, and on the other line Korshunov and even Petro Melekhov are farther from being fully human. All of them know too well what to do and what they want. They seem never to err. They are drawn simpler, more schematically. Their attitude to life is more dogmatic, while Grigorii's attitude is pragmatic. It is, perhaps, because of this that we feel closer, nearer to Grigorii.

All Soviet Sholokhovists assert that Grigorii perished, that indeed he had to perish, because he refused to accept the new beginning of life, the new direction which came to the Cossacks with the Bolsheviks, and thus he had turned a renegade to the Cossacks and to the whole Russian people. In regard to this it must be said that this appraisal of the novel's main hero contains much of the dogmatic attitude to him. On the other hand how could he, and why should he have to accept the new beginning. He was not alone. As a matter of fact he was by far not in the minority among his fellow Don Cossacks who took the same attitude to the new life.

Many years after the struggle of the Civil War, when there was no other choice possible, it might seem easy to say that it could not have been otherwise, that there was no other way, but just to accept the new life, and that the struggle against the new way was in vain and doomed from the very outset. It is possible to say all this many years later. But it did not look so in 1917 and in the Civil War. Grigorii, like his fellow Cossacks, had genuine doubts about the new life. They had every right to fight the new and unknown life, which, they were afraid, would destroy their established ways.

Grigorii should be understood and judged not from the point of the victorious Revolution, but from his own time, when the Revolution was feared by the host of the Cossack masses. The conquerers of the new life in Russia of course assert that the truth of the new life has conquered the untruth and the lie of the old departing order of life. It is, of course, easy to make this one-way assertion. It makes it easy to interpret the most complicated character of Grigorii. It is easy to explain that he had to perish because he did not recognize his hour and turned away from the new, good life. This is a retributive attitude. We saw that this attitude to Grigorii was taken also by Mishka Koshevoi. But Koshevoi, in his attitude to Grigorii, was guided by fear. But more than fifty years have passed since Grigorii and his fearless rebellious Cossacks were fighting the new revolutionary truth. There can be no more fear of a counter-revolution among the Cossacks. Now is the time to start to breathe free and to look at Grigorii without fear.

Seeing Grigorii as a renegade, the Soviet Sholokhovists, it seems, would like to propose to Grigorii (if this could still be possible), that to avert his tragic end, all he had to do, was to submit to the will of the Bolshevik Party by not resisting or thinking for himself, and to accept the wisdom of the Party since the Party in any case is always right and knows everything better. This is what Sholokhov himself later has chosen, when he said that his heart belongs to the Party. But his hero tried to retain his heart for himself. Exactly this, however turned out to be his tragedy. He tried to search, to think, to doubt, and finally, to err, because all this is human, all this is what makes man human.

There is no need to say that *The Quiet Don* is a great novel, indeed one of the greatest of Twentieth Century literature. It is great because its author has presented the truth of life, the truth uncovered and cruel as life itself. Sholokhov was able to penetrate into the truth of the Revolution through his revolutionary characters on one side and into the truth of the Cossack hosts through his Cossack characters on the other. By the word of his convincing art, the author has drawn the way the Revolution had conquered life in one part of the world after the terrible weariness of the German and the Civil Wars. It is not the geographical limitations which define the significance of the novel, but its two-way implicated and perplexing truth which reaches a universal level.

NOTES AND REFERENCES

1. *The Quiet Don,* Part Seven, Chapter X.
2. Part Six, Chapter LI.
3. Part One, Chapter XX.
4. Part Two, Chapter X.
5. *Ibid.*
6. Part Two, Chapter XXI.
7. Part Three, Chapter V.
8. *Ibid.*
9. *Ibid.*

10. Part Four, Chapter IV.
11. *Ibid.*
12. Part Five, Chapter II.
13. *Ibid.*
14. Part Five, Chapter XXIII.
15. Part Five, Chapter XXX.
16. Part Six, Chapter II.
17. *Ibid.*
18. Part Four, Chapter IV.
19. Part Six, Chapter X.
20. *Ibid.*
21. Part Six, Chapter XVI.
22. Part Six, Chapter XVII.
23. Part Six, Chapter XXI.
24. Part Six, Chapter XXVIII.
25. *Ibid.*
26. Part Six, Chapter XXXIV.
27. *Ibid.*
28. *Ibid.*
29. *Ibid.*
30. Part Six, Chapter XXXV.
31. Part Six, Chapter XXXVII.
32. *Ibid.*
33. Part Six, Chapter XLII.
34. Part Six, Chapter LVIII.
35. Part Six, Chapter LI.
36. Part Six, Chapter LXIV.
37. Part Seven, Chapter X.
38. Part Seven, Chapter XV.
39. Part Seven, Chapter X.
40. *Ibid.*
41. *Ibid.*
42. *Ibid.*

43. Part Six, Chapter XLII.
44. Part Seven, Chapter XVII.
45. See *Anna Karenina,* Part One, Chapter XXVII.
46. Part Seven, Chapter XXVII.
47. Part Eight, Chapter I.
48. Part Eight, Chapter VI.
49. *Ibid.*
50. *Ibid.*
51. Part Eight, Chapter I.
52. Part Eight, Chapter VI.
53. *Ibid.*
54. *Ibid.*
55. *Ibid.*

THE REVOLUTION AND ITS CHARACTERS

As Sholokhov had brought the Melekhov family into the focus of events in order to present the Cossacks' life, in like manner he introduced a number of revolutionaries in order to personify not only the forces of the Revolution but also to represent the Revolution itself, as it was in all its nature and system. The characters, who appear as symbols of the Revolution and its ideology, are Bunchuk, Stockman, Podtëlkov, and the Cossacks from the Tatarsk hamlet, Ivan Alekseevich Kotliarov and Mishka Koshevoi.

Bunchuk, in his brief appearances in the pages of the book, is probably the most important among them. He does not occupy a prominent part in the novel; his part in the Revolution, however, is of prime importance. He belongs to the Revolution. One could say about him and maybe about Stockman that they themselves were the Revolution.

Let us start with Bunchuk and see through him how Sholokhov visualized the Revolution. Chronologically, Bunchuk is not the first to appear in the book. But since, as we said, he is the most important embodiment of the Revolution, we shall start our discussion with him.

The reader's first acquaintance with the volunteer Bunchuk occurs at the time when he was a soldier in one of the Cossack Army's regiments on the front in

September of 1914. The author, as usual, neither reveals any of Bunchuk's characteristics, nor paints his
portrait. We learn about Bunchuk only from casual
conversations of the other characters, his colleagues in
the regiment. Thus, we hear that he is a remarkable
chap, and that he is a Russianized Cossack, who for a
long time lived in Moscow. We also learn that although
he is an ordinary factory worker, he is nevertheless
experienced in various ideological questions, and that
he is a daredevil and an excellent machine-gunner. He
impressed the officers of his regiment by his unbending
will, elusive reticence and reservation.[1]

Sholokhov's intention was to present the attitude of
the Cossack masses to the Revolution. Nevertheless,
he did not make the revolutionary Bunchuk, the former
Cossack and now a Moscow proletarian, one of the
principal characters of the novel. After this brief acquaintance, from which the reader does not learn much
about Bunchuk's inner world, he disappeared from the
novel for a long interval.

He appeared again two years later at the time of his
desertion from the front. He was now an officer. In
his conversation with his colleagues in the regiment,
Bunchuk revealed the truth about himself. He startled
his officer friends with the revelation that he was not
what they thought him to be, or what he had pretended
to be. He was a Bolshevik defeatist, a member of a
secret underground organization, working illegally while
serving in the Army. He fully subordinated his personality and his work to the program of the Party: "It
would be ridiculous, if I, the Bolshevik, should not share
the political platform of my Party faction," he declared

to the officers of his regiment.[2] He volunteered for
the front in fulfillment of his Party's assignment in order
to spread Bolshevik ideas and propaganda among the
soldiers.

Bunchuk's behavior can be evaluated in various ways.
He could be understood as an expression of the highest
and most noble aspect of his personality—his consistency and sacrificial service to the cause, of the truth of
which he was unshakably convinced. Or, in view of his
deception and desertion, he can be interpreted as an expression of the lowest form of baseness. The fact that
the soldiers loved him could be interpreted as having
a double significance: he was able to ingratiate himself
with the soldiers not because of his good nature, but
in fulfillment of the Party's requirements.

Sholokhov, the artist, did not pronounce any judgment upon Bunchuk's behavior. He remained neutral.

An officer from Bunchuk's regiment, the monarchist
Listnitskii who plays a greater part in the novel than
Bunchuk, gave him an unequivocal hint: "But how many
German workers, your class brothers, did you kill with
your machine-gun detachment?"[3] The author preferred
not to give an answer to this question. The irony of
the hint, however, remains undiverted.

In the same conversation with his colleagues from
the regiment, Bunchuk read them a long passage from
a brochure, where Lenin delighted himself with the
description of contemporary armies. Lenin praised army
discipline for its ability to organize and to command
the indivisible will of millions of people. The indivisible
will of the multitude—this was what not only delighted
the Bolshevik Bunchuk, but also what became his
program for action.

On the same night that he spoke to his friends, Bunchuk deserted from the front.

The novel does not reveal why and when Bunchuk became a devoted Bolshevik. The reader may make a probable conclusion that Bunchuk came to the front as a staunch Bolshevik. It was thus not the horrors of the war that brought him to the Bolsheviks, into the camp of the defeatists. He did not oppose the war as a pacifist. The goal toward which he worked was a civil war. His recollections of the past, which the author timed to be late summer of 1917, do not tell anything about his life. The fragments of the recollections are too general and indefinite.

> Involuntarily he recalled an episode during an attack in 1915, and as if rejoicing to find itself on the beaten track again, his brain insistently began to conjure up fragments of memory; the faces and hideous postures of dead Russian and German soldiers; snatches of talk, colourless, time-faded scraps of scenery; unspoken thoughts; the faint sputter of machine-guns and the rattle of the belts; a blaring melody, beautiful almost to pain; the faintly outlined mouth of a woman he had once loved; and then again scraps of the war; the dead; the low-settled mounds of the common graves. . . .
>
> He sat up and said, or perhaps only thought: "Until I die I shall carry these memories, and not I alone but all who come through. Our whole life has been mutilated, cursed! Damn them. . . .Damn them. . . .Not even with death will their guilt be wiped out. . . ." (*Part Four, Chapter XVII.*)

This is Bunchuk during one sleepless night in the late summer of 1917, where he suddenly found himself among the soldiers with whom he had served earlier, before he had deserted. His reminiscences of the war episode of the year 1915 do not reveal very much about his personality. Every soldier who once took part in an attack could have had those recollections. His curses could probably be attributed to the system as a whole, and not only to the Russian society. He could have had in mind any society which cannot prevent the massacre of war.

Another incident which equally does not furnish any clues as to Bunchuk's inward world is his recollection about a twelve-year-old girl, Lushka, the daughter of Bunchuk's friend, a Petersburg factory worker. Lushka's father was killed in the war and she, remaining all alone, had to earn her livelihood through prostitution. Bunchuk met her per chance on the street. The text of this meeting, especially Bunchuk's hate and anger in connection with Lushka's fate, however, is unclear. Above all, it is not clear from the text whether Bunchuk's anger refers to that time in the past when he met Lushka, or to the present time, i.e. in the late summer of 1917 among the Cossacks as they were approaching Petrograd, and at which time Bunchuk was thinking of the meeting with Lushka.

> Then he recalled Lushka, the twelve-year-old daughter of a friend of his, a metal worker killed in the war. One evening he had been walking along a boulevard. The girl— an angular, sickly child—was sitting on a bench, her thin legs flung daringly forward, smoking a cigarette. Her face was faded, her eyes tired, her painted lips, pinched with bitterness at the corners, were prematurely ripe. "Don't you know me, Uncle?" she asked with a professional smile, and rose. Then she began to cry, bitterly and helplessly like a child, stooping and pressing her head against Bunchuk's elbow.

He gnashed his teeth and groaned, almost choking with
the poisonous hatred that filled him. He sat rubbing his
chest, feeling that his hatred was seething in his breast like
hot slag, preventing him from breathing, and causing a
sharp pain under his heart. (*Part Four, Chapter XVII.*)

Bunchuk's personality and his inward world, as simple
as they were, were revealed only during the Revolution.
It was again accomplished not by the author's direct
description and external reference, but by the hero's
own actions.

After Bunchuk had fled from the front in the fall
of 1916, we meet him in the novel again in late summer
of 1917 among the Cossacks at the approaches to Petrograd. Bunchuk was sent by his party to spread propaganda among the soldiers in Kornilov's armies. Here
Bunchuk met one of his former colleagues from the
regiment, the officer Kalmykov. When Kalmykov tried
to oppose Bunchuk's propaganda and reminded soldiers
of their duties, Bunchuk decided to deal with Kalmykov on his own. He shot Kalmykov with his own hand.
This violence puzzled the Cossacks very much. The
Cossack who happened to witness the killing tried to
talk Bunchuk out of the violent act. When the killing
had nevertheless taken place, the simple Cossack could
not grasp why it had to happen. "Why did you kill
him?"[4] Bunchuk did not give an answer to the question
of the startled Cossack. Neither did Sholokhov. But
the reader cannot help but conclude that such is the
violent nature of the Revolution. And, indeed, the
reader will of necessity return to this conclusion many
times in the course of the novel.

The incident of Bunchuk's short shrift with his ideological opponent appeared to be only a small episode

in the long chain of his service to the Revolution. While serving the Revolution, Bunchuk had to work in its interests, striving to preserve and maintain the Revolution by any and all means available to him. From his point of view Kalmykov's death was a necessary one. Victims were not counted. Bunchuk subordinated all his behavior to the causes and ideas of his Party, and thus he had to act accordingly.

Following the August event below Petrograd, Sholokhov sent his Bunchuk to Rostov, his native city, in order to establish there the new revolutionary regime. In March, 1918, we find him serving in the Revolutionary Tribunal of the Don area. He was entrusted with the commandant's office. In that capacity he had the power to annihilate the counter-revolutionary physically.[5] Every night he commanded a Red Guard detachment to shoot those sentenced to death by the Revolutionary Tribunal. Bunchuk understood and felt with all his being that the physical annihilation of the counter-revolutionaries was not only necessary, but was moreover, a useful service to the cause of the Revolution.

He understood that since violence was the very nature of the Revolution, every revolutionary who had seized and firmly held the power of the Revolution had to perform this service. He justified his work. Even though it was dirty work, it served the future.

> "I won't give up this work! I see, I feel positively that I am being of service here. I shall rake away the filth, I shall dung the earth, so that it will be more fertile. More fruitful. Some day happy people will walk on this earth.... Perhaps my own son, that I haven't got, will walk here too!" He laughed gratingly and joylessly. "How many of these serpents, these ticks, have I shot! The tick is an insect

that eats into the body. I've killed dozens with these hands." He stretched out his long-nailed, blackhaired hands, clenched like a vulture's talons, then dropped them onto his knees and said in a whisper: "To hell with it all. We've got to burn, burn so there'll be no smoke to foul the air. . . .Only, I'm tired. . .that's true. A little more, and then I'll go off to the front. . . .You're right. . . ." (*Part Five, Chapter XX.*)

It is to Sholokhov's merit that he was able to present the life of the Cossacks and their attitude toward the Revolution from the point of view of the Cossacks who opposed the Revolution, and the Revolution as it was seen by the forces of the Revolution itself. Thus, there are two different points of view on the Revolution.

In any case, there can be no doubt that the above quoted words of Bunchuk reveal the nature and the world of the Revolution as Sholokhov wanted it to be presented. Bunchuk was convinced that his Party, and only his Party alone, could establish the desired and really just future Great Society. To realize this goal, Bunchuk's Party needed the power. Having seized the power, the Party was neither willing to share it with, nor to be checked in its power by any other force. In order to establish the just future society, the Party had to annihilate those who opposed or simply did not approve of the Party's power. Neither Bunchuk personally, nor his Party ever gave thought as to how many counter-revolutionary "serpents" they had to liquidate in order to establish the social justice for which they aspired, or just who were included in the group of counter-revolutionary "serpents" to be liquidated. Who would determine and how to determine the adherents or simple sympathizers of the counter-revolutionary "serpents"—these questions did not exist for Sholokhov's Bunchuk. Neither did there exist for him the problem of how to preserve some semblance of humaneness in his relations with other people under the conditions created by the Revolution. But he well knew that among those whom he had to shoot as counter-revolutionary "serpents," there were not only aristocrats, the natural enemies of the Revolution, but also toilers whose hands were as hard as book leather and covered with calluses.[6] These could not have been the inveterate enemies of the Revolution. However, no sacrifice of human lives, including his own, seemed to him too great a price to pay in order to save the Revolution and its glorious promises.

Sholokhov did not let his Bunchuk live long enough to see the end of the Revolution, but the physical annihilation of the counter-revolutionaries which he had started continued on and on. There was no end to the annihilation. Bunchuk was dead, but the machine of terror, of which he was one of the initiators, continued its function. But Bunchuk did not think of this, either. All he knew was that the Revolution had to liquidate all its opponents.

While saving the Revolution, Bunchuk himself turned out to be only a small screw in the big and impersonal machine of the Revolution. After the loss of the woman he loved, Bunchuk himself became lost, sank inwardly and suffered. He seemed to have lost his revolutionary zeal, and was utterly confused.

> In the days that followed, Bunchuk lived as he had in the delirium of typhus. He still went about, did things, ate, slept, but always as if in a stupefying, narcotic daze.

With frantic, swollen eyes he stared uncomprehendingly
at the world around him, failed to recognize his friends,
and looked as though he were heavily intoxicated or only
just recovering from a wasting illness. From the moment
of Anna's death, feeling was temporarily atrophied in him:
he wanted nothing, and thought of nothing. (*Part Five,
Chapter XXVI.*)

Sholokhov's presentation of his hero in his personal
loss appears to be more humane and warm: Bunchuk
is no longer devoid of the feelings inherent in all people.
The loss of a beloved woman was a bitter lot. Bunchuk
learned of the misfortune, and experienced it as all
people would do. He is no longer that ideal revolutionary who followed only one thought and lived only for
one goal—how to better serve the Revolution. He is
crushed by his personal grief and seems to be helpless,
as anyone might be in a similar situation. When the
expedition with which Bunchuk was sent away was
captured by the uprising Cossacks and all its members
were threatened with execution, Bunchuk refused to
think of escape. At first he thought of fleeing, but the
idea of escape in secrecy and of desertion was sickening
to him.[7] He had deserted from the German front without even a moment of hesitation, leaving his soldier
friends behind to fight the war. But now, having experienced personal sorrow, he had no more strength or
energy for escape. He seemed to remain indifferent to
his fate and to that of the Revolution. He was killed
by the Cossacks as an insignificant, nameless, and unknown man. He refused to even disclose his name.

Sholokhov did not bring Bunchuk to the end of the
novel. He did not even bring him to a point where his

mood could have changed in the direction of the heroic pathos of the revolutionary—a trait Bunchuk once possessed. In his tragic ending, Bunchuk was more human and less schematic.

Sholokhov's Bunchuk had little contact with the Cossacks. Though Sholokhov created him as a Cossack, made him serve in a Cossack Army regiment, and let him perish among the Cossacks on the Don at the hands of the rebellious Cossacks, he had little influence in the affairs of the Don Cossacks. Bunchuk's part in the novel was developing apart from the other principal Cossack characters.

In regard to the structure of this Cossack-peasant novel with its elemental way of life, Bunchuk himself does not make up the organic structure of the novel. Neither has Sholokhov created for him and with him a second line independent of the novel's parallel plot. Seen as a whole, Bunchuk's part in the novel is only an insertion in Sholokhov's magnificent Cossack novel. True, he represents the Revolution—a Revolution which the Cossacks neither understood nor accepted, but his part among the Cossacks was only a minor one.

The second character who personifies the Revolution is the professional revolutionary Stockman. Stockman, though painted as pale and colorless as Bunchuk, had more personal contacts with the Cossacks from the hamlet Tatarsk. He exercised noticeable influence on two of them, helping them to form their Soviet ideas.

Stockman first appeared in the lost Cossack hamlet in the fall of 1912, the time ascertained in the chronology of the novel at the beginning of this discussion. He settled there upon assignment of his Party, for the purpose of spreading propaganda among the peaceful Cossacks. The Cossacks met the strange settler in their midst cautiously and curiously. But when the stranger interfered in the fight between the Cossacks and the neighboring Ukrainians, their curiosity had turned into open hostility.

Stockman, like Bunchuk, is not revealed to us in the multiformity and multivariety of human nature and thoughts. We learn nothing from the novel about Stockman's personality, his aspirations, hopes, and despairs, nothing of that which makes human life so rich and indefinable. Stockman is drawn in a simple manner, as if according to a scheme—he is a man of one thought and of one goal. He is created without any weaknesses, human doubts, or sympathies.

About his work as propagandist, Sholokhov wrote briefly and factually as if it had been taken from official records:

> After long sifting and testing, a little group of ten Cossacks began to meet regularly in Stockman's workshop. Stockman was the heart and the soul of the group and he worked straight towards a goal that only he fully understood. He ate into the simple understandings and conceptions like a worm into wood, instilling repugnance and hatred towards the existing system. At first he found himself confronted with the cold steel of distrust, but he was not to be repulsed. Even that could be worn away. (*Part Two, Chapter IX.*)

This is the style of the author's resume. Sholokhov told two things in this brief fragment. First, the goal of Stockman's propaganda remained unknown to the Cossacks. Only Stockman knew why he conducted the discussions with the Cossacks. He did not reveal his purpose to anyone. And second, Stockman evoked in the Cossacks an aversion and hatred toward the system and order of their life. This was a very destructive mission indeed. This was a hatred that was obscure and vague, although premeditated, but undefined by any positive goals. It was impossible for the Cossacks to see and know what the enlightened Stockman felt and knew. He was devoted to his Party's program and principles. The Cossacks' hatred was void of any positive political foundation. There was, of course, always the opportunity of finding in life more than enough reasons for blind hatred.

At the beginning of the war in 1914, Stockman was arrested and disappeared from the pages of the novel. He reappeared in the novel in the village Tatarsk after the Revolution, as suddenly as he had the first time, as a *deus ex machina*. At that time, he related what had happened to him since his arrest. We learned thus that he was tried and sentenced to exile and hard labor. The Revolution set him free.[8]

Stockman is a professional revolutionary. As a character in the novel, he is deprived of the wealth and depth of the inner life which Sholokhov allotted to his other characters, especially those from among the Cossacks.

He appeared in the hamlet Tatarsk where the Revolutionary Committee ordered the arrest of the most well-to-do Cossacks. According to the chronology of the novel, it must have been toward the end of the winter of 1919. Seven men were arrested at the selection of the local committee, brought to the Cossack *stanitsa* Veshenskaia, and shot there. The coachman who drove the arrested to Veshenskaia brought this terrible news back to the hamlet. The Cossacks in the hamlet refused to believe this news. They could not understand how innocent people could be made such a short process of. Ivan Alekseevich Kotliarov, the chairman of the local revolutionary committee and himself a Cossack from the hamlet Tatarsk, at first refused to believe that people could be shot so quickly. He came with a complaint to Stockman.

> "We sent some prisoners to Veshenskaia today and they've shot them!" he exclaimed. "I thought they would just keep them in prison, but this is different. This way we'll never do anything. The people will turn away from us, Osip Davidovich. Why did they kill them? What will happen now?"
> He expected Stockman to be as agitated and indignant as himself at what had occurred, but as he slowly drew on his shirt Stockman answered: "Now, stop shouting!" (*Part Six, Chapter XXII.*)

With these words Sholokhov has revealed the attitude of the local Cossacks toward the violence of the Revolutionary Tribunal. In the eyes of the Cossacks it was violence indeed, if not exactly a mob law; but in any case, it was not a justice of the Revolution.

An investigator from the Revolutionary Tribunal demanded to remove all of the most hostile Cossacks.[9] The local committee, composed of native Cossacks, could not possibly know what it meant to remove the most hostile elements from among the Cossacks. The committee prepared a list of those whom they believed to be most dangerous to the Revolutionary powers. But the local Cossack committee did not know what would happen to the arrested. Such an outcome was therefore quite a shock. The unexpected end of the arrested had frightened the local revolutionary Ivan Alekseevich very much. This was in his eyes an unnecessary and senseless cruelty. He was afraid that through this cruel act, the Cossacks would disalign themselves from the Soviets. His misgivings were fully justified a few days after the event. The Cossacks not only withdrew their passive support from the Soviets, but rose against the young Soviet power in the Don area.

Stockman's answer to Ivan Alekseevich, which Sholokhov placed upon Stockman's lips, proved to be a stereotyped one. He referred to the closeness of the front, the necessity of the class struggle. Trying to justify the senseless killing, he referred, among other things, to Lenin who allegedly must have said that a Revolution cannot be fought in clean white gloves.[10] Sholokhov, faithful to his position as artist, did not take the side of either camp in this event. Nor did he try to interpret Stockman's words. He left it up to the reader himself to understand them.

Indeed, Stockman's answer is phased in such a way as to lead one to realize that here more than one correct answer is possible. His words can be understood in various ways. To the revolutionary Stockman, these words undoubtedly meant the same that they could have meant to Bunchuk: the physical liquidation of all enemies of the Revolution, not only of those actual but also of those potential, is a necessity of the Revolution. The seven Cossacks from the hamlet Tatarsk were shot without having first been proven guilty. This was done only with the purpose of intimidating the rest. In this way, anyone could be regarded as a potential enemy of the Revolution, and could be shot without trial.

While justifying the cruelty of the Revolution as necessary, Stockman undoubtedly had it in mind to strengthen the Revolution and the Soviet power. Undoubtedly, this was also Sholokhov's intention when he attributed these words to Stockman. It should be said once more that Sholokhov repeatedly showed his artist's ability to see events with the eyes of one directly participating in them—the Cossacks or the Revolutionaries— without his author's interpretation.

Stockman wanted to strengthen the Revolution, but the events on the Don shown by Sholokhov proved just the opposite to be the case. The unceremoniousness and unscrupulousness of the revolutionary authorities antagonized the Cossacks and pushed them away from the Revolution. Thus, Lenin's words found quite a different reflection among the Cossacks. The Cossacks became more frightened than before.

As to the Cossacks' attitude to the Revolution, Stockman was given the answer a bit later by one of the Cossacks, an Old Believer, when the Cossack uprising against the Revolution was in full swing.

> "I'll tell you how you've gone wrong. You've squeezed the Cossacks and made a lot of blunders; if you hadn't, your government would last forever. There are a lot of fools among you, that's why you've had this uprising."
>
> "How have we made blunders?"
>
> "You know as well as I do....You've shot people. Today it's one man's turn, tomorrow another's. And who's going to wait for his turn to come?" (*Part Six, Chapter XXXIX.*)

This was what the Cossacks thought of the Revolution.

This Cossack-Old Believer, who spoke with Stockman, was not from the hamlet Tatarsk. But he, too, spoke of the unnecessary execution of innocent people. He, in no way, could have had in mind the execution of the seven Cossacks in the hamlet Tatarsk. It is as if Sholokhov wanted to say that there must have been many executions. The execution in the hamlet Tatarsk was not merely one accidental excess of the Revolution; it was not just one innocent case of the misuse of power by those who were given this power by the Revolution. It was the system and the nature of the Revolution. The Revolution needed victims and had to find them.

The Quiet Don reflected the revolutionary epoch, when a man's life became cheap, and when the Cossacks of the Don did not know who had the right to make arrests and executions. Stockman himself barely escaped arrest and probable execution by a young commissar who accidentally happened to travel through the hamlet Tatarsk.[11] The insignificant episode with the young commissar in the novel was needed by Sholokhov for no other purpose than to stress the chaos of the Revolution in the turbulent and stormy Don.

With this we can finish our discussion of Stockman. There is nothing more in him that would shed new light on the Revolution or add a new feature to his personality. Sholokhov made Stockman die at the hands of the rebellious Cossacks, for whose happiness Stockman wanted to give his life. His sacrifice, like that of Bunchuk, was unwanted by and unacceptable to the Cossacks.

Among the other characters who represented the Revolution in the novel, we have to give some attention to

Podtëlkov. The Soviet critics often noticed the weakness and vagueness of Sholokhov's Communists. This was especially referred to in discussions of the character of Podtëlkov. Even such a benevolent Sholokhovist as Iakimenko, who sees everywhere in Sholokhov an objective approach to reality and the broadest interpretation of the characters of the Communists, has stressed the author's weakness in presenting Podtëlkov's character.[12]

Podtëlkov was one of those, who at one time exercised a great deal of influence on Grigorii Melekhov, who, as usual, was constantly wavering. In spite of the fact that Podtëlkov is in reality pictured weak, in him and through him, more than through any other character of the Revolution, the attitude of the Cossack masses to the Revolution was reflected.

The first time we learn of Podtëlkov in the novel is when Grigorii Melekhov met with him in November 1917. From their conversation we learn that Podtëlkov, as Grigorii himself, was a Cossack. As usual, Sholokhov did not present his portrait, nor did he tell of this character's past life. Grigorii saw a stout Cossack with the shoulder-straps of a cavalry sergeant-major in the Guard's battery, who was sitting on an officer's folding-bed.[13]   They discussed how best to arrange for the governing of the Don Cossack land after the Revolution. As usual, Grigorii wavered and did not firmly know to which opinion he should subscribe. At the present time, he seemed to believe that the political independence of the Cossacks would be the best form of government for them. In the process of the conversation he said, "The war will be finished soon—and we shall start a new life. The Ukraine will be governed by the *Rada,* and we by our Cossack Military Circle. And so we will be living as our ancestors lived in the old times."[14] Podtëlkov, however, objected to Grigorii on the ground that Russia would not permit this to happen. He also said that he was against General Kaledin and against all other elements of the nobility and added: "We have to strive in order that the power should be in the hands of the people."[15] To Grigorii's although unsophisticated, but in reality very essential question about the form of government (by whom shall we be governed?), Podtëlkov answered that "we will be governed by ourselves."[16]

We learn nothing more here about Podtëlkov's political credo. He is not yet presented as a Bolshevik. His character was evolving slowly and gradually. We learn about Podtëlkov's influence on Grigorii from the author's brief note, which is placed at the beginning of their conversation. Sholokhov remarked briefly to the effect that Podtëlkov's truth prevailed over Grigorii's hesitations.

We find Podtëlkov again in January of 1918 at the Cossack *stanitsa* Kamenskaia, in the center of the Revolutionary activity of the Don Cossacks. The Conference of the Cossack veterans elected Podtëlkov as chairman of the Don Revolutionary Committee. In one of his speeches, Podtëlkov declared that he is not registered with the Bolshevik Party, but that he strives for the same goals as the Bolsheviks do: for justice and happiness, for brotherly union of all the laboring people, that there should be no oppression, no rich, no bourgeois, and that everybody should live free and unrestricted.[17]

Podtëlkov made several appearances in the novel in the short duration of the power of the Don Revolutionary Committee, and each time we learn of a new feature of his personality. As if by chance, the author dropped a remark that Podtëlkov was dressed in a new leather jacket.[18]   This is very characteristic of a commissar of the early Revolutionary years. In his negotiation with the Don's Military Circle, Podtëlkov spoke for the direct and naked violence of his power.[19]   People who stood close to Podtëlkov noticed a visible change in him, and that he was assuming a certain note of superiority and arrogance.[20]

One of the brightest moments in the portrayal of Podtëlkov's character was his execution of the captured White officers and soldiers, which finally repulsed Grigorii Melekhov away from Podtëlkov and the Revolution. In the scene of the execution, Podtëlkov is not drawn bleakly or as a weakling, but as a person who knows his worth, power, and influence. This scene was discussed in connection with Grigorii Melekhov. (See above, page 196f.)

We find Podtëlkov in the novel again only before his death, when he was appointed to head the Extraordinary Revolutionary Commission, and when he was found to be a politician without a country, without people and without anybody's support. The power of the Revolutionary Committee on the Don had a duration of only three or four months. In the early spring of 1918, the Cossacks rebelled against the Revolutionary Committee and ended the Revolution in the Don region.

Here is how Sholokhov described the appointment of Podtëlkov's Extraordinary Commission and its departure:

An Extraordinary Mobilization Commission of five, with Podtëlkov at its head, was appointed; ten million rubles in gold of tsarist money were withdrawn from the exchequer for the needs of the mobilization; a detachment consisting mainly of Cossacks from the Kamenskaia district was hastily scraped together to act as guard, and on May 1st the expedition set out northward, already under fire from German aircraft. (*Part Five, Chapter XXVI.*)

These are the author's words. They are timed at the end of April, 1918, and reflect the haste on the expedition, its foreboding of doom: "the detachment was grabbed in a hurry."

And then came Podtëlkov's death. The rebellious Cossacks captured the expedition, hurriedly established a People's Tribunal, and having tried the expedition, sentenced all its members to death. In his death, Podtëlkov exceeded all his former activities. Several Soviet critics noted that Podtëlkov's only deserving deed was his death.[21]

As a footnote, we must add here that it was in this expedition that Bunchuk also found his death.

Among the other characters representing the Revolution, we have to mention briefly Mishka Koshevoi, the Cossack from the hamlet Tatarsk, who was Grigorii Melekhov's friend. Ivan Alekseevich Kotliarov, the Cossack from the same hamlet and the second revolutionary character from among the Cossacks was mentioned before in connection with the character of Stockman. Sholokhov did not say anything more about Ivan Kotliarov's revolutionary activity that would be characteristic and intrinsic only to him. So, we too, cannot say more than what was said by the author.

Mishka Koshevoi, though appearing in all eight parts of the novel, was not among the novel's main heroes, according to the original concept of the author. Were it not for his role in the last, the eighth part, the reader would hardly take note of Mishka's existence in the novel. Mishka's inner world and other facets of his personality remained unexpressed until the last part of the novel. In no way was he distinguished among the many other secondary characters such as Duniasha, Grigorii's sister, and others. Even the inner world of such a secondary character as Mit'ka Korshunov, who did not, and in the author's concept should not play a decisive part in the novel, was outlined more clearly and was featured more brightly than Mishka Koshevoi. Mit'ka Korshunov was an unscrupulous adventurer, and a cynical and cruel executioner. This is how he is portrayed every time he appears on the pages of the novel, from the very beginning to the end. But it is impossible to find out what part and significance Sholokhov had assigned to Mishka Koshevoi.

Then suddenly in the last part of the novel, Mishka Koshevoi emerges as a strong character, in the sense that he begins to play a full part as the opponent to Grigorii. But this is a new Mishka Koshevoi, whom we did not know before. He is no longer that unimportant and uncertain character that he was before. He is transformed at once into the role which Bunchuk, or Stockman, could and should have played until the end, had they not found premature death. We do not know how it happened that Mishka's character was transformed from an average Cossack into the most vigilant and conscientious representative of Communist power among the Cossacks. The author as usual preferred to hide the process of the transformation.

Mishka Koshevoi first appeared in the pages of the novel in Stockman's circle. He, however, did not distinguish himself here in any way. The author did not invest anything special in Mishka's personality in the way of characteristics unique to him. Then we find him in various fronts of the war. He was born in the same year as Grigorii, but for some reason, they were not drafted at the same time. Mishka was drafted directly to the front, while Grigorii started his service before the war. While a soldier on the front, Mishka began to think of the relationships among people, and especially the relations between the Cossacks and the Russians. These are the usual reflections common to peasants void of any ideological background, and void of any Bunchukovian or Stockmanovian revolutionary zeal and doctrines.

When the Cossacks of his hamlet rose against Podtëlkov's Revolutionary Power, Mishka Koshevoi decided to break through to the Reds. But he was caught by the Cossacks and sent to graze the village horses. Mishka had enough time there to think about his life. Contemplating on his life, his thoughts rather irresponsibly inclined towards the Reds.

In the winter of 1919 he was again in his native hamlet at the time when the Soviet Power was briefly established there for a second time. The Cossacks elected a new local government and Mishka was appointed co-chairman of the local committee, second in line to Ivan Alekseevich. It was in this capacity that he happened to witness Grigorii Melekhov's conversation with

Ivan Alekseevich about the nature of the Soviet Power. Grigorii came to the authorities to speak out on what was burning in his heart.[22] He had many doubts about the Soviet government. However, neither Ivan Alekseevich nor Mishka could give Grigorii a satisfactory answer. Grigorii could not accept the Revolution as the way for his Cossack life. From this time on, Mishka parted paths with Grigorii, not as a friend but as an inveterate foe. Each went his way separately. But we learn nothing about Mishka's ideology or his conscious attitude toward the new power. The only conscious manifestation of his personality was probably the fact that he ordered Grigorii's arrest. For him, Grigorii now became a most dangerous element, one who would go against the Soviets. But the Cossack uprising that soon followed prevented Grigorii's arrest. Mishka was nearly killed in this Cossack uprising. Only the extreme confusion and chaos among the rebels at the beginning of the uprising saved Mishka. This was the second Cossack uprising against the Revolution.

The execution of Petro Melekhov, Grigorii's brother, by Mishka, was more of a violent act and a mob trial over captured rebels than the carrying out of a just sentence. After the uprising, Mishka appears as if he were the people's judge and revenger. The bitterness on both sides at the time of the second uprising seemed to have reached utmost cruelty. On both sides, people believed that they had the exclusive right to revenge. And revenge it was; revenge that was both senseless and merciless.

Since the day he learned of Stockman's murder and heard the rumor that Ivan Alekseevich and Ielansk Communists had been killed, Mishka had been possessed by a burning hatred for the Cossacks. He no longer thought, no longer listened to the faint voice of mercy in his heart when an insurgent Cossack fell into his hands. Not to one of them did he show compassion. With blue eyes as cool as ice he would demand of the prisoner: "Had enough of fighting the Soviet Government?" and would ruthlessly cut the man down without waiting for an answer, without a glance at his stricken face. Not only did he kill his prisoners, but he set the "crimson cock" of an incendiary torch under the eaves of the houses in villages abandoned by the insurgents, and when the fear-demented cows and bullocks broke down the fences and galloped bellowing into the street, he shot them down.

He waged an irreconcilable, relentless war on the Cossack plenitude, on the Cossack perfidy, on all the inviolate and stagnant manner of life which had remained undisturbed for centuries under the roofs of those sturdy Cossack cottages. Stockman's and Ivan's death were as fuel to his hatred, and the words of the proclamation: "The nests of the dishonourable traitors must be destroyed, the Cains must be exterminated," clearly formulated his blind feelings. The same day that the proclamation was read to his company he and three other comrades burned down a hundred and fifty houses in Karginskaia alone. He found some kerosene in a merchant's warehouse and went round the square with a box of matches clutched in his hand. He left behind him a trail of pungent smoke and flame enveloping the smartly painted priests' and merchants' houses and the homes of the richer Cossacks, the habitations of those "whose scheming had driven on the ignorant Cossack masses to revolt." (*Part Six, Chapter LXV.*)

This is Sholokhov's picture of a revolutionary, painted

in his own words. This is how the author visualized Koshevoi's revolutionary activity. Koshevoi is here lacking any revolutionary idea, or ideological foundation. He is, rather, more a blind revenger than a devoted and conscientious revolutionary. This is not a very attractive picture, indeed. Such a merciless and blind reprisal Koshevoi also carried out in his native hamlet Tatarsk, where he burned down the Korshunov's house and killed old Grishaka, after having first mocked him. Old Grishaka's only guilt was that he was a Korshunov, and that his son was one of the richest Cossacks in the hamlet.

Koshevoi revenged the death of his Communist friends, those who were killed by the rebellious Cossacks. But his revenge is not conscious, not founded in ideological background and, of course, has no judicial legality. Innocent victims who were old and infirm, who could not escape or hide, suffered more from this kind of revenge than those who should be punished.

Sholokhov did not present Koshevoi's punitive executions as an ideological issue, nor Koshevoi himself as a fighter for an idea, as he had presented Bunchuk and Stockman. Bunchuk and Stockman also revenged in the novel, but their revenge, though being short shrift, was in their eyes justified because it was founded on class consciousness. They had to kill their class enemies who opposed the future just revolutionary society. But Mishka Koshevoi did not have this cause; old Grishaka was too old and infirm to be a danger for the Revolution. Koshevoi's killing was only a blind retaliation, which did not distinguish between the guilty and the innocent.

This senseless brutality gave occasion to the other side to revenge just as senselessly and cruelly. After Koshevoi's punitive visit to his native hamlet, the Reds again had to leave the area for a while. The hamlet Tatarsk was visited by Korshunov, one of the staunchest representatives of the Cossack counter-revolution. Mit'ka Korshunov carried out a parallel reprisal on the opposite side. He killed Mishka's mother, who did not have a chance to hide, and whose only guilt was that she was Mishka Koshevoi's mother.

It is to Sholokhov's merit that he allotted none of the revengers an idea. The revenge of Mishka Koshevoi, in equal measure to that of Mit'ka Korshunov, was senseless brutality.

On the occasion of his punitive expedition to his native hamlet Tatarsk, we learn of Mishka's sweetheart. In his own words, and as if by accident, the author revealed Mishka's secret to the reader. At once we learn that Mishka's love affair was already two years old. In these two years, Mishka only saw Duniasha Melekhov in snatches. During this time, both of them became bound by mutual feeling, of which they had not yet spoken in words.[23]   It can be discerned from the author's words that the feeling must be a mutual one. The author speaks about this feeling as of an old and long-held one. But he said nothing of this occasion about how each of them felt toward the other. He apparently preferred not to disclose such intimacies in his characters. In any event, we know nothing of Mishka's inner world.

After the terrible revenge in the house of Korshunov, Mishka Koshevoi appeared at Melekhov's and began a conversation with Il'inichna about his affairs of the heart, about his love for Il'inichna's daughter and about

his intention to soon send the matchmakers. If this is
not an irony in the author's device, then it must be a
light derision. It does not sound ironic, however. The
house burned by Mishka was still smoking, the corpse of
old Grishaka was still warm, yet Mishka speaks of his
affairs of the heart.

> Acrid smoke was still rising from the charred implements
> in the Korshunov's yard; the high stone foundations and
> the half-ruined stove lifting its sooty chimney to the sky
> were all that remained of the house. (*Part Six, Chapter
> LXV.*)

It looks as if at that time, Sholokhov did not want him
to think seriously of his love.

After this event, Mishka disappears from the novel
for a long period of time. We do not see him or hear of
him. He leaves again with the Reds, but the author does
not report his whereabouts or his activities.

He appeared again in his ruined native hamlet after
the Civil War, at the end of the novel. With his whole
heart he was ready to start farming anew. He married
his former sweetheart Eudokia Panteleevna, as he rev-
erently called her. It seems that Sholokhov led him in
such a way that Mishka Koshevoi, a reckless hero of
revenge, would become a good Cossack, a thoughtful
conscientious farmer. This would be more natural for
Mishka as we knew him earlier in the novel.

But suddenly he was transformed into a new Mishka,
one that we did not know before. After the death of
Il'inichna, Mishka's mother-in-law, and especially after
he was appointed chairman of the local revolutionary
council, Mishka, the most ordinary Cossack, such as we
knew him previously throughout the course of the en-

tire novel, reckless and often turbulent, suddenly became a most vigilant revolutionary professional. He became what Bunchuk and Stockman had been from the very beginning of the novel. He began to reproach his wife, saying that she spoke the enemy's language, and that the whole Melekhov breed had counter-revolutionary blood.[24]

Even long before Grigorii's return from the army, Koshevoi made a declaration to his wife that Grigorii must be tried by a Soviet court for his participation in the uprising, and that he would not live under the same roof with his wife's brother.[25] Because of this, their family's harmony was threatened with destruction.

His conversation with Grigorii resembled an official interrogation by security organs rather than a conversation with a relative. Mishka sternly warned Grigorii and threatened a reprisal of the Soviet law. One cannot otherwise but feel a false tone in the description of their conversation. One would like to say, it should not be like this; such a conversation is not possible between them.

No doubt, Mishka Koshevoi's final role in the novel was not in the author's original concept. But as Sholokhov approached the end of the novel, he saw that he needed an antagonist to Grigorii. He could not possibly finish the novel with Grigorii as he had become at the end of the novel. He could transform Grigorii into a new Soviet man and make him accept the Revolution as the only possible way of life for the Cossacks. This would mean, however, a great deal of strain on the novel and on the portrayal of Grigorii's character. Sholokhov must have recognized that he could not create a new

Grigorii Melekhov without an artificial twist in the novel. Obviously, there was a gap. And thus, Mishka Koshevoi had to come in and fill this gap. This is the reason for his transformation.

Besides these, so-to-speak, main characters of the Revolution, there are a few secondary characters—the common soldiers of the Revolution who are mentioned only once or twice in passing, as if accidentally. But strictly speaking, Sholokhov has no secondary characters. Even those most insignificant among them have a certain function. The insignificant are often featured more fully and outlined less schematically than some main heroes, as very often happens in great works of art.

One such character, whom Sholokhov made appear only a few times in the novel, is Maksimka Griaznov. Perhaps Maksimka Griaznov's only function in the novel was to demonstrate the complete absence of principles or ideals in a small man of the Revolution. Horse stealer, bitter drunkard and gambler, Maksimka Griaznov, Cossack from the Tatarsk hamlet, joined the Revolution and became a gunner in Bunchuk's detachment only because he then had the opportunity to do so. Had another opportunity presented itself, he, with equal success, would have joined the Whites.

Maksimka Griaznov did not play any part in the structure of the novel. He appeared in the novel as a little man, with many vicious passions. But in his death, on the other hand, is hidden something universally human. A certain warmth comes from the description of his death. The same attitude toward death was observed in connection with Valet's death (cf. above

p. 176). It is as though Sholokhov would like to say that in death all people are equal.

> He might have pulled himself together then, but in his very first battle a bullet struck him in the face, his blue eye dribbled on to his breast, and the blood spurted from the back of his head, that had been shattered like matchwood. Maxim Griaznov, Tatarskii Cossack, former horse-stealer and of late a drunkard, had departed this life. (*Part Five, Chapter XXV.*)

There is something pathetic in this description. The death of this simple Cossack seemed unnecessary.

There is one other character whom Soviet critics usually count among the Communist characters. But this character is featured in a manner so uncertain and unclear that it becomes impossible to say something definite about him. I have in mind Garanzha. Grigorii met Garanzha in Doctor Snegirev's eye clinic in Moscow, in the fall of 1914. As to who Garanzha was, where he came from, and where he went—we do not learn from Sholokhov. Equally, Sholokhov does not reveal Garanzha's world. According to his anti-war convictions he could be a Bolshevik-defeatist, but to an equal degree he could also protest against the war in the name of the Russian peasants' anarchism, which was always very popular among the Russian villagers. True, Sholokhov made Garanzha a Ukrainian, from the Chernigov area. But the popular Russian peasant anarchism can be equally applied to the Ukrainians. Garanzha's speech is saturated with Ukrainianisms. His concept of the Tsar and of authority is very popular. On the whole, there is nothing in his speech that would indicate his belonging to the strictly organized and conspiratory Bolshevik Party.

> "I'm not talking so quick as that, my boy. You think you're fighting for the tsar, but what is the tsar? The tsar's a grabber, and the tsaritsa's a whore, and they're both a weight on our backs. Don't you see? The factory owner drinks vodka, while the soldier kills the lice. The factory owner takes the profit, the worker goes bare. That's the system we've got. Serve on, Cossack, serve on! You'll earn another cross, a good one, made of oak."
>
> He spoke in Ukrainian, but on the rare occasions when he grew excited, he would break into pure Russian, generously sprinkled with invective. (*Part Three, Chapter XXIII.*)

With his peasant anarchism, Garanzha could not help but have a great deal of influence on Grigorii, a simple Cossack, who could not understand why he had to kill a man he did not know in the furious attack. But when Grigorii left the eye hospital, Garanzha, the smith from the village Gorokhovo, left the novel, and thus his influence on Grigorii came to a sudden end.

We included an example of Garanzha's conversation with Grigorii. But for the author it did not seem enough to have his hero speak directly. He seems to have no confidence in Garanzha, in that he might not say everything, or he might say something the author himself would not like to say. Therefore, in addition to the hero's direct speech, the author has written his own commentary on the conversation of his hero. He has recorded the proceedings of the conversation between Grigorii and Garanzha in his own words and thoughts. He summed up what was said by his characters, without

revealing details of Garanzha's arguments. This is one
of the novel's many common-place passages. Here is one
example of what the author has recorded about their
conversation:

> Day after day he revealed truths hitherto unknown to
> Grigorii, explaining the real causes of war, and jesting
> bitterly at the autocratic government. Grigorii tried to
> raise objections, but Garanzha silenced him with simple,
> murderously simple questions, and he was forced to agree.
> Most terrible of all, Grigorii began to think Garanzha
> was right, and that he was impotent to oppose him. He
> realized with horror that the intelligent and bitter Ukrain-
> ian was gradually but surely destroying all his former ideas
> about the tsar, the country, and his own military duty as a
> Cossack. Within a month of the Ukrainian's arrival, the
> whole system on which Grigorii's life had been based was
> a smoking ruin. It had already grown rotten, eaten up
> with the canker of the monstrous absurdity of the war, and
> it needed only a jolt. That jolt was given, and Grigorii's
> artless straightforward mind awoke. He tossed about seek-
> ing a way out, a solution to his predicament, and gladly
> found it in Garanzha's answers. (*Part Three, Chapter
> XXIII.*)

Besides Garanzha's bitter attitude towards his life, we
learn nothing here of his convictions and arguments.
Equally, nothing is said in concrete terms about Grigorii,
why he had to agree with Garanzha, and why he thought
that Garanzha was right. No more is said about Garanzha in *The Quiet Don.*

The Soviet critics firmly consider Garanzha as one of
the Bolsheviks.[26]   However, it seems that Sholokhov

had no reason to hide Garanzha's moral and ideological substance from his readers, if it were the case that he had one. He did not hide it in Bunchuk, in Stockman, or in others. If he did not present a political substance in Garanzha, it is probably because he wanted to make Garanzha something other than a Bolshevik.

Among the other characters who represent the Revolution there are Abramson and Anna Pogudko, Bunchuk's young friend and life companion who was prematurely killed. But what can we say about them that was not already said by the author? They hardly appear as paragons of individuality.

Soviet literary criticism quite often noted the weakness of Sholokhov's Communists, the so-called "our people." Serious rebukes were sent in Sholokhov's address—that his Communists are rare guests in the novel, that not one of them belongs to the principal characters. This is, according to Soviet literary standards, the main deficiency in the novel.

On one hand, it is impossible to disagree with these critical assertions. Even the most superficial perusal of *The Quiet Don* will affirm the thesis that the Bolsheviks speaking the language of the Sholokhovist Lezhnev do not frequently appear in the novel.[27] On the other hand, it is impossible to agree that this fact alone should constitute a serious shortcoming of the novel. An author should not be judged on the basis of what he did not present in his work, but only on the basis of how he has presented and what he has included. It was not Sholokhov's intention to create the central Bolshevik characters of the Don area. Having made it his goal to present the Cossacks' attitude to the Revolution, he pictured the Civil War on the Don from the point of view of the Cossack participation and resistance. He remained faithful to his intention, not digressing from it in the slightest.

A critic has no right to ask what would happen if Sholokhov had included in his novel several portraits of ideal Communists, the fighters for the future Revolutionary society. Whether the novel would gain or lose from this is an irrelevant question. Literary criticism should devote itself only to the problem of what is written and how the author has created his work.

But since we have mentioned the critics' rebuke, even though this rebuke is not valid, we would like to ask a further question: what do those critics mean when they speak of a deficiency in this novel? Do the critics expect that literary works be written according to a certain scheme, where certain features and devices can have only definite functions and meanings? If a device does not fit the scheme, they believe that they have found a serious deficiency in a work of art. However, what exactly the scheme should be, the critics never define.

The critics assert that the Communists do not occupy a prominent place in the novel because they are drawn as weak and vague. This deficiency in the eyes of the critics can probably mean first, that the characters of Bunchuk, Stockman, Podtëlkov, Koshevoi, Kotliarov and others are not sufficiently active, that they are deprived of leading roles among the Cossacks. No doubt, when literature is looked upon as only a reflection of the leading ideas of society, then this rebuke might be justified. The Communists have indeed little influence on the course of the Cossacks' affairs.

Secondly, the rebuke can also mean that the novel's Communists are weak people who are not developed in full, that they are narrow-minded and restricted, and that the author could and should have broadened their intellectual and emotional horizons and could have presented them as more human, more attractive people. Again, when literature is understood only as a sociological study, this rebuke can also be justified. The Communist characters in the novel are indeed what the criticism asserts. They are narrow-minded.

Thirdly, the rebuke can also mean that they are merely weakly presented, and that though in the novel they are positive characters and beautiful people, they did not, nevertheless, receive enough of the author's colors and attention in order to shine brighter and more vividly among the other characters, especially those among the Cossacks.

The third rebuke may appear justified when literature is approached from the point of view of the author's intention and realization, and also from the point of view of the linguistic means and devices which an author has, or can have at his disposal.

When literary criticism is restricted only to a few general sociological theses, when the study of the text remains untouched, it is hardly possible to find out what criticism really means when it speaks of the weak sides of Sholokhov's master novel.

No matter what the rebuke really means, one fact is clear: Grigorii Melekhov, the simple Cossack, coarse and often cynical, egoistic and often dissolute, but also tender and thoughtful, laborious and honest; Grigorii Melekhov who is constantly wavering and inconsistent, searching for something which he himself does not always know—this Grigorii came out more attractive, more winning, more charming and more human than those characters with ideal and firm principles who firmly knew what they wanted and who could always account for their actions and behavior, such as Bunchuk, Stockman, or the final Mishka Koshevoi. With his weaknesses and vices, Grigorii Melekhov is nearer and more approachable than many one-sided heroes. He is humanely more versatile and more diverse than Bunchuk or Stockman.

The fact remains that Sholokhov has succeeded in creating just such a character. It is that maybe while creating the characters of Bunchuk and Stockman, Sholokhov could not incorporate in them qualities which he did not find in life on the Don at that time. They came out as they were found, and reflected the author's concept.

NOTES AND REFERENCES

1. Part Three, Chapter XV.
2. Part Four, Chapter I.
3. *Ibid.*
4. Part Four, Chapter XVII.
5. Part Five, Chapter XX.
6. *Ibid.*
7. Part Five, Chapter XXVIII.
8. Part Six, Chapter XXII.
9. *Ibid.*

10. *Ibid.*
11. Part Six, Chapter XXIV.
12. L. I. Iakimenko, *Tvorchestvo Sholokhova,* Moscow, 1964, pp. 356-370.
13. Part Five, Chapter II.
14. *Ibid.*
15. *Ibid.*
16. *Ibid.*
17. Part Five, Chapter IX.
18. Part Five, Chapter X.
19. *Ibid.*
20. Part Five, Chapter XII.
21. Cf. Iakimenko, *op. cit.,* pp. 357ff.
22. Part Six, Chapter X.
23. Part Six, Chapter LXV.
24. Part Eight, Chapter V.
25. Part Eight, Chapter IV.
26. Cf. Iakimenko, *op. cit.* p. 319.
27. Cf. Lezhnev, *Mikhail Sholokhov,* Moscow, 1948, p. 222ff.

IN LIEU OF A CONCLUSION

There is no need of a conclusion in this book. If we have to write one, it would be only a repetition of all that was said in various passages and statements throughout the book. This should be self-explanatory to a sufficient degree.

A few thoughts, however, should be recapitulated from various passages in order to stress their evidence once more. We believe that this work has adequately shown that Sholokhov often acted as a participant in the life which he had created so vividly and colorfully. His novel is based neither on fantasy or fiction about life, nor on its facts. It represents, rather, his personal vision of reality. As a participant, no matter how neutral he tried to be, he could not abstain from his interpretation of reality. What marks his novel in a special, we would like to say "Sholokhovian" way, is that he tried to present his reality without a particular ideology. In the life of the novel, there was, as he put in his own words, "much bustle and disorder." It is as if he wanted to say that there is not much sense to this life of ours.

Nor did he try to solve any mysteries or riddles of life. He did not search for new ideas, or seek to find any unknown truths in life. He accepted life as he observed it around him. But his life is not without reflection. His novel is, if it would be possible to say so, full of life. His Cossack characters display irrepressible vitality and strength. Spontaneous force and natural dynamism are as if inescapable and come through nearly every line. The life he portrays might seem strange, and as if of illogical impression. One never knows what might happen and why it happens. All this makes this life, even in the time of depression, very much alive. There is a violent uproar in this life, and a high level of emotions and sensitivity abounds throughout.

One of the definite features of his presentation is that he seems to have no interest in the end result of the events that he described. His emphasis lies rather on the process of an event, that is, in the individual progression of a given event; hence his interest in detail.

Grigorii Melekhov is the central figure of the novel. He is the pivotal around which the novel turns. The main issue of the novel is placed with him and around him. In this, there seems to be no disagreement among the critics. A major disagreement, however, is what is the issue, and what is the meaning of the novel. The Soviet critics seem to maintain that the main issue of the novel is Grigorii's tragic end that he did not find the way to the new life offered by the Revolution. His errors appear then to be the main issue of the novel. Grigorii should have found the way to the Revolution and its universal human truth. Thus, the critics would say, Sholokhov has shown the negative way of the main character. He perished because he persisted in his errors.

This is, however, not the main issue intended by Sholokhov. The critics, stressing Grigorii's errors as the main issue of the novel, seem to forget that the author did not show how and what the way of the Revolution should be. The author did not point out and apparently had no intention to show why and how Grigorii should find his way to the Revolution. The Revolutionary truth did not appeal to him. On the other hand, Grigorii had no reason to be particularly hostile to the Revolution. As a matter of fact, he was made out of material of which revolutionary forces could be formed. All he needed, was that the author let some one show him the way.

But apparently Sholokhov from the very outset, waived off his hero's claims to the Revolution. The author's attitude toward Grigorii is not didactic or pious. He did not want to teach his hero the right way of life. Grigorii has no other function in the novel than to exist in his own rights and to express what he was. He always felt envious of men like the young Listnitskii or Koshevoi. Everything was clear to them from the very beginning, but nothing was clear to him.*

The final note of this conclusion should concern the characters of the Revolution. It should not be considered as the author's weakness that his Communist characters are drawn pale and schematically. True, they are presented as if lifeless, as if they were inserted in somebody's place which did not belong to them. They are displaced persons. But this hardly can be the author's weakness. He has presented them where he saw them. On the other hand, the unrelenting doubting and unsteady Grigorii is always presented in his own place.

---

*Part Eight, Chapter VII.

SELECTED BIBLIOGRAPHY

Aleksandrova, Vera. *Literatura i zhizn.* Ocherki Sovetskogo obshchestvennogo razvitiia. New York, Russian Institute of Columbia University, 1969.

Blagoi, D. *Literatura i deistvitel'nost'.* Voprosy teorii i istorii literatury. Moscow, 1959. Chapter on Sholokhov "Ideinost' i masterstro," pp. 506-574.

Brukhanskii, A. "Sholokhov v Zarubezhnoi Kritike" in: *Russkaia Literatura.* February, 1965, pp. 218-230.

Carlisle, Olga A. *Voices in the Snow.* New York, Random House, 1963.

Gura, V. V. *Zhizn' i tvorchestro M. A. Sholokhova.* Moscow, Seminarii, 1962. Second revised edition.

Hallet, Richard. "Soviet Criticism of *Tikhii Don,* 1929-1940" in: *The Slavonic and East European Journal.* Vol. XLVI, no. 106, January, 1968, pp. 60-74.

Iakimenko, L. "Novoe izdanie *Tikhogo Dona*" in: *Literaturnaia Gazeta.* No. 10, August, 1954, pp. 3-4.

―――――. *Mikhail Sholokhov Literaturnyi Portret.* Moscow, 1967.

―――――. *"Tikhii Don" M. Sholokhova.* O masterstre pisatelia. Moscow, 1954.

―――――. *Tvorchestro M. Sholokhova.* Idei i obrazy. Tvorcheskii Metod. Zhanry. Stil'. Masterstro. Poetika. Moscow, 1964.

Khmel'nitskaia, Tamara. "The Realism of Sholokhov" in: *Soviet Press Translations.* Vol. IV, no. 10. May 15, 1949, pp. 301-314 from the Russian monthly *Zrezda,* no. 12, December, 1948.

Khvatov, A. "Obraz Grigoriia Melekhova i Kontseptiia romana *'Tikhii Don'"* in: *Russkaia Literatura,* no. 2, 1965, pp. 3-33.

Lezhnev, I. *Mikhail Sholokhov.* Moscow, 1948.

————. *Put' Sholokhova Tvorcheskaia Biogratiia.* Moscow, 1958.

Lukacs, Georg. *Der Russische Realismus in der Weltliteratur.* Vol. 5 in the Work. *Probleme des Realismus.* Berlin (OST), 1964. Chapter on Sholokhov, pp. 378-416.

Lukin, Iu. *Sholokhov.* Kritiko-biograficheskii ocherk. Moscow, 1962.

Michail Sholochov. Werk und Wirkung. Materialien des Internationalen Symposiums. Leipzig. 18-19. März, 1965. Karl-Marx-Universitat, Leipzig, 1966.

Muchnic, Helene. "Sholokhov and Tolstoy" in: *The Russian Review.* Vol. XVI, April, 1957, pp. 25-34.

Pankov, V. *Na strezhne zhizni,* Moscow, 1962. Chapter on Sholokhov: "Gody i knigi," pp. 3-59.

Rühle, Jürgen. *Literature and Revolution.* A Critical Study of the Writer and Communism in the Twentieth Century. New York, 1969. Translated from German (West) edition of 1960. Chapter on Sholokhov: "The Epic of the Cossacks," pp. 58-77.

"Das Schicksal eines Kosakenromans. Michail Scholochov und "Der Stille Den" in: *Der Monat,* no. 90, March, 1956.

Stewart, D. K. *Mikhail Sholokhov.* A Critical Introduction. Ann Arbor, Mich., University of Michigan Press, 1967.

————. "The Textual Evolution of *The Silent Don*" in: *The American Slavic and East European Review,* Vol. XVIII, April, 1959, pp. 228-237.